# RUSSIA AGAINST JAPAN, 1904–05

# RUSSIA AGAINST JAPAN, 1904–05

*A New Look at the Russo–Japanese War*

J. N. Westwood

State University of New York Press

First published
in USA by
State University of New York Press
Albany

For information, address State University of New York Press.
State University Plaza, Albany, N.Y., 12246

Printed in Hong Kong

Library of Congress Cataloging in Publication Data
Westwood, J. N.
Russia against Japan, 1904–05.
Bibliography: p.
Includes index.
1. Russo–Japanese War, 1904–1905. I. Title.
DS517.W48 1986 952.03'1 85–22112
ISBN 0–88706–191–5

# Contents

# List of Illustrations

**Plates**

With two exceptions, all the photographs were first published during or soon after the war in Russian, British and American periodicals. After so many years it has not been possible to identify those to whom credit should be given for some of these pictures. It is known that on the Russian side many photographs were made by Viktor Bulla, whose work was used by the magazine *Niva* and syndicated abroad. Other photographs were copyrighted by Underwood & Co., H. C. White & Co., and *Collier's Weekly*, but the individual photographers were not identified. Some pictures were retouched to suit them for publication. Where considerable artwork was used the words 'from a photograph' have been included in the captions.

**Map**

The war zone

# Preface

Every decade or so a new book appears about the Russo–Japanese War, usually fatter than this one. So the appearance of yet another volume on the subject needs to be explained, if not excused.

Until August 1914 put it into the background, this war attracted enormous interest. First came the newspaper accounts, then the first memoirs translated from Russian or Japanese, or written by western attachés, correspondents and freelances who had followed the campaigns in person. In the military and naval world, painstaking analyses were made, sometimes for the interested public and sometimes for restricted circulation. It was felt at the time that this war, with its combination of advanced technology and massive human involvement, was a precursor of things to come. By 1914 the military and naval staffs of all the great powers were well advanced in the publication of multi-volume official histories of the war that were intended for the education of their officers. Of these, the British *Official History* is probably the best, and has served as a basis for subsequent, more popular, accounts.

However, apart from its justifiable neglect of the non-military aspects of the war, the *Official History* makes over-confident use of questionable Russian and Japanese sources. As with most wars, the first books to be written (and translated) were not the best; the more thoughtful and reliable accounts too often came after intense public interest had subsided, and they were not translated. Subsequent general books for general readers relied on the *Official History*, memoirs of doubtful reliability and, worst of all, contemporary newspaper accounts. Most writers accepted that unreliable sources make the most exciting narratives.

In this volume a few examples will be noted of distortions that have long been treated as historical evidence, but the main purpose is to draw upon the enormous stock of neglected, mainly Russian-language, material. The result is a book which omits, as unreliable, much anecdotal and hitherto unchallenged material recycled in previous works, and which at the same time seeks to view the events of 1904–05 from new or long-forgotten angles.

*Bristol*                                                   J. N. WESTWOOD

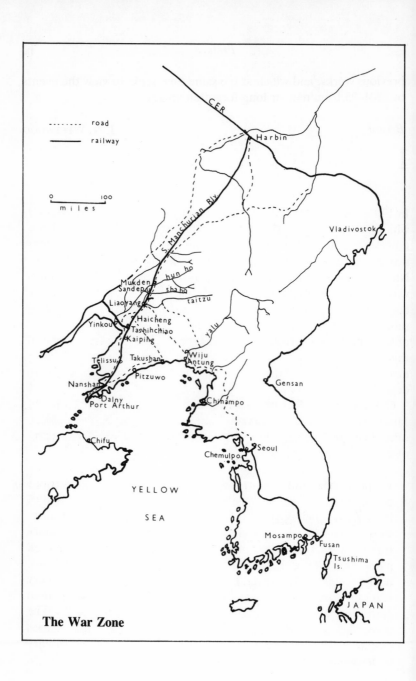

The War Zone

# 1 The Inevitable War?

In 1904, most Russians knew Japan simply as a small distant country which had recently emerged from barbarism. That Japan's inhabitants were puny yellow men from whom Europeans had little to fear was an impression which Russians shared with their Tsar. As heir, Nicholas in 1890–1 had seen the Orient during an official tour which was intended to emphasise Russia's interest in the Far East. During his stay in Japan he was attacked by an assassin, whose first sabre-blow gashed his forehead and whose second was parried by one of his companions, Prince George of Greece. The long-term result of this excitement was a scar on the imperial forehead, and Nicholas's hostility towards the Japanese, whom, in private, he was pleased to describe as 'monkeys'.

One prominent Russian who did not share the accepted view of Japan was General Kuropatkin, who as war minister had paid an official visit to Japan in 1903. In his memoirs he described, with a hint of envy, conditions there:

> I saw a beautiful country with a numerous and industrious population. There was activity everywhere. The joie de vivre of the masses, their love of country, and their faith in the future, were great assets. . . . In all the schools of the country military training had an important place, and children and young men took part with pleasure. Military walks involved problems of fieldcraft, deployments, surprise attacks, movements at the double. In every school the study of Japanese history must have helped strengthen patriotism and the conviction that Japan was invincible. The successful wars of Japan were emphasised, and their heroes glorified. The Japanese learned that every Japanese military undertaking had been a success.[1]

Whatever the motives of Nicholas's Japanese attacker, the assault symbolised the dawning realisation that Russia was the main threat to Japan's territorial ambitions. The conflict of 1904–05 had its origins in

1

the 1860s when Russia and Japan, each in its own different way, broke with their past and began to emulate the more advanced nations of the West. In Russia, during the 1860s, serfdom had been abolished, opening the way for the development of an expansionist economy. In Japan in the same decade the Meiji Restoration had led to the abandonment of Japanese exclusiveness; henceforth, instead of shrinking from foreign contact, Japan sought to preserve her independence by imitating the western powers. She too industrialised, armed herself, and sought spheres of influence abroad.

For both Russia and Japan the obvious region for expansion was the territory of the ever-weakening Chinese Empire. Japan was especially interested in Korea, whose nearest cape was only 100 miles distant. Japanese nationalists liked to describe Korea as a foothold which, once gained, would be a key to further expansion into the Chinese Empire. Pursuing their ironmongery analogy, they warned that if Korea should fall into the sphere of another expansionist power, this foothold and key would be transformed into 'a dagger pointed at Japan's heart'.[2] Thanks to this kind of propaganda, well before the turn of the century the ordinary Japanese citizen seemed hypersensitive, even irrational, whenever the future of Korea was in question. For Russia, meanwhile, Manchuria, Korea, and perhaps Mongolia were the main interest; all three adjoined Russia, and the political and military weakness of the Chinese government made them tempting targets.

In the last quarter of the nineteenth century both the Japanese and Russian governments were convinced that a carve-up of the Chinese Empire was imminent. Britain, France, the USA and Germany were all penetrating in the same way that the European powers had penetrated Africa earlier; they were building railways, sending traders, and signing commercial agreements. What Russia and Japan feared was that the carve-up would take place before they were ready. Indeed, the Russo–Japanese War occurred because both governments believed they had no time to lose in establishing themselves in Korea and Manchuria, and in their hurry they were in no mood for compromise when it became clear that the aims of one jeopardised the aims of the other.

Russia's eastern policy in the 15 years preceding the war with Japan was largely the work of Sergei Witte. Regarded at the time as one of the world's great statesmen and as the best adviser the Romanov dynasty had ever had, his stature has not diminished with the years, even though the veracity of his memoirs has been increasingly questioned. He had many enemies and was the object of almost continuous intrigue, but in the game of smear and counter-smear he probably gave as good as he got. Because of this lack of objectivity, because there were other influential Russians with their own views about the Far East, and because ultimately the will of the Russian government was the will of the Tsar, whose opinion was changeable and not always explicit, it is sometimes impossible to know what Russia's eastern policy was at any given moment. Foreigners, not realising that there were always contending influences within the government and within the Tsar's private circle, were often surprised by the resulting inconsistencies of policy as one opinion ousted another from the Tsar's favour. For most, these inconsistencies were simply proof of Russian duplicity.

Witte had been a railway administrator who had once been sentenced to imprisonment for negligence after one of his troop trains had plunged into a ravine when railway workers forgot to replace a lifted rail. He was later brought to St Petersburg to work out a new tariff structure and then became minister of transport, rising rapidly to the key post of finance minister. He soon became the trusted adviser of Tsar Alexander III, but after the accession of Nicholas II in 1894 his position slowly weakened. Alexander III was sometimes called Alexander the Peacemaker, because he never took Russia into war. It was Alexander the Peacemaker, however, who laid the foundations for the Romanovs' two final and disastrous wars; by moving from friendship with Germany to friendship with France he sowed the seeds of August 1914, and by seconding Witte's Far Eastern ventures he put Russia on the rails which led to the disastrous war against Japan.

What became known as the 'Witte System' was Witte's attempt to transform Russia into an industrialised state on the western model. Like the Soviet governments which later pursued the same aim, he relied heavily on crippling taxation of the peasantry, but he also resorted to an inflow of capital from foreign investors and to the creation of a market in the Far East for the goods which his new industries would produce. While Witte was very successful in his industrialisation, achieving growth rates which match those of Stalin's five-year plans, each strand of his policy brought trouble: peasant revolts, loss of independence because of the need to please foreign investors, and conflict with Japan. When Witte was dismissed from the ministry of finance in 1903 he blamed intriguers, but basically the cause of his dismissal was that his 'System', at a time when its achievement was not quite evident, had brought difficulties which were all-too-evident.[3]

One of the ways in which Witte anticipated his communist successors was his creation of what was virtually a planned economy in Siberia.[4] With his Trans-Siberian Railway as the key element, a careful scheme of development was drawn up and applied, with entire new townships created by planners and built with state funds. But Siberia, important though it was for absorbing surplus population and for supplying European Russia with food and materials, was only part of Russia's eastern policy, a policy which led one American financier to describe Witte as the Cecil Rhodes of the East.

✗ In 1860 China's weakness had enabled Russia to obtain, by treaty, Chinese territory on the Pacific, which became the Maritime Province. Here the naval base of Vladivostok was built and here the Russian Empire found itself adjacent to Korea. With this acquisition Russia was well-set to expand her influence, and perhaps her territory, into the Chinese Empire. With the accession of Alexander III and the ascendancy of Witte this expanion became an accepted policy; the creation of a new Russian navy and of the Trans Siberian Railway (begun in 1891) may be regarded as the two arms of a pincer movement designed to close around those two weakly-held Chinese territories, Manchuria and Korea.

Witte's motives were commercial. His critics condemned his imitation of western models but this did not deter him. He had seen how the Canadian Pacific Railway had bound British Columbia to the British Empire. He had seen how the Suez Canal had not only brought India closer to London, but had facilitated European commerce with China, and he feared that, unless Russia acted, western trade and influence would spread northwards through China right up to the Russian border. He saw no reason why Russian ships from the Black Sea should not trade via Suez with China alongside the freighters of other countries, and it was not long before his ministry of finance was operating a sizable merchant navy (the 'Volunteer Fleet') in those waters. He also believed that since British tea from India had ruined the China tea market, the Chinese would be glad to use the new Trans Siberian Railway to transport their tea to Europe, where it might re-establish itself at the expense of the British.

For Alexander and many Russians, however, commerce was not the main object. They had loftier motives. In the 1880s a famous Russian explorer, Przhevalski, had popularised the idea that many peoples on the Chinese side of the Russo–Chinese frontier would be only too glad 'to become subjects of the White Tsar whose name seems in the eyes of the Asian masses to be encircled by a halo of mystery and power, just like that of the Dalai Lama'. Przhevalski was probably right, even though those peoples regarded the Russians simply as the lesser of two evils. At about the same period several professors were advancing the theory that Russians, because they were partly Asian anyway, could expand in Asia as liberators, not merely as conquerors. As one St Petersburg professor said, it would be 'a crime before humanity if we renounced our sacred duties and refused to aid the oppressed' by expanding into Chinese territory. Striking a different chord, the celebrated Russian Christian philosopher Soloviev was not alone when he claimed that Russia should advance in Asia in order to defend Europe against 'yellow power', and that if inferior races refused to submit to superior they must simply disappear from the face of the earth.[5] Witte, though certainly an 'easterner', was not enthusiastic about the concept of inferior yellow races. He was in fact one of the least race-conscious of Russian officials, and his marriage to a Jewess and his sympathy towards Jews in Russia made him many enemies. Nevertheless he was not averse, sometimes, to using racial arguments; knowing the Tsar's strong opinions he spiced his reports on occasion with phrases about Russia being 'a bulwark against the sea of the yellow race.'

Another well-known and notoriously uninhibited figure had no hesitation in appealing to Nicholas II's racial instincts. Kaiser Wilhelm combined sincerity with self-interest when he wrote to his cousin 'Nicky' about Russia's divine mission 'to defend Europe from the inroads of the Great Yellow Race . . . in the Defence of the Cross and the old Christian European culture . . .'. This was sincere advice, because 'Willy' really believed in the Yellow Peril. It was also self-interested, because deployment of the huge Russian army towards the East would have been a dream-come-true for the German general staff. Wilhelm's notorious 1902 telegram to Nicholas, 'The Admiral of the Atlantic salutes the Admiral of the Pacific', was one of several calculated moves designed to turn Nicholas's attention towards the East; the Kaiser well knew the value of flattery. But even though Nicholas was unaware that the Kaiser was simultaneously warning Washington of Russian designs in the East, he probably paid less attention to Wilhelm's advice than some historians have assumed. On the other hand, the Kaiser's implicit assurance that Germany would not threaten Russia's rear while Nicholas was engaged in his holy mission against the yellow hordes removed one argument which might have been raised against Russia's involvement in Asia.

While Russia was strengthening her position in Siberia and the Maritime Province, Japan was entrenching herself in Korean affairs. Korea was a Chinese vassal state, although in practice Peking was too weak to enforce its authority. In the 1870 many influential Japanese had wanted to invade, but in 1876 Tokyo instead made a treaty with Korea; such a treaty at least implied that Japan regarded Korea as independent of China. Cultural links led eventually to the maturing of a class of young Japanese-educated Koreans who favoured reform, modernisation, a break with China and closer ties with Japan. But the growing pro-Japan trend provoked a revolt in the capital, Seoul, and the inmates of the Japanese legation had to fight their way to safety at Seoul's port at Chemulpo, and it was Chinese troops that came to restore order. In the 1880s Korea signed commercial treaties with all the major western powers. These established missions in Seoul which, from time to time, were 'protected' by foreign warships stationed at Chemulpo. Another measure to reduce Japanese influence, an invitation to Russia to train the Korean army and to establish a Russian naval base in Korea, came to nothing because of Britain's strong opposition to strengthening Russia's position in the Far East. In 1884 a new revolt, this time instigated by 'reformers', captured the king and tried to reintroduce close cooperation with Japan. However, the Chinese garrison in Seoul recaptured the king. There were more anti-foreigner riots, Japanese and Chinese troops entered Korea, but a treaty between China and Japan averted war.

In 1894 another anti-foreign revolt broke out in Korea and the Korean government asked for Chinese troops. By this time the Japanese army and navy were more fully developed, and the Japanese government decided that the time had come to fight China for dominance in Korea. So Japan sent her own troops into Korea, and demanded that the Korean government should declare its independence from China. In the ensuing war Japan thoroughly worsted the Chinese forces; in the naval victory in the Yalu estuary, and in the storming of Port Arthur, Japanese officers gained valuable experience that would stand them in good stead when they fought Russia ten years later.

This Sino-Japanese War of 1894–5 came at a time when Japan was in its most imitative period. Indeed, its concern with overseas expansion can be partly explained by its compulsive desire to do what the western powers had done. In its conduct of the war against China it imitated in several ways the conduct of the Prussians against France in 1871–2. This was especially evident in the treaty which Tokyo imposed on the defeated Chinese. Not only did Japan demand a free hand in Korea, plus the cession of Formosa and the Liaotung Peninsula, but also a sizable indemnity.

The Liaotung Peninsula is a southern extremity of Manchuria, projecting into the Yellow Sea. On it stood Port Arthur, a fortified harbour through which much of Manchurian trade was chanelled. The Japanese acquisition of Port Arthur would seriously threaten Russian ambitions in Manchuria. But other powers were anxious about Japan's threat to their influence in China, and St Petersburg was able to persuade France and Germany to join with her in presenting Tokyo with what was virtually an ultimatum. Although Britain, which was already viewing Japan as a potential ally against Russia, did not subscribe to the move, this 'Triple Intervention' was sufficient to persuade Japan to relinquish her demand for the Liaotung Peninsula, and hence for Port Arthur. Ordinary Japanese resented this surrender of what they regarded as a rightful reward for their heroism and self-sacrifice, but for the time being they vented their wrath against their ministers and stored up their resentment against the Russians.

As time passed, it seemed to the Japanese that the main beneficiary of their victorious David-and-Goliath struggle against China was not Japan, but Russia. Witte had not been slow to take advantage of the new situation that seemed, superficially, to be so advantageous for Japan. Tokyo's stern demands on China gave Russia the opportunity to act as China's friend. The massive war indemnity, which the hapless Chinese government had somehow to find, was provided by Russia (in fact the funds were French, but Russia arranged the transaction). In exchange, China allowed Russia to lay the eastern section of the Trans Siberian Railway through Manchuria. The reduction of that railway's length by about 400 miles was not the only advantage that Witte thereby obtained. In order to house the railway workers, Russian settlements were founded across Manchuria and at Harbin, the main railway town, a Russian city was established which remained a thriving Russian community right up to 1949. As protection against bandits, railway protection troops were permitted to live along the belt of land allotted to the railway. These troops, sardonically termed 'Matilda's guards' by Witte's enemies (Matilda being Witte's wife), were controlled by Witte's ministry of finance. To conceal the truth that a strip of Chinese territory had in effect been handed over to the Russian government, a private company was established as the ostensible owner of the line. Although this company, the Chinese Eastern Railway (CER), had an office in Paris, the true power behind the line was Witte and his ministry. Its managing director was a colonel, who also commanded the railway troops. Russia could now dominate the trade of the region and possessed the most effective local military force. And all this had been achieved in the territory of the Chinese Empire without recourse to threats or violence; the brute force needed for this advance had been supplied by the Japanese.

The CER was linked with another of Witte's powerful establishments, the Russo–Chinese Bank. This, again, was ostensibly a Franco-Russian company but in reality an instrument with which Witte intended to monopolise Manchurian finance. Its managing director was Prince Esper Ukhtomski, an 'easterner' trusted by both Nicholas and Witte. Finally, in 1896, when China's leading statesman was in St Petersburg for Nicholas's coronation, a Russo–Chinese treaty cemented the new relationship. This treaty virtually made Russia the guarantor of China's territorial integrity. Against whom this treaty was directed was clear to all literate Japanese, whose resentment of Russia intensified in consequence.

As a result of the unique Japanese political system, foreign relations were affected by several influences.[6] Nominally the making of treaties and the declaring of war were the prerogatives of the Emperor, but in practice such decisions were reached by the Emperor's advisers. The popularly-elected western-style Diet had little direct say in foreign affairs, although it was increasingly important in domestic matters. The Emperor's advisers included the elder statesmen, mainly high military and officers from leading clans who, after backing the winning side in the troubles of the 1860s and 1870s, had become the Emperor's trusted executives until advancing years limited them to an advisory but very powerful role. Rivalling and slowly replacing the elder statesmen were the cabinet ministers, largely men of a younger generation but still mainly confined to members of a few major clans. Then there were the military and naval chiefs of staff, and the ministers of the army and of the navy, all of whom reported directly to the Emperor. Finally there were the privy councillors appointed by the Emperor.

Thus there was a variety of people who could advise the Emperor, but this variety was misleading because almost all the influential voices belonged to an oligarchy of men of similar high birth, men who had started life in the Samurai tradition as members of powerful clans. For intelligent men born outside this circle, only the unlikely patronage of a well-born superior could open the door to real influence. For the most part such men tended to form the opposition to the government, practising careers in fields like journalism, university teaching and the professions. They were the mainstay of the political parties, and some participated in the Diet. But the Diet was excluded from foreign affairs and tended to be uninformed, or misinformed, because the government refused to share its information. However, the Diet was not entirely powerless in external policy; the government needed its goodwill and, after all, the Diet politicians did in a loose sense represent the Japanese people who had elected them. Clearly, the Japanese man-in-the-street had a choice of scapegoats whom he could blame for Japan's failure to gather all the fruits of victory after the war against China. The one person who was never blamed was the Emperor, a personage whom the Japanese people had been deliberately schooled to regard as a divine figure.

In 1896 the Japanese patriotic press had yet another cause for wrath; evidently the government had failed even in Korea. Following the defeat of China, Japan had seemed strong in Korea, but the arrogant behaviour of her diplomats and soldiers there had aroused strong opposition. The Japanese representative in Korea, feeling that it was the queen who was the inspiration of the anti-Japan movement, hired professional thugs who successfully decapitated that lady. Her widowed husband, the king, was then held in his palace and forced to issue a pro-Japanese statement. But the Russian diplomats in Seoul excelled themselves in this crisis. One dark night, huddled behind a woman sitting in a lady's traveling chair, the king slipped out of his palace and took refuge in the Russian legation. From here he issued a proclamation inviting his loyal subjects to decapitate the leaders of the pro-Japan faction and to deliver the heads to him, care of the Russian minister. Realising that they were beaten for the time being, the Japanese soon agreed with the Russians that the king should go back to his palace, that the Japanese thugs should be controlled, and that both countries should limit the armed forces that they kept in Korea as legation guards.

All this was very satisfying for Witte. In time, he believed, Russia would dominate not only Manchuria but Korea as well. The only danger was that things would come to a head before he was ready. This in fact happened in 1897, when two German missionaries were murdered in China. The Kaiser used this as a pretext to occupy Kiaochow, and this in turn persuaded the French and British governments to stage their own march-ins. But in this episode Russia once more profited most. Abandoning her chosen role as China's best friend, she forced the Peking government to lease her the Liaotung Peninsula with Port Arthur, and to concede the right to build a branch of the CER southwards from Harbin to Port Arthur. Witte opposed this advance. He believed it to be premature, and also realised that the transformation of Port Arthur into a Russian naval base would bring the Russian army and navy into Manchura; once the war ministry was involved, Witte's ministry of finance would lose its monopoly of power and influence in Manchuria. The certainty that the seizure of Port Arthur would enrage the Japanese, who had been forced to reliquish it after the Sino–Japanese War, did not at this time worry many Russians.

That the Tsar should overrule Witte and take Port Arthur was one of the earliest portents that Witte's influence was on the decline. The appearance in St Petersburg of entrepreneurial groups favouring a bolder policy was another sign. Notable among these groups was the so-called Bezobrazov clique. Bezobrazov is typically called an adventurer by subsequent historians, but in fact he was simply an enthusiast who became temporary spokesman for a group of prominent Russians who advocated a bold Far Eastern policy. They argued, perhaps correctly, that it was better to risk war with Japan than to delay too long the consolidation of Russia's potential gains in the East. They were especially hostile to an agreement reached in 1898 between Japan and Russia, which implied that at least for the time being Japan should have a free hand in Korea while Russia should have a free hand in Manchuria. They believed that Russia, if only to protect her gains in Manchuria, had also to be strong in adjoining Korea. The navy, too, was anxious to establish a base on the coast of Korea facing Japan. Mosampo, near Fusan, was the favoured location. Without such a base, said the admirals, Port Arthur was useless because the Japanese could dominate the sea route connecting that port with the second dockyard at Vladivostok. The concession that the Japanese had obtained to build a railway from Fusan to Seoul was regarded with great suspicion, and this anxiety was only partly mollified when the French builders of a railway northwards from Seoul into Manchuria were persuaded to adopt the Russian 5ft gauge. There was already talk of dividing Korea into a north under Russian influence and a south under Japanese. The 39th Parallel was regarded as the logical dividing line, just as it would be in 1945.

✶ The Japanese government, ever since the humiliation of 1895, had been deliberately preparing for an eventual war with Russia. At the end of that year an expensive rearmament plan was adopted that was largely financed by the funds which Russia had raised to pay off China's war indemnity. But the Japanese leaders could not agree on whether Japan should fight soon, or later. Meanwhile, in 1900, yet another upheaval in China upset the status quo on which Russian and Japanese policies both relied.

✶This upheaval was the Boxer Rebellion. Instigated by a secret society, the revolt was directly against foreigners in China. Although the Chinese government ostensibly stood on the side of law and order, in practice its officials encouraged the Boxers. There were a number of incidents on the border with Russia; Cossacks massacred the too-trusting Chinese inhabitants of the Russian town of Blagoveschensk, and Chinese troops shelled the CER. An international operation was launched to relieve the foreign legations in Peking, besieged by the rebels. Because of her common frontier with China, Russia took a leading role in this operation. When the European and Japanese forces reached Peking, it was the Russians who took the initiative in entering the capital. Led by General Linievich, the Russians approached quietly one night, bayonetted the sleeping Chinese sentries outside the walls, and then brought up two guns to batter down the gates. A lucky shot eventually sprang the bolt of these, and the Russians fought their way in.[7] The Japanese, not relishing the Russian monopoly of glory, by the next morning had launched their own attack on one of the other gates. The Americans arrived two hours after the Japanese, but instead of assaulting the gates which had been assigned to them they asked the Russian gunners to make a convenient breach in the walls. This done, the Americans rushed in, but met no opposition. They then wished to hoist their flag on the wall, but found all suitable spots already occupied by Russian flags, and were last seen by the Russians trudging off, still in search of a fitting location for the Stars and Stripes. Meanwhile, the Russian and Japanese forces were encountering stiff resistance inside the city walls. While they were overcoming this, at the price of many casualties, the British, who had not hitherto been very active, sneaked into the city by way of a dry riverbed and, unnoticed and unharmed, reached the British legation.

Thus it was not the weary Russians or Japanese who had the glory of first reaching the legations, but British officers and Indians soldiers.

In their campaign against rebellious Chinese troops in Manchuria, the Russians had won easy victories, and it was not surprising that they became convinced that one Russian soldier was worth ten orientals. Over the next few years, therefore, Russian officers had little fear of the Japanese army. At Peking they had been so impressed by their own exploits that they failed to notice that one breed of oriental, the Japanese, produced soldiers far smarter and more effective than those of the Chinese. There was an additional factor that invalidated the Russian belief in their superiority; in the Boxer campaign the Russian soldiers, inspired by thoughts of white Christians being butchered by Chinese rebels, fought bravely, willingly and energetically. In a war against Japan they were unlikely to have this incentive, especially if the war was fought for the terrority of Manchuria or Korea, territory that had no attraction for the ordinary Russian.

The intervening governments agreed that, with the Boxers crushed and the Chinese government secure, their armies could withdraw. The foreign troops were in any case already indulging in atrocities. Probably the Russian troops behaved no worse than those of their allies.[8] Even during the savage fighting in Manchuria, eyewitnesses had reported how the Tsar's soldiers had taken great trouble to protect christianised Chinese. Early in 1901 the Russians were distributing food and clothing to the Chinese needy, while Russian officers made collections in aid of the poor in their garrison towns. However, the world did not wish to notice these things in 1901, when it had a much bigger preoccupation: the Russians, it seemed, were not going to evacuate Manchuria after all.

In 1900 the Russian government had had no intention of keeping its army in Manchuria, but within a few months, spurred by the urgings of Bezobrazov and his circle, Russian Far Eastern policy was in a turmoil from which it did not emerge with clear-cut goals until 1902, if then.[9] Even without the intervention of rivals, Witte's policies would have been undermined at this period, for both the Witte System as a whole, and his Far Eastern enterprises in particular, were passing through a difficult period. In the Russian economy, a depression coincided with what seemed to be an upsurge of peasant discontent. In Siberia and the Far East the casual observer might have thought that Witte was still running an empire within an empire, but in reality he was on the defensive. Nicholas II had never really

liked him and was becoming more self-assured (or, as Witte expressed it, fell more completely under the sway of intriguers). Second, the
powerful war ministry, now that its troops were in Manchuria, had a
growing voice in Far Eastern affairs. Third and more fundamentally,
Witte's policy suffered from internal contradictions that were becoming more evident. Because Russian industry was not competitive with
western industry, both in terms of prices and enterprise, the only way
by which Manchuria could become a market for Russia was the
raising of artificial barriers against the trade of other countries. But if
this were done, there would be an immediate decline of commercial
activity because Russian trade was not ready to fill the gap. Such a
decline would reduce the traffic of the CER, which was already
hopelessly unprofitable. Witte had earlier promised that the CER
would bring in great profits, but it was now a serious drain on the
Treasury. What Witte wanted was to secure, slowly, a monopolistic
position for Russian trade in Manchuria, preferably by signing
exclusive trade agreements with China. Eventually with government
encouragement, Russian trade might establish itself firmly. However,
all this required time and a compliant Chinese government, and
because of the opposition of other trading nations Witte was unlikely
to enjoy either of these prerequisites.

Britain and America in particular were opposed to a Russian
monopoly in Manchuria. Confident in the competitiveness of their
own commerce, they demanded the 'open door' for trade. Japan,
whose long-term aim was to impose her own monopoly in Manchuria,
took care to give the impression that she, too, was for the open door.
Although at times even Russian diplomats expressly approved the
principle of the open door, in private they sometimes acknowledged
the true facts. In 1913, for example, the British ambassador to Russia
reported to the foreign secretary that the Russian ambassador to
Britain had appealed to him not to be too hard in the matter of
tariffs, because it was obvious that Russian goods could not compete
with British in a free market.[10]

Apart from foreign suspicion, Witte faced criticism at home. His
CER was even criticised because, it was said, it was bringing masses
of Chinese settlers into the Maritime Province, where they would
soon submerge the local Russians. More serious were the successes of
the Bezobrazov group. After several false starts this group had set up
its East Asian Development Company. Bezobrazov had frankly
described this company as modelled on that of the old British East
India Company, and its aim was to exploit a concession in north

Korea, just south of the river Yalu which divided Korea from Manchuria. The concession involved an extensive belt of timberland, but although some profit was expected from woodcutting, the main object was not commercial. The Bezobrazov group, unlike Witte, believed that Russia should move quickly and decisively, that Japan was too weak to oppose Russia by force in Korea, and that if Russia did not exert herself in that kingdom, then Japan would. Moreover, said Bezobrazov and his friends, Korea was essential for the security of Manchuria; if Japan took Korea, sooner or later she would have Manchuria too. Conversely, a Russian presence in the area of the timber concession could be a foothold for a further advance, with the aim of eventually annexing all of Korea. If this were done, it was claimed, Japan would never be able to rival Russia but would be condemned to remain as she had always been, a mere string of Pacific islands. It was not surprising that among the influential proponents of the Bezobrazov scheme was a contingent of admirals.

By 1902 Witte was able to force the dissolution of the East Asian Development Company, an organisation over which he had no control and which had already made serious inroads into his monopoly of commercial power. He replaced it with his own Manchurian Mining Company. But this was almost his last success; he was on the defensive and would be dismissed in 1903. Nicholas II was already impressed by the claims of the Bezobrazov group. Bezobrazov himself, who until this time was only the spokesman of the group, was given the rank of state secretary to provide the status he needed (until then, he had been merely a retired guards officer).

Nicholas's indecision, about whether or not to abandon Witte's cautious Far Eastern policy, was connected with the pressing short-term problem of whether or not to withdraw Russian troops from Manchuria. When the Boxer Rebellion ended, Russia had close to 200 000 troops in Manchuria and China. At first, Nicholas intended to withdraw these troops in conformity with the intentions of the intervening powers, but he was persuaded to think twice about this. From China proper the Russian troops did depart on schedule, but there was a genuine problem with the withdrawal from Manchuria. The CER had been badly damaged in the campaign, and its vulnerability was now obvious. In Manchuria the bandit gangs had grown during the rebellion and, moreover, there were bands of disaffected Chinese troops still roaming about the countryside. A Russian withdrawal would therefore risk further damage to the railway. Not only would Russian lives be in danger, but also those of the native population. Although at the time most of the British and American press ridiculed the Russian claim that the local Chinese wanted the Russians to stay, this claim was probably true. Privately, but only privately, even the Japanese government acknowledged that Russian troops might be needed in Manchuria for some years.

In 1901 the temptation of using its military presence in Manchuria as a threat was too much for the Russian government. It tried to persuade Peking to sign an agreement giving Russia exclusive trading rights in certain key Manchurian centres; unless the Chinese signed, Russian troops would stay. The Chinese government quietly appealed to other powers for support, and in consequence the Russian proposal came to nothing. In 1902, feeling isolated in a hostile world, St Petersburg acted in a way that only provided its critics with ammunition. Instead of saying frankly that Russian troops would stay in Manchuria as long as they were needed, the Russians announced a timetable for their withdrawal by stages, a withdrawal that was scheduled to be completed by 8 October 1903. When the dates set for the second and the final stages passed without any movement of troops, Russia's position was hard to defend.

In 1902 and 1903 the Russian government held several conferences to evolve an agreed policy. Represented at these conferences were the ministries of finance, foreign affairs and war, together with a number of important individuals. The latter included some members of the Bezobrazov group. Witte was no longer in a position to lay down policy, even though at first he still had an influential voice. Gradually the proponents of a more aggressive policy overcame the cautious officials, and in 1903 Witte was dismissed. This came as rather a shock to the once all-powerful minister, but it enabled him years later to claim that it was not his fault that in 1904 Russia entered a war against Japan.

Russia had become more and more isolated. Japan, realising that her quarrel with Russia had no hope of success unless the other powers were on her side, or at least benevolently neutral, played her cards carefully. Her most significant diplomatic success was the signing of the Anglo–Japanese Alliance in 1902. This was the first alliance which Japan had ever signed with a major power, and it had a great moral effect among the Japanese, too. For the British, the Anglo–Japanese Alliance came as a welcome sharing of burdens, and as a useful stroke against Russia.

For decades Russia and Britain had regarded each other as inevitably hostile. The press of the two countries, and hence popular opinion, reflected this hostility; in the British press and Parliament 'Russian scares' were as frequent in the nineteenth century as 'red scares' would be in the twentieth. These fears were partly justifiable, but were inflamed by those politicians and newspaper owners who thought they could profit from them. Some newspapers even hinted that Russia had instigated the Boxer Rebellion so that she might benefit from it. British credulity reached perhaps its peak when the Admiralty, persuaded that a Russian invasion fleet was about to set sail for Australia, sent an ironclad to Melbourne (where she has remained ever since). But whereas Australia was never threatened by the tsars, the alleged Russian threat to India was more serious. A Russian invasion through the Himalayas was not envisaged, but there were army officers who, in the cafés of St Petersburg, would talk of such projects in the earshot of journalists. Russia's expansion into Central Asia did bring the Russian army closer to India, and at least one prominent Russian, the celebrated General Skobolev, advocated continuing pressure there to make Britain more amenable to Russian requirements in the Balkans.

Towards the end of the century Russian expansion in the Far East had brought another area of conflict; Britain had developed extensive trade with China, wished to develop it still further, and was worried by Russian ambitions. Russia, after all, had the advantage of a common frontier with China, and a railway too. It seemed to the British government that the best check to Russian ambitions in the East was a strong Japan. From the British side the Anglo–Japanese Alliance seemed to promise that Japan would, in the Kaiser's sardonic words, act as Britain's soldier in the East. While the claim of Russian historians that the Alliance was deliberately intended to push Japan into war against Russia for the benefit of Britain is unconvincing, the Alliance certainly was an important factor enabling Japan to make war at a time of her own choosing.

The main terms of the treaty included a recognition that Japan had a special interest in Korea, and the promise that if either of the signatories were at war with two or more other powers, the other would come to its assistance. These terms meant that in 1914 Japan would declare war against Germany and Austria. More immediately, they meant that in a Russo–Japanese conflict Russia's friend, France, could not come to the aid of the Tsar without in turn finding herself at war with Britain. As things turned out, in 1904 the treaty did confine the Russo–Japanese War to just two belligerents, which was what both Russia and Japan preferred; the intervention of other powers would have threatened the monopoly position that each intended to occupy in Korea and Manchuria after the war.

The treaty was the result of secret negotiations in London. When it was revealed to the British Parliament there was some anxiety expressed by the Liberals, who suggested that it might involve Britain in a war which basically had no relevance to her interests. But as all politicians realised that the treaty was implicitly aimed at Russia, and as all good Liberals would accept anything directed against the Russian autocracy, misgivings never grew into opposition.

The position of the USA was equally important to Japan. The Japanese government realised that America would hardly go to war over Manchuria, and that America had no territorial ambitions in the region (the American plate was already full with the rebellious Philippines). But the USA was very sensitive to any attempts to close that 'open door' which she regarded as so important for her economy. Exploiting this situation, and aided by the repulsion felt by the American public at the concurrent *pogroms* which the Russian administration was inflicting on Russian Jews, Tokyo persuaded Washington to join her in a commercial treaty with China. The essence of this treaty was that China promised Japan and the USA that three major towns in Manchuria would be open to the commerce of all nations; thus it would be difficult, if not impossible, for Russia subsequently to persuade China to close Manchuria to all except Russian trade. The treaty was pointedly signed on 8 October 1903, the date by which the Russians had promised to complete their evacuation of Manchuria. On that same day, again deliberately, the Russians held a massive military parade in Port Arthur. Meanwhile the Japanese socialists, not the most bloodthirsty of Japanese parties, chose 8 October to protest noisily against the continued Russian occupation of Manchuria and to ask what their government was going to do about it.

The anti-Russian excitement in Japan during October 1903 was only a phase in a campaign that had its beginnings in 1895 when Russia 'robbed' Japan of Port Arthur. In 1900 the People's League had been founded to persuade the government to do something about Russian intentions in Korea. By means of meetings, pamphlets and demonstrations this association did much to arouse popular feeling. In April 1903 the People's League was renamed the Comrades' Society for a Strong Foreign Policy. Later the same year it hoisted its true colours, renaming itself the Anti-Russia Comrades' Society. At a more sophisticated level, patriotic professors published learned pamphlets to influence the Japanese policy-makers. Just as Russian proponents of a strong line were arguing that Russia would never be safe in Manchuria if Japan was entrenched in Korea, so the Japanese professors and their friends argued that Korea would only be safe for Japanese exploitation if Russia was kept out of Manchuria. Both views, of course, were correct; the Russo–Japanese War was an inevitable war, because neither of the two governments had the moral strength, or even desire, to draw back from its expansionist aims. While Russian publicists were talking of Russia's civilising mission in the East, a mission she could not abandon without losing her honour, Japanese publicists were convincing their audiences that Russia in Korea would sooner or later mean Russia in Japan, and that in any case Japan's rising population could only be accommodated on the mainland.

In 1901 the Amur River Society was found by a Japanese national-ist who, having visited Russia several times, believed that the Russian Empire was corrupt and easily defeatable. The aims of the Society were to propagate Japan's own civilising mission: that is, to check the western powers, to fight Russia and defeat her, and then to establish a Japanese economic sphere embracing Manchuria, Mongolia, Korea and Siberia. Some of the Society's members were basically friendly to Russia, but acknowledged that Japan could establish friendly and fruitful relations with her only after defeating her in war. The founder of the Society concurrently founded a Japan-Russia society to develop friendly relations after the hoped-for war had been won. However, the Tokyo language school which the Society established to teach the Chinese and Russian languages was not designed for post-war friendship, but to supply the spies and interpreters who would be needed in wartime.

Most of the Japanese senior officers regarded war as inevitable, and felt that it should be started immediately, while Russia was still relatively weak in the Far East. But the army chief of staff, Oyama, was not in favour of war, and reminded those who tried to change his mind that Russia was a very powerful nation. As for the navy minister, Admiral Yamamoto, he was regarded with contempt by the activists, who felt he was impossibly soft. When he was confronted with the Korea-as-a-dagger-pointed-at-Japan argument, Yamamoto retorted that Russia would never be able to land an army in Japan. This infuriated his critics, partly because it was an unfashionable truth and partly because it came from the person best qualified to make such a judgement. It was in order to change the minds of men like Oyama and Yamamoto that the more aggressive officers joined with like-minded officials of the foreign ministry to found the Kogetsukai, an alliance which took its name from the restaurant in whose pantry the first secret meeting was held. The participants worked to put their point of view before their superiors at every possible opportunity. In the event, although both Oyama and Yamamoto continued to have doubts, once the decision was made for war they responded energetically, Oyama being among those who advocated an early start of hostilities.

Negotiations with Russia had started in 1901, but when the senior Japanese negotiator arrived in St Petersburg he found the Russians unwilling to get down to business. In the two following years Japanese proposals were kept for months without reply, and the replies which did come seemed designed to promote further delay. This behaviour was really only a sign that the Russian government was uncertain how to handle the situation, but viewed from Japan it seemed like prevarication, especially as the Russian troops were sitting tight in Manchuria. At first there had been those on both sides who thought there might be a compromise, with Japan being acknowledged as supreme in Korea and Russia in Manchuria. But too many influential Russians and Japanese opposed such a compromise. Even those who wanted peace acknowledged privately that such a peace could only be temporary.

Several additional factors worked against the cause of peace. The Japanese foreign minister, Komura, ever since his days as Japanese minister in St Petersburg, had been convinced that war with Russia was both inevitable and desirable. It was he who had been largely responsible for obtaining the Anglo-Japanese Alliance, making it so much easier for Japan to go to war against Russia. On the Russian side, an obstacle to peace was introduced when negotiations were at a critical stage. Nicholas created the Viceroyalty of the Far East; Admiral Alekseev, the local commander in chief, became Viceroy and henceforth, said the Russians, the talks with Japan would be conducted through the Viceroy at Port Arthur. Although some diplomats were attached to the Admiral's staff, Alekseev was not the best man to conduct negotiations; he had long regarded war as inevitable, and the sooner the better. The transfer of the negotiations from St Petersburg to Port Arthur also reinforced the suspicions of the Japanese, for it seemed to downgrade the talks while at the same time emphasising the permanence of the Russian presence in Port Arthur. In reality the main purpose of the Viceroyalty was the coordination of Russian policy, which since the decline of Witte's private empire had been split confusedly between several ministries and the Tsar's advisers.

In June 1903 the Russian minister of war, General Kuropatkin, made an official visit to Japan. This was portrayed as a peace mission, but in reality was more in the nature of a reconnaissance. He arrived in June, and was housed in a Tokyo palace. He was received not only by the prime minister and the foreign minister, but also by the imperial family. From the cordial dinners, military reviews, and other ceremonies which he attended it would have been hard to realise that both he and his hosts were contemplating war against each other. For the optimists, a compromise still seemed possible, but in his conversations with Komura it was evident that neither side could give way on the basic issue dividing them, the question of Manchuria and Korea. They agreed, though, that a war would be undesirable, not because wars were bad but because a war might involve other powers and lead to a carve-up of the Chinese Empire; they wanted not a grand carve-up, but a cautious vivisection. In personal attendance on Kuropatkin during his visit was Colonel Tanaka Giichi. Tanaka had been a military attaché in St Petersburg and, an enthusiastic proponent of immediate war with Russia, had falsified the figures which he sent to Tokyo about the carrying capacity of the Trans-Siberian Railway; he had felt that his superiors would be more aggressive if told that the railway was hardly able to maintain the existing Manchurian forces. Tanaka was obviously a man with a future, and he did in fact become prime minister in the 1920s.

Kuropatkin returned to St Petersburg quite impressed with the state of the Japanese army. He had never been in favour of war, and at one time had urged that Russia should content herself with just the northern part of Manchuria. However, after his visit he reported that war was unlikely provided Russia took care not to intervene in Korea, about which Japan was highly sensitive. Unfortunately his visit coincided with renewed Russian interest in Korean timber. In June the irrepressible Bezobrazov was involved in a newly-formed Russian Far Eastern Lumber Company. Already, in April, Russian foresters and settlers had been observed along the banks of the Yalu in the area of the Russian timber concession. Significantly, Witte in his last months of power had approved this new company, which was correctly regarded by the Japanese as an agent of the Russian government. The Japanese did not know that the Company had been allowed to protect its concession with reservist detachments dressed as forestry workers, but they were aware that there was now some kind of Russian military presence in northern Korea.

In 1903 both sides knew that Japan's armed strength was approaching its peak, whereas Russian strength in the Far East would grow more slowly. Hence Russian aims would be furthered by a postponement of the showdown with Japan, whereas for the Japanese the shrill now-or-never urgings of the patriotic societies had an ever-wider appeal. These pressure groups, together with the majority of newspapers, had succeeded in creating an intensely aggressive public opinion. Thanks to Japan's system of state education, which perhaps better than any other country's had trained new generations to use their brains but not to ask awkward questions, the Japanese masses were literate enough to respond to patriotic propaganda. From this they had absorbed that peculiar Japanese patriotism which assumed that loyalty simply means fighting against a foreign country. The Japanese public was devoted to its Emperor, and was prepared for sacrifice in the cause of a greater Japan. Compared to the Russian public, the Japanese were much more receptive to expansionist propaganda. They had been made aware of their Emperor's vulnerability to bad advisers and they had been persuaded that a Russian triumph in Korea would mean not only an end to prosperity but also a threat to Japanese independence; hence by the end of 1903 they were almost unanimously demanding war. That the expected victory would bring not only glory and security, but also the riches of an indemnity and of a conquered territory, was also not far from their minds. The peace movement, centred on socialists and Christians, was so weak that even after the war started the government found no need to take drastic action against it. On the Japanese side, therefore, the Russo-Japanese War would belong to a category hardly recognised by modern historians, that of the people's imperialist war.

In December 1903 the latest Russian counterproposals still excluded Manchuria as a subject for discussion, while containing unacceptable Russian conditions for Japanese activity in Korea. The Japanese government decided at this point that war must be regarded as inevitable and any further negotiations should be merely to gain time. Foreign observers in Tokyo believed that if the government made concessions to Russia the war-fever of the population would explode into riots and even perhaps civil war. One newspaper, regarded as pro-government, had warned that if the government seemed to be making further concessions Japan would resemble a broken hive of angry bees. In December the Diet convened to hear the usual message from the Emperor. The Speaker, instead of reading the reply to the throne which had been prepared for him, pulled out of his pocket a reply of his own composition and read it to the house. Parliamentarians being Parliamentarians, most dozed through this peroration and then voted their approval without realising that it was an appeal to the Emperor to be more watchful in his relations with his obviously incompetent government. To prevent this reply reaching the Emperor, the government hastily dissolved the Diet and thereby also freed itself from Parliamentary criticism in the final weeks before the outbreak of war.

In the first week of February 1904 the chief of staff, Oyama, told the Emperor that it was essential for Japan to strike first. An imperial conference was summoned on 4 February to hear the opinions of the Emperor's various advisers. These indicated that because of her limited population and financial resources, Japan would stand a doubtful chance in a war against Russia, Oyama thought that there was only 50–50 chance of military victory, while the navy thought that it might master the Russian Pacific squadron, but only at the cost of losing at least half its ships. Nevertheless, it was decided that war was the only possible choice; negotiations were leading nowhere, the Russians seemed determined to have Korea sooner or later, and it was considered that Russia in Korea would threaten Japan herself (Yamamoto, irritatingly level-headed, expressed his doubts about Russia's capacity to invade Japan, but he made little impression). All agreed that the war would need to be short, because Russia with her vast resources could always win a long war. A defeat was not regarded as unlikely, but was considered as something less than the end of the world; at worst, Japan might lose Formosa and be forced to pay a war indemnity, but she would survive and after 100 years could tackle Russia once again. Because of the crucial fact that only a short war could bring victory, and that a long war would be disastrous, peace-making preparations were made simultaneously with war preparations. Among other moves, an old Harvard acquaintance of the US President was despatched to cultivate good relations in the USA, for that republic would be useful as a go-between in starting peace negotiations when Japan approached the end of her resources.

Meanwhile, on 3 February, new Russian counterproposals had been sent from St Petersburg, via Admiral Alekseev, to Tokyo. It has been alleged that the Japanese telegraph service delayed the delivery of these to the Russian ambassandor in Tokyo, preventing their presentation before the outbreak of hostilities.[11] But since the counterproposals contained only one minor concession, it is doubtful whether they would have averted war. Nevertheless the fact that they only reached the Russian ambassador on 7 February does raise the question, never satisfactorily answered, of where and how they were held up, and by whom. On 5 February the Japanese government informed St Petersburg that 'Further prolongation of the existing situation being unacceptable, the Imperial Government has decided to terminate the pending negotiations and to take such independent action as it considers necessary to defend its menaced position and to protect its rights.' Diplomatic relations were broken and the Japanese ambassador left the Russian capital.

# 2  The Contenders

In 1903, a Russian entering Manchuria by rail would have found the frontier station named Manchuria little different from hundreds of other Russian railway stations. Moreover, the CER, which took him eastward from this station, had trains, stations and red-capped stationmasters that were clearly Russian, and struck the same familiar three bells to signal the departure of each train. Along this railway the traveller would see settlements built for the railwaymen and their families, settlements whose dwellings and inhabitants were typically Russian yet cleaner, tidier, and more prosperous than those he had known back home. Indeed just as Russian villages in Siberia seemed more spacious and less squalid than those of European Russia, so did the dwellings of the Russians in Manchuria exceed in their comfort those of Siberia.

When the traveller reached Harbin, the junction for the lines to Vladivostok and Port Arthur, he found a flourishing Russian town where a few years earlier had been merely a Chinese village. From Harbin, Russia's 'capital' in Manchuria, passengers for Vladivostok would continue eastward to Pogranichnaya. From this frontier station the Ussuri Railway wound down through six tunnels to the coastal plain of Russia's Maritime Province and terminated on the western side of the Golden Horn, a four-mile bay on which Vladivostok had been founded in 1860. Vladivostok was already taking the aspect of a Russian provincial city, with its handful of restaurants, a museum, an electric tramway from the station along the main street, and an oriental institute. It also had a memorial to the explorer Admiral Nevelski, on which were inscribed some portentous words of Tsar Nicholas I, 'Wherever the Russian flag has once been raised, never must it be lowered.'

Passengers from Harbin southward to Port Arthur had a longer journey. Their train would run over the CER for a while, and then move on to the tracks of the South Manchurian Railway. The latter was essentially under the same management as the CER, namely the Russian government, but the fiction was bravely maintained that these were two independent and private companies. To emphasise their separation, the CER timetables used St Petersburg time (6 hours 26 minutes behind local time) while the South Manchurian Railway used Chinese coast time (22 minutes behind local time).[1]

The 189–mile line from Harbin to Mukden traversed a fertile region growing soya bean and tobacco as well as the ubiquitous kao-liang. The latter, a species of millet which grows to ten feet or more, was a favourite crop in Manchuria and in 1904–5 provided superb conceal-ment for the opposing troops. Mukden, whose 150 000-odd population was contained within an 11-mile mud wall, was the ancient capital of the Manchurian emperors and was still regarded by the Chinese as a sacred city. South of Mukden the terrain was more mountainous. In general, rather bare mountains flanked the railway on its eastern side, while towards the west there was flat low-lying land which in season was covered with kao-liang. This pattern continued almost all the way to Port Arthur, with the railway and the old Mandarin Road skirting the mountains in a successful compromise between the difficult terrain of the mountains and the floods of the plain. The Mandarin Road was bumpy, and in places positively dangerous, but it was Manchuria's only road; the other roads shown on maps were little more than tracks.

Forty miles south of Mukden was the town of Liaoyang. Of about the same size and antiquity as Mukden, its most prominent feature was a gigantic stone pagoda. After another 60 miles the railway entered the Liaotung Peninsula, and the mountains began to close in. At 430 miles from Harbin the six-mile line to Dalny diverged, while the Port Arthur line continued for another 31 miles along a river valley before swinging eastward along the water's edge for the last stretch to the terminus at Port Arthur.

Most passengers had the misfortune of arriving in Port Arthur during the small hours. This was especially depressing in winter which, though often snow-less, was bitterly cold. An initial un-pleasantness was the descent from the train; there was no station apart from a barrack hut, and passengers alighted directly on to a cobbled street. Those who arrived at night were met by an oppressive silence. Everything seemed dead and empty and the few passers-by appeared preoccupied and unhappy. Occasional military patrols challenged pedestrians with the time-honoured summons of a great bureaucratic empire, 'Your documents, please!' In the background, very close, towered the dark shapes of battleships.

When the sun rose things looked more cheerful. The first rays of the sun would play on the peak of Golden Hill and, as the sunshine spread downwards over the brown mountain sides, an intent observer could discern the glint of gun barrels pointing out to sea. This observer would already have noticed that the town, about one-tenth the size of Mukden, was situated on one side of a large natural harbour. Access to this harbour from the sea was through a passage less than a quarter of a mile wide and more than half a mile long. The town itself was divided into two parts. The New Town, containing the official buildings, was to the west of the station, while to the east was the Old Town, where most of the Chinese lived. From 1898 the Russians had been converting some of the Chinese buildings for their own use. To dissuade sailors from ruining their health with Chinese vodka, a Chinese theatre had been converted into a European theatre with a sailors' tea house attached. While the sailors drowned their sorrows in tea the local high society (that is, officers, officials, and their families) would gather for various social events in the adjoining theatre.

Although the ordinary Russian did not consider that Manchuria was worth fighting for, visiting Russians were often proud of what their fellow–countrymen had achieved in this remote part of the world. Even Russians who at home were critical of the petrifying interference of government officials felt a glow of pride when they saw what those same officials were doing in Manchuria. Foreign travellers, hostile in principle to the Russian presence in Manchuria, often admitted that the Russians were indeed a civilising influence. An American senator, one of many US politicians who at this time regarded a visit to Siberia and Manchuria as part of their political education, commented with some admiration that the CER witnessed Russians, Koreans and Chinese travelling together on the same crowded freight cars without any suggestion of racial division: 'Superior to all the world, as the Russian believes himself, he shows no offensive manner towards the other races with which he so picturesquely mingles.'[2] In the towns many Chinese had found it worthwhile to acquire a kind of pidgin Russian. The Russian railway settlements compared well with the Chinese villages, being clean and pleasant. Russian soldiers had embellished the settlements with newly-planted trees, paved streets, parks and gardens.

Meanwhile the Russian army and Russian officials, building on their experience of colonial management in Central Asia, ensured a well-ordered and fairly secure life for the local inhabitants. In accordance with Russian colonial practice of earlier (as well as subsequent) periods, native governors were retained and native laws enforced. But behind the governors, somewhere in the background, stood the Russian officials whose supervision and armed force guaranteed that things would be done in accordance with Russian interests. The local Chinese hardly realised that they had lost their independence; those few who did understand that their local administrators were only puppets could still appreciate that it was probably better to be ruled from St Petersburg than from Peking, and that Manchuria was a part of China where Chinese laws were actually enforced in a fair way, and where ordinary people were less at risk from thieves, murderers and bandits.

Despite the clamour of the world's press and the pronouncements of subsequent historians, the Manchurian population was better off under Russian occupation, and knew it. This did not prevent the Russian presence in Manchuria being the ostensible cause of the Russo–Japanese War. Indeed, there was no reason why it should, for although the war was fought on Chinese territory amid a large Chinese population, neither the Chinese government nor the Chinese people had any influence on the course of events. In any case the Russian presence was not perhaps the real cause of the war, and it was certainly not the determining factor in its timing. It was the military balance of power which persuaded the Japanese to attack when they did. Russia was several times stronger than Japan on land and sea, but in the Far East theatre this situation was reversed, and in 1904 the gap between Japan's strength and Russia's eastern weakness was as wide as it would ever be. If the war was short, Japan could bring her entire strength to a bear on just a fraction of Russia's armed forces.

At the beginning of 1904 the strength of the Japanese army was about 850 000, but the standing army was only about 380 000, the remainder being reservists of various degrees of readiness. Compared to these figures the Russian strength seemed overwhelming, even when the elderly ex-conscripts of the national militia were not counted.[3] The active Russian army totalled about 1 100 000 men, and this was supported by a reserve of 2 400 000 young ex-conscripts. Both armies were based on conscription; in Russia a conscript was liable to five years with the active army, although he usually served only four. After this he transferred to the reserve for 13 or 14 years, and then for a few more years up to the age of 43 he was in the national militia.

In Japan the conscripts served three years in the active army and nine years in the reserve. Neither Russia nor Japan called up all men who were theoretically liable. In Japan many men of each age group escaped entirely, while others (the First Division of the Conscript Reserve) served only for a few months. In Russia there were many exemptions on grounds of health and family circumstances. Moreover, secondary and higher education qualifications entitled their holders to a considerably reduced term of service. This had certain economic advantages; it encouraged young men to study, and it meant that educated men were withdrawn from productive civilian life for shorter periods. But on the other hand it meant that those men who tended to become officers spent insufficient time in the active army to gain the experience required of officers in wartime.

Japan's army really dated from the 1868 abolition of feudalism. With the Emperor as national figurehead and his advisers as national administrators, and with the disappearance of feudal lords and their private armies, the way was open for a national army. The Samurai warrior class transferred its allegiance to the Emperor, and when conscription was introduced in 1871 the profession of arms became the right of all classes. However, the Samurai, with their military tradition and peculiar code of behaviour, provided most of the professional officers and greatly influenced the development of the army. As was pointed out delightedly by journalists in 1904, many of the highest Japanese officers had started their military careers as Samurai, mounted on horseback wearing armour, and wielding a battleaxe.

When it was decided to create a modern army it was realised that while the martial spirit of the Samurai was worth cherishing, their military technology was not likely to ensure victories over foreign enemies. Accordingly French, and later Prussian, assistance was obtained. The Prussian General von Meckel arrived in 1885 and, lecturing through an interpreter, taught the Japanese how to organise an effective general staff.[4] Later, visiting foreign officers were dispensed with, and it became the practice to send the most promising Japanese officers for training in Prussia. By 1904 there had been created a highly competent, brave and devoted stock of officers for the new divisions.

The Russian officers were very different from the Japanese. In terms of courage they were perhaps equal, but not in terms of energy and initiative. They were a mixed lot. Some were highly trained in military academies. Other were army officers because in their youth this seemed an honourable career for incompetent sons of the nobility. Traditionally, army officers came from the gentry, but reforms of the late nineteenth century had eased the path of the non-gentry so that a considerable number of middle-class men had received commissions and thereby joined the gentry (commissioned service automatically brought conferment of nobility). Since warfare was becoming more technical, bright young men from the middle class were essential, especially in artillery and engineering with their demand for mathematical talent. It is perhaps no coincidence that in the Russo–Japanese War it was the Russian artillery and sapper units which appeared to enjoy the most competent competent leadership, and the cavalry which suffered the worst kind of officer. The gentlemen of the old school, who predominated among infantry and cavalry officers, tended towards inertia; they seemed to regard battle as a game like hunting in which they could indulge when they felt like it. Unlike the Japanese, they could not realise that war demanded a sustained and maximum effort. The relationships between these gentlemen-officers were peculiar in that junior officers did not invariably regard the wishes of their superiors as unquestionable. Officers requiring assistance from subordinates in battle tended to issue not orders, but appeals.[5]

Russia was a centralised and bureaucratic state, and it was natural that officers of bureaucratic temperament should reach the top. The bureaucratic approach does have its virtues when practised by energetic and intelligent men, but in the hands of below-average men it does not win wars. Probably a majority of the Russian generals in the war could be described as 'bureaucractic'. What this meant, among other things, was that they consciously or unconsciously placed great stress on avoiding situations where they might attract criticism from above. In a bureaucratic system it is the person who never appears to fail who gets to the top. Thus risk-taking (that is, initiative) was perilous for an ambitious officer; a failure brought about by his action was many times more damaging than a continuous lack of success induced by inertia. Therefore the typical Russian officer seemed more at peace within himself when it was the enemy who had the initiative. He was happier in defence than in attack; failure in the first could be ascribed to the actions of the enemy, whereas failure in attack might seem to be more the result of his own decisions. When a Russian attack was mounted, it was never delivered until every possible factor had been planned. Thus time after time Russian attacks were cancelled because some minor but unexpected factor had intervened. During the war the Russian commanders seemed almost unwilling to win a victory, but they were very successful in the rearguard actions which avert disasters. Bureaucratic centralisation also implied that the centre (that is, the senior command) was unwilling to allow the periphery (the junior commanders) to act independently even if the latter had wished. Both in and out of battle, headquarters would send its officers in the field a succession of lengthy written orders which, by the time they arrived, might be completely outdated.

For most of the war the commander of the Russian land forces was Kuropatkin, a bureaucrat's bureaucrat.[6] Distinction in his military career had come early, in the Russo–Turkish War of the 1870s. In this he had been chief of staff to General Skobolev, regarded as one of Russia's outstanding generals. In this capacity Kuropatkin had been superb; detailed planning, the handling of information, and organisation were his strong points. As a decision-taker he was less adequate. He rose rapidly. He was a guest of the French army in its North Africa campaign, and he developed this experience of colonial warfare with action in Turkestan as Russia extended her empire in Central Asia. When the Russo–Japanese War started he was minister of war, but was soon sent to take over the Manchurian armies. He wrote to the Tsar that he realised that his appointment was due not to his military qualities but to the lack of any more talented generals, and this modesty was probably not false; he had a fairly accurate appreciation of his value as a competent but by no means great general. In the war his greatest handicap was his fear of defeat, which enabled the Japanese more than once to steal victory from potential disaster. After his failure at the Battle of Mukden, Kuropatkin was replaced by General Linievich. Linievich had little opportunity to display his qualities, but it is unlikely that he would have proved any more competent than Kuropatkin. The latter, despite his faults, had certain intellectual qualities whereas Linievich, risen from the ranks and liking to regard himself as a soldier's soldier, was primitive in his ideas, as his diary demonstrates.

Kuropatkin's opposite number was Oyama, assisted by a very competent chief of staff (Kodama). Like other Japanese officers, Oyama was imbued with the idea that attack is the best guarantee of success. Certainly, against the Russians, this doctrine was proved true. At the Battle of the Sha ho, for example, Oyama went into the attack even though he did not know Kuropatkin's dispositions or intentions. As soon as the Japanese began to attack, they had the initiative, for Kuropatkin immediately abandoned his own offensive intentions and adopted the favourite Russian tactic of passively waiting for the enemy's blow to fall. Oyama had been with the Prussian army, and was a great admirer of that army's encirclement and defeat of the French at Sedan. In his Manchurian campaign he was evidently trying to bring off his own Sedan, but never quite succeeded, being defeated by his inability to coordinate the movements of his enormous army properly and by the wariness of Kuropatkin, who had himself been at Sedan as an observer with the French army. None of the Japanese leaders was a great general. At the time they were greatly praised in the West, but their successes were gained only at the expense of enormous casualties. In this as in other ways the Russo–Japanese War did provide a glimpse of future wars, with overrated generals ordering attack after attack against impregnable positions. Possibly the Japanese generals would have done better if their infantry had been less willing to sacrifice itself.

Encouraged by their press, the people of the West were fascinated by the rival generals. In Britain and America the Japanese leaders were clear favourites. Excursion boats, pet cats and dogs received the names of Japanese leaders, and British horticulturists unveiled the new Oyama gladiolus. Details of the generals' personal lives, sometimes fact and sometimes fiction, were presented to newspaper readers who seemed to prefer this kind of material to hard news from the battlefronts; thus when, in March 1904, Kuropatkin was appointed to command the Russian Manchurian armies, the Associated Press was soon (22 March 1904) off the mark: 'General Kuropatkin's war horse is a bay stallion named le Marechal, son of Lohengrin, an English thoroughbred. ... He was trained to the report of firearms, even when occuring close to his ear, and taught to lie down and rise at the word of command.'

The weapons of the two armies were similar. Although the Russian infantry was trained to revere the bayonet as the supreme weapon, it was nevertheless supplied with a good magazine rifle. Both the Japanese and Russian magazine rifles were of recent introduction, unfamiliar to the older reservists. The Japanese rifle was of .256 inch calibre, against the Russian .299 inch, and this difference inspired a fatuous comment from one of the many intellectuals who visited the front. The world-famous theatrical director Nemirovich–Danchenko had this to say:

Japanese bullets are so noble. They are small and fine. When they penetrate the body it is hard to see their entry and exit. So long as there is no blood poisoning you don't die from their wound. That is, so long as dirty rags or sweaty linen is not taken in with the bullet. If they don't kill you on the spot, you will survive.[7]

Both armies were equipped on a limited scale with machine guns. The Russian Maxim was probably somewhat superior in action to the Japanese Hotchkiss, but both armies underestimated this weapon until the war showed how destructive it could be. At first it was regarded as an artillery weapon by the Japanese, being organised in batteries, but its virtues as an infantry weapon were soon realised.[8]

The Japanese field gun was mainly the Arisaka 13-pounder of 2.95 inch calibre and 5000 yards range. It was not a true quickfirer, although it could fire more 'rapidly than previous models. The Russian artillery was being re-equipped with a new three-inch quickfirer, which fired a 13 lb shell up to 6000 yards. In 1904 the Russian gunners were still unfamiliar with this new gun, and were unable to use it to its full advantage. In fact after the first unsuccessful battles some officers complained that they would like their old guns back. But as the war progressed it became clear that the Russian gun outclassed the Japanese, and this was only partly compensated for by the great superiority of the Japanese in mountain guns.

The war witnessed the large-scale use of many new items of equipment. Of these the most important was the field telephone. This was exploited, especially by the Russians, in defensive works, with each strongpoint connected to headquarters. It was soon realised, too, that telephone communication between the various batteries and between the batteries and headquarters enhanced the effectiveness of gunfire, especially of indirect gunfire. Telephone and telegraph operations were entrusted to special sapper companies, but both sides soon found that wire communications were never quite as adequate as they would have liked. The Russians, at least, were also troubled by line breaks caused by troops chopping down poles for their campfires, tethering their cattle and horses to posts, and using the wire for their own purposes. Kuropatkin in November 1904 had to issue an order condemning these practices, and noting additionally that many lines had been found with notches where their insulation had been cut away by inquisitive soldiers. Both sides possessed balloons, but made little use of them. At Liaoyang and Mukden effective balloon observation might have saved the Russians from the surprises which led to their defeat, but Russian staff officers did not have much faith in these monsters. The British *Official History*, describing the Battle of the Sha ho, mentions that one Russian balloon was torn from its moorings by a sudden gust of wind, to the secret delight of the staff officers who had to make daily ascents. The balloon careered off towards the Japanese lines, but a change of wind carried it northwards. Just possibly, this may have been the origin of later reports of a mysterious 'Japanese balloon' that was terrorising the population in faraway Siberia.

To a degree which still remains uncertain the Japanese army was aided by a spy network that had been established in Manchuria before the war. No doubt the Russians exaggerated this, because spies and treason are favourite explanations of military defeat. But undoubtedly the Japanese Amur River Society's training programme for Chinese and Russian linguists was inaugurated with spying in mind. According to a British clergyman long resident in Mukden, Russian-speaking Japanese spies, masquerading as Chinese, wore their hair long and in a pigtail and spoke passable Chinese. One of them was employed as a barber at the Russian staff headquarters in Mukden, while others had found positions as officers' tailors and valets.[9] From Mukden there was a runner service connecting with the advancing Japanese army. Another source, a Russian officer, mentions that among the Japanese officers who entered Port Arthur after the fall of that fortress was a man whom, before the war, he had known as a local watchmaker.

At the turn of the century Russia was clearly stronger at sea in the Far East, having a squadron based on Port Arthur and Vladivostok which had more heavy ships than the entire Japanese navy. But the war indemnity which China had paid to Japan after the Sino–Japanese War enabled Japan to place large orders in England for armoured ships. By 1904 these new ships had enabled Japan to catch up with Russia; by that year Japan had six modern battleships and six modern armoured cruisers. All but two of these units were British-built. Russia meantime had been acquiring ships from both her own and from foreign yards. Delivery from home yards was exceptionally slow, which was one reason why Russian naval power was beginning to be overtaken by Japanese.[10] Another reason was that Russia's naval effort was divided between the Baltic, the Black Sea, and the East. In theory, so long as war in Europe was unlikely, Baltic ships could in emergency be transferred to the Pacific, although in wartime this would be difficult because the laws of neutrality would prevent coaling at foreign ports en route. As for the Black Sea, although the Russian government in 1904 made diplomatic efforts to enable its warships to pass the Straits en route to the East, British opposition prevailed.

When the war started Russia had seven modern battleships in the East, against Japan's six; four armoured cruisers against Japan's six; five first-class but no second-class cruisers against Japan's twelve second-class; two modern light cruisers against Japan's four; and 42 torpedo craft against Japan's 104. In auxiliaries and older ships Japan was superior. Both countries were awaiting reinforcements. The Russians had sent from the Baltic a battleship (*Oslyabia*) and 13 smaller vessels, but because the battleship had run aground in the Mediterranean this detachment had been delayed. When the war started it had only got as far as French Somaliland, and the navy ministry ordered it home; in view of British hostility, the risks of proceeding seemed too great. On the way home one of the torpedo craft sank and three others broke down.

As the crisis in the East had deepened, the Russian navy ministry had energetically tried to purchase battleships from South American countries. An American entrepreneur almost succeeded in selling to the Russian government some battleships which in reality did not exist. Two Chilean battleships which were completing in Britain and were surplus to Chile's requirements following an agreement with her potential enemy, Argentina, were hastily bought up by the British Admiralty to prevent the Russians buying them. The Japanese, enjoying British support, had better luck. Two armoured cruisers being built in Italy for Argentina, and redundant for the same reason, were purchased by Japan and taken East with the help of Royal Navy officers and men. They had just passed Singapore when the war started, and joined the Japanese navy as *Kasuga* and *Nisshin*; they brought the total of Japanese armoured cruisers up to eight, which more than compensated for the Russian seven to six superiority in battleships. However, Japan could not receive reinforcements once war had started; neutral shipyards were not allowed to deliver new warships to belligerents, and Japanese shipyards could not build ships larger than small cruisers. Russia, on the other hand, had a strong Baltic squadron, and her Baltic shipyards were completing a class of five powerful battleships. Thus the overriding care of the Japanese admirals was to avoid loss, for such losses could not be made good. The somewhat half-hearted tactics often adopted were probably the consequence of this situation. Fortunately for the Japanese, the Russians did not adopt the appropriate policy of taking risks in order to sink Japanese ships.

The Japanese navy had been modelled on the British. Although some small ships were built in Japan, the majority still came from

Britain. Many of the Japanese admirals had been trained in Britain, while other less senior officers had spent time in Britain supervising the construction of Japanese warships. Like their contemporaries in the army, they had recent battle experience, having routed the Chinese navy during the Sino–Japanese War.

Undoubtedly the greatest celebrity of the Russo–Japanese war was Japan's Admiral Togo, whom the British press liked to describe as the 'Nelson of the East'. As a naval cadet Togo had arrived in England in 1871 at the age of 23. He lived for a time with an English family, then spent two years on the training ship *Worcester*, cruised to Australia, supervised the building of a Japanese warship in a British shipyard, and returned to Japan. He married a girl of the same Samurai stock and despite the early onset of crippling and chronic rheumatism, rose rapidly in his profession. On the eve of the Sino–Japanese War the cruiser he commanded sank a British ship chartered by the Chinese to carry troops; thus he was already something of a specialist in the surprise attack carried out before a declaration of war. On this occasion, his act was condemned by the British press even though he had carefully rescued the British crew of the freighter before turning his machine guns on the Chinese soldiers struggling in the water. This incident accelerated his promotion, and by 1900 he was commanding Japan's active fleet.

The Russian naval officers were the products of a bureaucratic society in which avoidance of blame was more important than technical competence or imaginative enterprise. Yet there were in the Russian navy a few outstanding officers, and even among the undistiguished there were those who, in different circumstances, would have performed well. The several groundings, collisions, and other self-inflicted injuries suffered by Russian ships during the Russo–Japanese War are not by themselves proof of gross incompetence, for other navies, including the Japanese, suffered similar mishaps. The ships of that time, with their reciprocating engines and vulnerable boilers, were not easy to handle. However, it must be admitted that Russian officers were less well-trained in handling their ships than were the Japanese. This was largely because the Russian ships spent their winters iced up, with their crews ashore; the year-round cruising possibilities of the Pacific station were not fully exploited, partly because for reasons of economy the ships had to spend too much time in harbour with their fires out. Also, a measure which made promotion dependent on sea-time meant that a large proportion of the officers in the Far East were newly appointed, accumulating their sea-time. As for the Russian gunnery, which was widely believed to be bad, a careful reading of the evidence suggests that at least in the beginning it was little worse than the Japanese gunnery. The gunnery of all navies was bad at that time. On the eve of the Battle of Tsushima, Togo's flagship aimed 64 six-inch shells at a stationary target 100 ft long, and in easy conditions at a range of 2500 yards scored only 16 hits.[11]

Japan was well equipped with naval dockyards, there being four well-protected yards with dry-docking facilities. Of these, Maizuru was the most useful, being closest to the scene of action. Additional bases were on the island of Tsushima, suitable for the smaller ships, and after the war started a fleet base was established at Mosampo in Korea (see map, p. x). The Russian bases were less convenient. Vladivostok, the former main base, needed an icebreaker in winter to keep a channel open. It did offer dry-docking to ships of battleship size, but the repair facilities were not generous; in 1904 a number of ships that were nominally part of the Pacific squadron had returned to the Baltic for reboilering and major refits. As for Port Arthur, which by 1904 was regarded as the main base, this had a good harbour but its narrow entrance was passable by heavy ships only at high tide. Its dry dock could not take ships larger than average-sized cruisers. There were grandiose plans for developing Port Arthur, but little progress had been made because few funds had been allocated. In 1904 three armoured cruisers were based on Vladivostok, mainly because the build-up of Russian naval strength had resulted in overcrowding at Port Arthur. Strategically, in a war against Japan, Vladivostok was defective because of its distance from the probable scene of hostilities, while Port Arthur was defective because it could easily be isolated. On the other hand, possession of Port Arthur did enable Russian ships to threaten any movement of Japanese troopships from Japan to Korea or Manchuria. It was this threat which dominated Japanese naval thinking in the first months of 1904.

# 3 Admiral Togo Strikes

The few Japanese residents of Port Arthur, shopkeepers and traders, had long anticipated an outbreak of war. In 1903 many of them began to close their businesses and go home. By the end of January 1904, a dry but bitterly cold month, the remaining Japanese stalls in the Old Town began one by one to disappear. One enterprising Japanese, hoping to attract buyers for his shop, wrote in Russian on a big sign 'I am scared!' On 8 February the Japanese consul, accompanied by his secretary in tails and top hat, went to the Russian authorities to make final arrangements for evacuating the last of the Japanese. War was only a few hours away and Admiral Togo's Combined Fleet was already steaming towards Port Arthur.

Since war seemed inevitable, Tokyo had decided to start it at a moment of its own choosing. Febrary 1904 seemed to be the best time; 1904 because by 1905 Russia would have five new battleships available for eastern service, February because that was when the ice would begin to melt in west Korean ports. A quick victory depended on full utilisation of the campaigning season, which began with the thaw. The war might have started a few days earlier if it had not been felt necessary to wait until the two new cruisers had cleared Singapore.

The Japanese war plan envisaged striking heavy and early blows at the Russian army in Manchuria before Russia's huge military reserves could be mobilised and transported East. For this, secure lines of communication between Japan and the mainland were essential. If Russia could dominate the sea communications, Japan would be defeated. In fact, the Russian navy was confident that it could beat the Japanese. The Viceroy in the Far East, Admiral Alekseev, who had overall command of the land and naval forces, distributed in 1903 a report drawn up for him by Admiral Witgeft in which, among other things, it was stated that 'our plan of operations should be based on the assumption that it is impossible for our fleet to be beaten, taking into consideration the present relationship of the two fleets, and that a Japanese landing is impracticable.'[2]

On the day Japan broke off diplomatic relations with St Petersburg, Admiral Togo summoned his officers and gave orders for two immediate operations designed to assure Japan of those early successes so essential for her war prospects. The main part of the navy was to make a surprise attack on the Russian squadron, known to be anchored outside Port Arthur, while a cruiser squadron was to escort troop transports to Chemulpo (now Inchon), land troops there which would march to the nearby Korean capital of Seoul, and destroy the Russian naval detachment stationed at Chemulpo. It was this second, less spectacular, operation which began first, but it was news of the Port Arthur attack which first reached Europe and aroused the Russian government to the shocked realisation that it was at war.

To deliver what he hoped would be the war-winning blow at Port Arthur, Togo on the evening of 8 February had taken his ships to about 50 miles east of the Russian base. According to the latest reports, the Russian heavy ships were anchored just outside the harbour; because of the time needed to move them through the narrow harbour entrance, too shallow except at high tide for the battleships, it could be assumed that they would still be outside the harbour when the attack went in. The only possibility to be guarded against, it seemed, was that the ships might for some reason have moved to nearby Dalny. For this reason Togo divided his torpedo crafts: ten destroyers were to be sent against Port Arthur and eight against Dalny.

Since Togo emerged from the Russo–Japanese War with the reputation of a Japanese Nelson, his tactics have been largely protected from critical scrutiny, but in this action he does appear to have misjudged the situation. This was going to be the most crucial operation of the war. It was the only operation which could expect to achieve complete surprise, and it was the best chance of putting the Russian squadron out of effective action. Yet Togo, in effect, committed only ten small craft. It is true that Togo used all the destroyers he had, but he could have instructed the eight which were sent to Dalny to proceed to Port Arthur in the event of Dalny being empty (as indeed it was). These eight would then have formed a second wave of attackers against a Russian squadron which would certainly have been alerted by the first attack, but which could be expected to be already damaged and confused. Also, Togo could have committed some of his light cruisers, which carried four torpedo tubes. It may be assumed that Togo, like other naval officers, had an exaggerated appreciation of what torpedoes could do; ten destroyers, after all, would at short range fire 20 of these terrible weapons into the closely anchored Russian squadron. As things turned out, his surprise attack did not bring the results he had anticipated.

The Japanese attack began about midnight. The destroyers, orientating themselves by the Russian searchlights, approached their targets unseen. The lights of two patrolling Russian destroyers were seen, and the Japanese took evasive action during which their three flotillas lost contact with each other, and two of their destroyers collided. According to Japanese accounts this evasion was successful, but some Russian eyewitneses claimed that the Russian destroyers did observe their enemy, and, following instructions, returned to report to the commander of the squadron, but were too late. The Japanese, less one destroyer which had been put out of action by the collision, pressed on, but because of their confusion could not make the planned mass attack. Only four destroyers took part in the first strike, the others following later, It seems that the four approaching attackers were observed by the cruiser *Pallada*, which was on searchlight duty, but they were not recognised as hostile until it was too late. These first four destroyers passed close to the outer Russian line, and soon after midnight launched their torpedoes at the indistinct shapes of the armoured ships. As they made off at full speed Russian gunfire commenced sporadically, with some ships opening up immediately but others not commencing until the fourth destroyer was well away. This first attack lasted about five minutes, and was followed by an attack by four destroyers which had earlier become detached from the leaders. These met more opposition; blinded by searchlights and the spray from near misses, they had more difficulty launching their torpedoes. Then, about an hour later, a stray destroyer made an individual attack, followed by the final destroyer which, having been damaged by collision, managed to limp quietly towards the Russian ships and launch a torpedo against the shape of a four-funnelled vessel.

When Togo's force, according to plan, approached Port Arthur the next morning to take advantage of the shattered state of the Russian squadron, it found that the latter was distinctly unshattered, materially if not morally. Of all the torpedoes fired during the night, only three had exploded against the targets (these three, apparently, were fired by the first wave of attackers). Unluckily for the Russians, however, their two most modern battleships, *Retvizan* and *Tsesarevich*, had each suffered one hit. The other torpedo had struck the cruiser *Pallada*. By morning these three vessels were grounded near the harbour entrance, attempts to take them inside having failed. The other Russian ships remained at anchor, with their boilers lit.

The outside world was as astonished as the Russians by this attack. Although in some countries, notably France, the newspapers were critical of the Japanese action, in Britain and the USA the press and politicians did not hesitate to voice their approval. The London *Times* described the attack as 'stunning' and 'masculine'.

How the Russians had allowed themselves to be taken so completely by surprise was discussed endlessly throughout the world, but even now it is hard to say who was to blame. Russian accounts differ about the situation at Port Arthur that night. Some say that many of the ships' officers were enjoying themselves on shore at a party given by the wife of the Russian commander, Admiral Stark. Others deny this. The most likely version is that there had indeed been some kind of social gathering at Madame Stark's, but that ships' officers had returned to their posts by nightfall. These circumstances, so easily dramatised by a little journalistic licence, gave rise to lurid stories, willingly believed, of the Russian officers being surprised in their cups. But an entry in the diary of a Russian diplomat at Port Arthur suggests that all the officers were aboard, with the exception of the Admiral:

> All our squadron has gone out to the anchorage. More than twenty units, not counting destroyers. After sundown nobody is allowed ashore. I met Admiral Stark at dusk. He was going home for dinner (it is his wife's name-day). He tells me that he is 'contraband', and then asks me, 'Well, mister diplomat, how are things?' I reply, 'Our work is finished. It's your turn now.'[3]

Admiral Stark, in view of the deteriorating situation, had ordered his ships to be in a state of readiness against possible torpedo attacks, but each ship reacted differently, most officers regarding the order as an exercise rather than a genuine warning. None put out their torpedo nets; it was said later that officers who suggested doing so were criticised for being alarmists. Some ships' gun crews slept fully clothed by their weapons, but others did not. There had not, after all, been a declaration of war. The news that Japan had broken off diplomatic relations with Russia had arrived by telegraph, and the cruiser *Pallada* had been ordered to raise steam preparatory to leaving for Japan to remove the Russian embassy staff. Whether the ominous wording of the Japanese note had been conveyed is not clear, nor is it clear how many officers were aware of the break. Some accounts allege, not implausibly, that in the Russian bureaucratic tradition of giving subordinates as little information as possible, few officers were even aware that diplomatic relations had been broken. On the other hand, it seems that the whole town knew that a Japanese ship had that day removed the last of the Japanese residents.

Each night a seaward watched was kept by a cruiser's searchlights, and further out at sea each night a pair of destroyers was on patrol. Apparently the latter had been ordered to investigate suspicious vessels but not to open fire; in the event of trouble the destroyers were merely to return to report to the squadron commander. All this accorded with the spirit of a telegram which Admiral Alekseev had received from the Tsar. The morning after the attack, one of Alekseev's staff was allowed to see this telegram:

> The Admiral showed me in confidence a telegram received from the Tsar yesterday ... The Tsar mentions his desire for peace: 'If there should be a conflict, let it be the Japanese who start it' (I was reading it aloud and interposed, 'How precisely the Japanese have obeyed his Gracious Command'). The telegram continued that if the Japanese should land in Korea they should be met with military opposition only if they moved northwards above the 38th Parallel.[4]

Admiral Stark, generally regarded as responsible for the defeat, was soon dismissed from his command. However, there is some evidence that Alekseev was more blameworthy. Some officers believed that Stark had accepted the role of scapegoat on the understanding that he would not be court-martialled; if he kept quiet, he could expect to retire at full rank and with a pension. The same sources allege that Stark knew that Alekseev bore the main share of responsibility; Alekseev had ordered the ships to anchor outside the harbour so that they would be ready for immediate offensive action as soon as war was declared, Alekseev had failed to make clear the true nature of the diplomatic crisis, and Alekseev had rejected the idea of putting out torpedo nets (like Stalin in 1941, he rejected defensive precautions as likely to provoke the enemy). It is hard to evaluate this evidence; it certainly accords with Alekseev's character but on the other hand his general unpopularity must have generated many unfounded allegations against him. An extramural son of

Alexander II, throughout his life he occupied posts demanding greater talents than he possessed.

For his concurrent Chemulpo operation, Admiral Togo had despatched five cruisers, eight torpedo boats, and three transports under the command of Admiral Uryu. On 8 February this detachment appeared off Chemulpo. To protect foreign nationals in Seoul, as violence of some kind was expected, Britain, France, the USA and Italy had each stationed a warship there. There was also a Korean gunboat, the Japanese cruiser *Chiyoda*, and two Russian warships. The main purpose of *Chiyoda* was to observe the movements of the Russian ships. The elderly gunboat *Koreets* had been the Russian guardship at Chemulpo, but a few days previously *Varyag* had steamed in from Port Arthur. This modern US-built cruiser had been put at the disposal of the Russian envoy in Seoul, and had already landed a small detachment to strengthen the defence of the Russian legation.

The Korean telegraph service was under Japanese 'protection', and the Russian legation began to find that its messages were not getting through. For this reason the Russian envoy requested *Koreets* to carry despatches to Port Arthur and to discover what was happening in the outside world. Lack of information was equally an embarrassment to the commander of *Varyag*, Captain Rudnev. His orders had been explicit: he was not to leave Chemulpo without instructions, and in the event of a breakdown in communications he was told 'we shall find one way or another to inform you.' According to the later testimony of Rudnev (which is corroborated) he had been ordered not to interfere with any Japanese troop landings so long as war had not been declared.[5]

*Chiyoda* had slipped out of Chemulpo at midnight and met Uryu's ships with the information that *Varyag* and *Koreets* were still at anchor. In the afternoon of 8 February the transports, accompanied by cruiser and torpedo boats, approached the harbour to land the troops. As they approached, *Koreets* emerged on her way to Port Arthur. Seeing the Japanese detachment, the captain of the *Koreets* decided to return, but he was immediately approached by the Japanese torpedo boats, which moved in as though intending to make a torpedo attack. During this manoeuvre one of the torpedo boats ran aground, and *Koreets* fired two shots before regaining the harbour. After this the Japanese landed their troops in sampans and at daybreak on 9 February, having finished this work, moved out. *Chiyoda*, however, re-entered the harbour with letters for the foreign naval commanders. The letter addressed to the captain of *Varyag*, written in English, was as follows:

His Imperial Japanese Majesty's Ship *Naniwa*
8 February 1904
Sir
As hostilities exist between the Government of Japan and the Government of Russia at present, I respectfully demand you to leave the port of Chemulpo with the Force under your command before the noon of the ninth of February 1904. Otherwise, I should be obliged to fight against you in the port.
I have the honour to be Sir, your most obedient servant.
S. Uryu
Rear Admiral commanding a squadron of the Imperial Japanese Navy

The foreign naval captains received an equally polite letter from Uryu, informing them that hostilities had begun beween Russia and Japan and advising them to leave the port to avoid damage if the Japanese were obliged to attack the Russians in harbour. The British, French and Italian captains (but not the American) sent a reply protesting at the violation of Korean neutrality. Meanwhile Captain Rudnev addressed his crew. He told his men that he had received a Japanese challenge to fight, and that although it was quite clear that *Varyag* had no chance against such an overwhelming enemy force they would nevertheless go out, rather than surrender their ships to the enemy. 'Let us put our trust in God, and go bravely into battle for the Tsar and for the Motherland – Hurrah!' The crew returned the cheer in the time-honoured manner, and the ship's band struck up the national anthem, 'God Save the Tsar'. *Varyag*, followed by *Koreets*, weighed anchor and passed out of the harbour. Her band was still playing, her crew were dressed in their best uniforms, and she was cheered by the crews of the other foreign warships.

*Varyag* mounted 12 six-inch guns, while *Koreets*'s guns were too old to be taken into consideration. Against these the Japanese disposed of a total of four eight-inch and 36 six-inch guns. Although *Varyag*'s designed speed was a little faster than that of the Japanese cruisers, the state of her boilers meant that she could hardly move faster than half-speed. Thus Captain Rudnev was not over-pessimistic when he concluded that his ship did not stand a chance.

*Varyag* was assailed as soon as she appeared outside the harbour. One of the first shells struck her bridge. The midshipman at the rangefinder was blown to pieces, together with his instrument. The second rangefinder was also an early victim of the fight, and it was partly for this reason that of the 1105 six-inch, 12-pounder and 3-pounder shells fired by *Varyag* not one found a target. It was not long before the cruiser was reduced to a flaming shambles on her upper deck. Rudnev was wounded, and the steering gear put out of action. The Japanese took advantage of this to close the range. An eight-inch shell holed her at the waterline, causing a list. More fires were started. She limped back towards Chemulpo, firing with her two after six-inch guns (the only guns still workable). Two hours after leaving Chemulpo the Russian ships, *Varyag* crippled and *Koreets* unscathed, anchored once more in the harbour. The cruiser had lost 31 killed and 91 seriously injured. The sentry who had stood at the flag throughout the battle was only slightly injured; his clothing and one shoe had been torn, his rifle butt smashed, but he himself was only bruised.

The foreign ships sent their doctors to help the *Varyag* wounded. Meanwhile Rudnev had decided to open the Kingston valves of *Varyag* and to blow up *Koreets*. This was done after the crews had been transferred to the British, French and Italian warships (USS *Vicksburg* refused to take any). Subsequently the Russian crews gave their parole to refrain from further participation in the war, and were returned to Russia in neutral ships. In Odessa and St Petersburg they received a heroes' welcome with celebrations, parades, presents and banquets.

Back at Port Arthur the morning after the surprise attack, Togo's ships approached within range of the Russian squadron. The Russians had been informed of the Japanese movements by the cruiser *Boyarin*, which had been sent out to reconnoitre. When the Japanese were reported, the unfortunate Admiral Stark was again absent from his post; he was ashore, reporting to Alekseev about the damage already received. He managed to catch up with his ships in a steam cutter just as Togo opened fire at about 9000 yards range, with the Russians staying under the cover of their shore batteries. Some hits were scored by both sides, and the Russian light cruiser *Novik* distinguished herself by dashing at the enemy armoured cruisers and unsuccessfully discharging a torpedo at 3000 yards. Togo withdrew when he began to suffer damage from the Russian guns, especially from the increasingly accurate fire of the shore batteries. However, this retirement was hardly an acknowledgement of defeat, as the

Russians made no attempt to pursue. Evidently, although the surprise torpedo attack had done less damage than had been hoped, the Russians had been sufficiently demoralised to adopt a passive attitude. Although Togo could not yet claim to have won command of the sea, he could certainly claim to have won the initiative.

*Novik*, whose damage needed ten days to repair, was docked immediately. The same day *Pallada* and *Tsesarevich* were brought into the harbour, but for the time being *Retvizan* seemed immovably fixed in the harbour entrance. Meanwhile the minelayer *Yenisei* was sent to lay a protective field in Talien Bay, to guard against a possible landing. The captain of *Yenisei* was somewhat inexperienced, having recently been appointed from a post ashore. During the laying in fairly rough weather, trouble with a faulty mine caused the minelayer to strike one of her own mines. She sank in a few minutes, taking her captain and 92 others with her. This was a serious loss, for minelaying was a strong department in the Russian navy, and the 500-mine *Yenisei* and her sister *Amur* had been the mainstay of the mining work. In Port Arthur it was believed that *Yenisei* had been attacked by Japanese destroyers, and a force led by the cruiser *Boyarin* was sent to the scene. There was some confusion about the precise position of the mines laid by *Yenisei*, and it was not long before *Boyarin* came to grief. After the mine exploded her captain gave the abandon–ship order, and the crew was transferred to the accompanying destroyers. *Boyarin*, however, remained afloat. Her captain, now on a destroyer, ordered another destroyer to torpedo her. This destroyer's commander twice queried the order, but eventually complied (or at least went through the motions of complying). His first torpedo appeared to be jammed in its tube, and the second missed. After thereby exhausting its torpedo armament, the destroyer followed her consorts home. The next day, other destroyers were sent. *Boyarin* was boarded, her anchor dropped, and her wardroom silver removed, but a storm in the night sent her to the bottom. Her captain was subsequently court-martialled for this sorry affair, and sentenced to be deprived of command for one year. Russian minelaying continued, supervised by the newly-arrived Admiral Loshchinsky. About 800 mines were laid in bays thought to be possible landing points for Japanese troops.

Togo was well aware that Port Arthur had no dry-dock that could take the battleships torpedoed on 9 February. Nevertheless, Russia still possessed enough serviceable ships to threaten Japanese communications. In view of this, and of the pressing need to bring troops from Japan to southern Manchuria, Togo decided to bottle up the Russian squardron by blocking the narrow entrance to Port Arthur. Five blockships were prepared, manned by volunteers who were proudly convinced that they were going to certain death. On the evening of 23 February, after the crews' farewell meal, the blockships set off for Port Arthur, escorted by torpedo boats that were to attempt to take off the crews at the last moment. Shortly before dawn the gallant five ran in at full speed, but were soon picked up by searchlights. Gunfire disabled some of the blockships and the others were scuttled well away from the ship channel, having lost their way amid the dazzle and spray. The Japanese at first thought that the channel had been blocked, but later it became clear that the expedition had been a complete failure, although Japanese casualties were small. A number of minor attacks were then made: destroyers tried to torpedo *Retvizan*, still aground in the harbour entrance, and Togo's armoured ships bombarded Russian cruisers outside the harbour, inflicting little damage. The Russian threat to Japanese transports was still in being, and Togo knew that if Russia sent out her Baltic squadron to reinforce her Pacific squadron the resulting combination would be overwhelming. Somehow, by blocking the harbour, by defeating it at sea, or by capturing Port Arthur, the Russian squadron had to be neutralised.

Meanwhile, the Russian squadron seemed to be emerging from the depression into which it had been thrown by the torpedoing of its two newest battleships. Admiral Stark had been replaced by Russia's most competent admiral, Makarov.[6] Although Makarov was subsequently credited with a genius which he may not have possessed, he was certainly Togo's equal, and perhaps more. He was an energetic leader, unlike the majority of his colleagues, and could inspire confidence among his subordinates. He was an intellectual among admirals, with an interest in science, Arctic exploration and naval theory. It was he who had been mainly responsible for the introduction of icebreakers, which did much to ease the situation of a navy operating in icy waters. His arrival in Port Arthur coincided with the arrival of skilled shipyard workers from the Baltic, and the refloating of *Retvizan*. Repairs to *Retvizan* and *Tsesarevich* were soon under way; as substitutes for dry-docking, cofferdams were laboriously built around the ships' sides, allowing workers to repair the wide holes beneath the waterline.

Most naval action at this time was confined to destroyer operations. Russian destroyers were frequently sent out on reconnaissance, and from time to time were intercepted by Japanese destroyers. Some spirited actions took place. On one occasion four Japanese destroyers fought four Russian at ranges which at time were as short as 50 yards; great damage was done but all ships survived. But on two occasions a Russian destroyer was sunk after encountering superior Japanese forces.

A new initiative was soon taken by Togo, still worried by the Russian battleships lying snugly but threateningly in Port Arthur. He took his battleships to within about six miles of the harbour and cruised in the cover of high ground outside the field of fire of the shore batteries. With his cruisers lying six miles from the harbour entrance to spot the fall of shot, the battleships fired high-trajectory shells over the hills and into Port Arthur. This bombardment continued for four hours, but only the cruiser *Askold* and the battleship *Retvizan* were hit, and they not grievously. However, as the Japanese 1st Army was landing at this time, the operation served to forestall any Russian attempt at interference. On 23 March a similar bombardment was undertaken, but this time the Russian ships came out. A few days earlier, Makarov had taken his squadron out for a few hours of much-needed training, and on this second occasion he fired a few shots at the Japanese. But he did not yet feel strong enough to venture outside the cover of his shore batteries, and after some sporadic firing the Japanese retired and the Russians returned to harbour. During this engagement *Retvizan* and *Tsesarevich*, still under repair, replied to the Japanese indirect fire over the hills with their own indirect fire guided by observers.

Makarov intended to build up the competence and confidence of his squadron by small sorties and skirmishes. He was certainly not willing to risk a fleet action at this stage. It was not simply a question of raising morale, but also of improving technical competence. During these training cruises those officers who seemed incorrigibly bad could be transferred to less important duties. For example, returning from one cruise two battleships came into gentle collision in clear weather, and this resulted in the replacement of *Sevastopol*'s captain by von Essen, a man who had Makarov's confidence and who later became a distinguished First World War admiral.

One consequence of the first Japanese attack on Port Arthur was a spy mania among the Russians. Probably, as so often happens, the attention paid to imagined enemies enabled the genuine spies to operate more freely. Britons in Manchuria were especially suspect. One British resident later wrote that 'The alliance between Britain and Japan made them suspicious, and the common soldiers, if they knew we were "Angliske", scowled at us openly.[7] In March a steamship that approached Port Arthur aroused suspicion. According to a Russian officer's report this vessel stopped only after a destroyer had fired a shot at her:

> On board her was a correspondent of the 'Daily Mail'. Although nothing suspicious was found aboard, and the correspondents gave the destroyer commander photographs of the 'Koreets' and 'Varyag' after scuttling, all the same I feel that there were spies there. This is not the first time that ships flying the German flag come up, and the next day there is a Japanese attack.[8]

Meanwhile, Togo prepared a second blocking attempt. Four freighters, each of about 3000 tons, were made ready. Although there was no lack of volunteers to man these ships, thirst for glory being as avid in the navy as in the army, it was wisely decided that the crews of the previous attempt should be used, because of their experience. But by this time the Russians were better prepared. *Retvizan*, with her powerful batteries of light guns, was no longer aground in the harbour entrance, but gunboats and destroyers were stationed behind booms and, together with the shore batteries, guaranteed a hot reception. When, early in the morning of 27 March, the Japanese expedition approached, it was picked up by searchlights when still two miles from its objective. It bravely proceeded, two blockships being torpedoed by Russian destroyers and the others sinking themselves. All but four of the Japanese sailors were picked up by the accompanying torpedo boats. Despite the opposition, this was destined to be the most successful of the blocking operations. Two of the blockships partly obstructed the channel; one more could have completed the blockage. As it was, Makarov was able to take out his ships the next day, attempting to lure a Japanese detachment over a previously laid minefield.

The increasing activity of the Russian squadron worried the Japanese command. Moreover there was the possibility that it might attempt to break through the Japanese screen and reach Vladivostok where, joined with the cruisers stationed at that port, it would be difficult to contain. Togo therefore intensified his reconnaissance and prepared yet another blockship attempt. His strength had recently been increased by the two new and powerful armoured cruisers, *Nisshin* and *Kasuga*. A plan to lay a minefield outside Port Arthur, where the Russian ships were in the habit of passing, was accepted, though not with great enthusiasm. Minelayers, mainly destroyers, were sent on this work during the night of 12 March. The Japanese ships were soon picked up by Russian searchlights, but Makarov apparently thought that they were his own destroyers awaiting daylight before entering harbour. However, when the Japanese had finished their minelaying they fired on the searchlights, and Makarov ordered that the area should be swept in the morning. The second part of the Japanese plan was to lure the Russians over the minefield. Since the minelayers had been observed, this part of the plan hardly deserved to succeed, but circumstances favoured the Japanese. At dawn, two Russian destroyers returning from patrol were attacked by Japanese destroyers. One was sunk, but Russian cruisers put to sea to fight off the Japanese. A Japanese cruiser division then appeared over the horizon, and a cruiser action began. Some Russian battleships were already in steam, and emerged one by one to support the cruisers.

The Japanese, having seen the Russian battleships emerge, withdrew. The Russians pursued, but at about 15 miles from Port Arthur the shapes of Togo's approaching battleships could be discerned through the haze. Outnumbered, Makarov turned and made for the shelter of his shore batteries.

So far, the Japanese had been disappointed. They had lured the Russians over their minefield but without success, and they had almost but not quite brought their armoured ships into action against a smaller number of Russian battleships. Why the normally cautious Makarov should have risked his ships in this way has never been satisfactorily explained. Some accounts suggest that he was so incensed by the loss of his destroyer that he threw caution to the winds. This seems somewhat out of character. It is more likely that this was simply not one of his good days; after all, he had not had much sleep that night and he may have forgotten about the probable presence of enemy mines.

Togo soon withdrew, realising that the Russians were safely covered by their shore batteries. But ten minutes after turning about the Japanese saw the Russian flagship *Petropavlovsk* strike a mine. A second explosion followed, perhaps caused by ignition of a forward magazine. A third, probably in the boiler room, produced dense clouds of white steam which merged with the thick yellow smoke already hanging over the stricken ship. When this screen of smoke and steam had lifted, the battleship had disappeared, taking all but 80 of her crew with her. An eyewitness later recorded that he had seen Makarov on the bridge take off his greatcoat and go down on his knees for a final prayer. This was the last time he was seen; in the icy water a man of his age would not have lasted long. Another distinguished figure, the artist Vereshchagin who was on board to gather material for his war pictures, was also lost. The Grand Duke Cyril (who in exile two decades later would become the self-styled Tsar Cyril I) was saved. Some years later Japanese divers entered the sunken battleship and were able to identify the bodies of some of the staff officers, but there was no trace of Makarov. What is said to be his peaked cap, picked up after the sinking, rests now in a glass case in Leningrad.

While the surviving Russian ships were searching for survivors, the battleship *Pobieda* struck another mine. A coal bunker absorbed most of the blast, and she was able to limp back to harbour. At this point the Russians appear to have been gripped by a collective hysteria; Japanese submarines were imagined to be everywhere, and the ships began firing on the surrounding water with all available guns. Fifty years later, surviving Russian officers could still be met who clearly remembered sighting periscopes on that disastrous day, but Japan possessed no submarines at that time.

Just as on 9 February the Russians had been unlucky in that the only two battleships torpedoed happened to be their best, so on this day they were unlucky in that the one ship destroyed happened to be carrying their best admiral. The ascent of Russian morale and competence which Makarov had achieved did not survive his death. Crews were dispirited, and there were no high officers fit to replace him. Moreover, most of his chosen staff officers had died with him. For a time the Viceroy, Alekseev, took over the direct command of the squadron, but the landing of Japanese troops further north, threatening to cut off Port Arthur, caused Alekseev to evacuate himself to Mukden. Admiral Skrydlov, who was sent out by train to take over the squadron, was unable to reach Port Arthur, and had to be content with hoisting his flag at Vladivostok. Thus the command of the Port Arthur ships devolved upon Admiral Witgeft. Witgeft was a devoted officer but, having spent most of his service ashore, was unfitted for his command. Like General Kuropatkin, he modestly admitted that he was not a great leader; on his appointment he confessed to his assembled captains, 'I am not a fighting sailor.'[9]

Although he had now reduced the Russian strength to a level significantly below his own, Togo was still not satisfied. He knew that he could not keep Port Arthur under observation every hour of the day and night. There was always a chance that the Russians would come out and destroy Japanese transports or, perhaps worse, slip out to Vladivostok. So preparations continued for the third attempt to block the harbour. This time no fewer than 12 freighters were taken from Japan's dwindling stock of commercial ships. The date of 2 May was chosen, so as to coincide with the landing of the 2nd Army elsewhere in Manchuria. That evening, the weather being good, the blockships' crews (new this time) received their final instructions. But en route the weather deteriorated and the commander of the expedition ordered its postponement. However, only two of his ships received his signal, and the rest struggled on to Port Arthur. The commander, realising that his order had been ignored, attempted to pursue his errant ships and bring them back. But evidently full speed in rough sea was too much for his steamer, for his steering gear broke down. Another blockship had also broken down, so only eight ships made the attack. These arrived in groups, having lost contact with each other, and were easily countered by the defences. Not one ship was sunk in the channel. Only a few crew members could be removed by the torpedo craft. The remainder stayed on their ships or made for the shore. Next morning they refused to surrender and most fought against Russian troops until they were killed.

# 4  The War in Manchuria

The Japanese army could not imitate Togo and attack before war was declared. On the other hand, whereas Togo faced a strong Russian squadron, the army faced an enemy who was weak and scattered. The first Japanese troops landed in Korea at Chemulpo on the eve of the war, and at the beginning of April the 1st Army under General Kuroki reached the River Yalu. It was on the line of this river, dividing Korea from Manchuria, that the first substantial land battle was fought. A Russian detachment on the north bank faced the three Japanese divisions on the south bank near Wiju. Kuroki's problem was to get his men across the river so that their preponderant strength could be brought to bear.

This problem he solved brilliantly. While his carefully concealed artillery waited silently on midstream islands, one of his divisions established a bridgehead on the north shore some six miles inland. This bridgehead, achieved by a few boatloads of soldiers against negligible opposition, enabled a pontoon bridge to be built, the first of several.

By dawn on 1 May the three Japanese divisions were on the north shore, unknown to the Russians. The Japanese occupied a position along the eastern bank of the Ai ho, a tributary of the Yalu, while parallel to them, stretching for six miles on the other side of the Ai ho and only about 2000 yards away, were the Russian defences. The Russians had only seven battalions guarding this stretch, and had already suffered some gloom and casualties from an artillery bombardment the previous day. During the night Russian outposts reported hearing the sound of wheels crossing bridges, but even at this late stage their commander, General Zasulich, still expected the main blow to come on his right or centre, not on his left. Activity near the river mouth by small Japanese ships, which exchanged shots with the Cossack cavalry, probably reinforced his opinion. He therefore sent only the machine-gun company to reinforce his left flank. It was not until the fog lifted on the morning of 1 May that he realised his mistake.

The fog dispersed from the valley of the Ai ho at about 0600, and the battle could begin. In fact the battle was decided before the fighting started, because Kuroki's main task had been to get his men across the river, and this he had already achieved. A preliminary artillery duel resulted in the outnumbered Russian guns soon being silenced. Kuroki, in view of the apparent weakness of the defending force, decided on a simultaneous advance across the Ai ho by all three of his divisions. Heavy gunfire was directed on the Russian trenches as the Japanese infantry advanced. The latter was in close order; the Japanese still accepted the Prussian view that the extra momentum of closely packed troops outweighed their vulnerability. The Japanese dark blue uniforms stood out well against the sandy background, and those Russian riflemen whose heads were not kept down by artillery fire could aim at clearly defined targets. The attackers had discarded or lightened their packs, but were still encumbered when they waded chest-high into the waters of the Ali ho. The Russians had held their fire until the range was down to 1200 yards, but heavy casualties were inflicted as the river was crossed, many wounded being drowned. However, most of the Japanese troops emerged from the water, disorganised but not disheartened, and began to return the rifle fire. They were still supported by heavy artillery fire and in places were able to push back the Russians. In this way, with now one Japanese unit and then another moving forward, by 0900 the first Russian line had been captured. The forces on the right of the Russian line had retired in good order, but those of the northern sector, under Colonel Gromov, were in disarray and had lost their six guns. The Russian troops held in reserve, and those defending the areas where Zasulich still expected blows to fall, had been kept back and took no part.

Gromov, in view of the pressures he was facing, decided not to hold a second planned position but to retire further. However, his message to this effect was not received by headquarters until late afternoon. The forces south of Gromov were successfully holding the Japanese with a spirited defence along a mountain stream, thus becoming a rearguard which enabled the other Russian forces, including the reserve, to retire safely along the planned line of retreat. However, the unanticipated retirement of Gromov's forces exposed the left flank of this rearguard, which was consequently unable to conduct an unscathed retreat. Cut off in a narrow defile, part of the rearguard was eventually compelled to surrender, losing all machine guns and 11 field guns. Casualties at this final stage were quite heavy; in fact it was only at this point that the Russians could be said to have suffered a defeat, for hitherto they had been conducting a successful retirement before an overwhelming enemy. In all, Russian casualties were around 3000, and Japanese about 1000. For the Japanese, the most costly part of the battle had been the advance across the Ai ho.

After the war Kuropatkin blamed Zasulich for this defeat, accusing him of trying to crush the Japanese instead of retiring gracefully as he had been instructed. This seems somewhat unfair. After all, Kuropatkin had also ordered Zasulich to put up a 'firm' resistance, and it was precisely when he did put up a firm resistance that he became involved in a battle from which he extricated himself only with heavy losses. Zasulich's main mistake was that when offence might have been worthwhile, he held back; that is, he did not interfere when the Japanese were consolidating their bridgehead on the northern shore of the Yalu. However, the main trouble seems to have been lack of communication between the different commanders. The failure to report promptly important events was to be repeated in later actions; sometimes it was a question of forgetfulness, sometimes a self-deceptive hope that the single messenger would somehow get through. Zasulich himself might have discovered what the Japanese were planning if he had been more adventurous in the use of his scouts; if he had sent his Cossacks to reconnoitre across the river they would have met opposition but some at least would have got back with information about the Japanese dispositions. In the search for scapegoats, Gromov was court-martialled. Later he shot himself.

At the time the Battle of the Yalu was regarded as a historic encounter; orientals had fought Europeans on equal terms and won. The significance of this was not lost on other Asians, especially those living under colonial regimes. In Calcutta a poet regarded locally as 'the Kipling of Bengal' began (in English) a five-part epic which would conclude with sentiments like:

> Japan! thy magnanimity like wild fire spread,
> The proudest European Powers thee now dread,
> Thou amazed all, all nations, thee the world adores,
> Magnanimous Japan! thy praise like a torrent pours![1]

Meanwhile, further west, Port Arthur was already under threat. The Japanese 2nd Army, under General Oku, had landed near Pitzuwo (see map, p. x) in early May. Its advanced detachments soon cut the railway linking Port Arthur with the north and henceforth Port Arthur's touch with the outside world was limited to occasional blockade-running ships.

To defend Port Arthur from the north the Russians had chosen a strong defensive position near Nanshan. Here there is a narrow isthmus separating the Kwantung Peninsula, on which stands Port Arthur, from the Liaotung Peninsula. According to the state of the tide the width of this strip of land varies from only 4500 yards to about 6000 yards. Low hills enabled the Russians to site their defences so as to cover all the approaches. They had constructed redoubts, and emplaced some old Chinese heavy artillery on the hills. Barbed wire entanglements and man-traps, together with electrically detonated mines, provided additional strength. A weakness of the position was that the Japanese, having command of the sea, might land in its rear. But this would be no easy operation, for the Japanese troops would land in clear view of the Russians and could be opposed by forces sent from Port Arthur. Another, self-imposed, weakness of the position was that the main trenches were not placed on the hill sides, but at their feet. This accorded with the doctrine that rifle and gun fire was most effective on a flat trajectory, and with the belief that men on the hill sides would be more exposed to enemy fire. However, there would have been less dead ground if the defences had been sited higher. Moreover, the often steep hill sides would themselves have been an extra obstacle to attacking infantry. Tretyakov, the lieutenant colonel commanding the 5th East Siberian Rifle Regiment which was defending this line, protested to his superior, General Fock, about this siting of the trenches. But, he wrote later, Fock's only response was a fit of irritation.[2]

General Oku had about 35 000 men and 215 guns. His opponent, General Fock, put into the line only the 5th East Siberian Rifles (about 4000 men, 65 guns, and 10 machine guns). The bulk of the Russian forces were kept back as a reserve. The Japanese attack began at dawn with an artillery barrage, followed by infantry attacks against the whole line. The Russian guns replied as best they could but, being placed in open position without concealment, they suffered badly.

In the western sector of the line the Japanese were supported by gunboats, whose gunfire, taking the Russian positions in the rear, was extremely destructive. The Russian artillery was fully occupied with the enemy's field guns and paid little attention to the ships because it was the infantry, not the artillery, which was suffering from this naval bombardment; orders to a battery to turn its guns towards the ships had no result, although this was probably because the orders did not get through. On the other side of the isthmus a solitary Russian gunboat, *Bobr*, laid some damaging fire on the Japanese infantry. But she soon steamed off and was not replaced.

Meanwhile the Japanese infantry attacks were defeated, thanks largely to the Russian machine guns, which had been skilfully positioned. Despite careful use of dead ground and cover, the Japanese assaults were dissipated before they could reach the Russian position. Scenes which later would be typical of the fighting in Manchuria was presented to the curious eyes of the Western war correspondents: lines of closely packed Japanese infantry shouting 'Banzai!' (the Japanese 'hurrah') rushing at the entrenchments and being cut down by small-arms fire, followed by fresh lines which would meet the same fate.

At about midday the artillery fire ceased; the Japanese needed to bring up ammunition and most of the Russian guns were out of action. The infantry attacks also died down, but after about an hour the battle was resumed. The Russian line, thanks to Fock's refusal to send in any of his ample reserve, was very thinly held. This meant that Japanese shrapnel shells did not kill many Russians while the latter, with their magazine rifles and machine guns, were still adequate to repel assaults. The attacks of the afternoon were fruitless, and the Russian commanders felt confident that they had little to fear from the Japanese infantry. But towards evening the western flank of the Russians was turned. Apparently some of the Russian defenders had been forced to withdraw by Japanese naval gunfire. Reinforcements had been requested, but Fock had refused to send them. Fock also refused to use his reserve to mount a counterattack. Since he was not willing to incur casualties in saving the situation, Fock ordered a general withdrawal. However, the local commander (Tretyakov) was not informed of this decision. When Tretyakov heard that his force was withdrawing, he rushed to the scene and tried to persuade his men to halt and resist the Japanese only to be told, 'Your Honour, we have been ordered to retreat.' At this point Tretyakov and his fleeting men came under Japanese shellfire. Tretyakov's horse was terrified by a piece of shrapnel which struck her ear, and as she and her rider careered madly off the men continued their flight. Thus by nightfall the western sector of the Russian position had been lost, and considerable casualties incurred. To avoid being taken in the flank, troops of other sectors had also to retreat. At least one company, having earlier being instructed to fight to the last man if necessary, did so, and refused to withdraw. Individual officers, too, stayed behind, swearing that they would never retreat. One of them, standing alone in his abandoned position, emptied his revolver at the oncoming Japanese before being killed.

The Russian retreat during the night was successful, mainly because the Japanese did not pursue. There were occasional panics. One such panic set in when an artillery battery rushed at breakneck speed along a track full of retreating infantry amid cries of 'Japanese cavalry!' In fact there was no Japanese cavalry, but the thought was sufficient to convert a retreat into a mad rush. Eventually Tretyakov managed to find his regimental band, and ordered it to strike up a march. This had the desired effect, the men fell into step and the band continued playing throughout the retreat. Arrived at a nearby railway station, where it had hoped to find the regimental baggage, the 5th Regiment discovered that this had already been despatched to Port Arthur, so it had nothing to eat. But its redoubtable commander soon found a few wagonloads of bread in a railway siding, and had this distributed. He himself went to the station buffet, which he found full of officers but with all its food supplies exhausted. Luckily, he wrote later, 'I succeeded in obtaining some salt with which to flavour my bread.' The next day the 5th Regiment began the march back to Port Arthur, accompanied by several hundred head of cattle; while fighting the Japanese at Nanshan it had also been fulfilling an order to round up all available local cattle and march the beasts towards Port Arthur.

A few days later Tretyakov's regiment was congratulated by the commander of the region, General Stoessel. Until then many men thought they were in disgrace, having abandoned their Nanshan positions to the enemy. Stoessel arrived with a bagful of St George crosses, intending to award them to those soldiers who had been wounded but who nevertheless had stayed in the ranks. But there were more than 300 of these, so the doctors were instructed to select the most badly wounded; 60 of these received the decoration. Thus many deserving men were unrewarded. Possibly the limited number of awards was a consequence of the criticism directed at the over-generous distribution of these crosses that had followed the Japanese navy's surprise attack on Port Arthur. On that occasion two crosses were given to each company, many of which had not even seen the Japanese. Company commanders, not knowing to which individuals the crosses should be awarded, had drawn lots for them, with the result that cooks and other non-combatants received the Empire's highest award for bravery. Thus St George crosses were losing their distinction. Equally valued by the soldiers would be the Tsar's instruction, in September, that each month of service spent at besieged Port Arthur was to be counted as one year of the soldiers' terms of military service.

The Russians claimed that Nanshan was a victory, because they had successfully withdrawn with little loss in face of a stronger force. Russian casualties were about 850, compared with about 4300 Japanese. From the point of view of causing the most damage to the enemy with the least damage to oneself, Fock's conduct of the battle had been highly successful. But his critics complained that whereas the position could have been held for weeks the way was now open to Port Arthur, whose defences were still incomplete. However, there is some evidence that Kuropatkin had made it clear that he did not want a long holding action at Nanshan.[3] If resisted too long at this point the Japanese might have decided to merely seal off Port Arthur and thus would have been able to send stronger forces northwards against Kuropatkin, who was not yet ready to fight a major battle.

Having captured the key Nanshan position, Oku and most of his troops moved northwards to join the forces facing Kuropatkin in Manchuria. For two weeks, unknown to the Russians, the Japanese left only one division to cover Port Arthur. They were still too weak to advance immediately against Kuropatkin but reinforcements were landing according to plan. A further army, the 4th under General Nodzu, landed in May at Takushan with the object of operating with Oku's 2nd and Kuroki's 1st Armies against Kuropatkin. Nearer Port Arthur, two fresh divisions were landed to join with the one division already in the Peninsula, thus forming the 3rd Army under General Nogi. It was this 3rd Army which was entrusted with the capture of Port Arthur.

Until the 3rd Army was fully assembled, the weakened Japanese force in the Peninsula advanced only slowly towards the south. But the port of Dalny, evacuated hastily by the Russians, was occupied on 30 May. Before the war Dalny had been developed as part of the commercial offensive in the Far East. Intended by Witte to become the principal port of Manchuria, it received extensive, and expensive, installations. Officers complained that the concrete used at Dalny would have been better expended to make Port Arthur safe, and as things turned out they were quite right. It was not long before the Japanese began to use the port as the main entry for troops and

supplies destined for the siege of Port Arthur. Being close to Port
Arthur, and having a rail link, Dalny was ideally situated for this
purpose.

By the end of May the deployment of Japanese troops on the
mainland was well under way, thanks to the Russian navy's inaction.
Russian land forces were divided between the Port Arthur defenders
and the Manchurian field army. The latter included the Eastern
Detachment under General Keller, holding the mountains which
separated the Japanese 1st and 4th Armies from the main Russian
centres of Liaoyang and Mukden; a Siberian corps, divided between
Yinkou, Tashinchiao and Kaiping, which covered the railway and the
Mandarin Road from the Peninsula northwards; and the reserve
forces and HQ services at Liaoyang (see map, p. x). In addition
there were cavalry forces filling in the gaps between the main groups.
Kuropatkin's strategy was to concentrate his forces around Liaoyang
and to stay on the defensive until his troops outnumbered his
opponents. Thus for the time being his advanced forces were to delay
the expected Japanese advance northwards, but were to retreat in
good time without getting drawn into full-scale battles with superior
forces. In the meantime, in accordance with the Russian predilection
for positional warfare, strong fortifications were built covering the
roads leading to Liaoyang.

The Japanese strategy was to leave Nogi's 3rd Army to invest Port
Arthur, and to move all other forces as soon as possible against the
Russian concentration in Manchuria. The roads northwards, which
were neither good nor plentiful, determined the positions and lines of
march of the Japanese armies. The three armies would move
northwards along roads which converged near Liaoyang. Until this
junction was reached there could be little communication between
the armies because of the intervening mountains. General Oku's 2nd
Army had the best road, the Mandarin Road, which paralleled the
railway from Port Arthur. It passed close to the western side of the
Liaotung Peninsula, over easy terrain, and north of the Peninsula it
followed the line dividing the mountains in the east from the plain of
the Laio River in the west. The 1st and 4th Armies, on the other
hand, had to move through a succession of passes, easily defended by
Russian detachments. The local climate was extreme; in summer it
would be very hot, but rivers might be flooded, while in winter it
would be bitterly cold but the ground would be firm.

Kuropatkin's strategy of gradual retreat was compromised in June,
when both Alekseev and St Petersburg urged Kuropatkin to do

something to relieve Port Arthur. Kuropatkin seemed content to let Port Arthur hold out until he had accumulated sufficient troops to defeat the main Japanese forces, after which the siege would automatically be ended. But his superiors, perhaps knowing that Port Arthur's defences suffered from past neglect, aware of its importance to the navy, and conscious of public concern, were not prepared to show the same careful patience. They ordered Kuropatkin to prepare an attack.

From the start Kuropatkin appears to have planned this operation with one main aim, to commit the minimum number of troops likely to satisfy Alekseev. He did not enjoy Alekseev's interference; indeed, as a general he could not be expected to appreciate fighting his battles under the supervision of an admiral. But he realised that he could not ignore Alekseev's instructions and therefore ordered General Stakelberg to take the 1st Siberian Corps southwards to Telissu, a town lying about 25 miles north of the Japanese 2nd Army's position. A cavalry brigade under Samsonov had already reconnoitred in that direction, and had encountered a squadron of Japanese cavalry, which it routed by a lance charge (the only occasion in the war when this much-practised movement was used).

On 7 June Kuropatkin issued to Stakelberg orders in which Stakelberg was told to avoid fighting the enemy when outnumbering the Japanese, and that the aim of his operation was the capture (that is, recapture) of the Nanshan position, and an advance on Port Arthur. It is hard to see how Kuropatkin could sincerely have believed that Stakelberg, who commanded only one corps, would be able to advance to Port Arthur without fighting superior enemy forces. What is most likely is that the orders were designed to please Alekseev, rather than to instruct Stakelberg. The latter was perhaps expected to read between the lines in the Russian bureaucratic tradition. Stakelberg had a meeting with Kuropatkin later; what was discussed on that occasion was not revealed but it probably had more relevance to actual circumstances than did the written orders.

Stakelberg took his corps southwards and selected a defensive position south of Telissu. Here he awaited the expected advance of Oku's 2nd Army, which he intended to hold and then to counterattack. Oku had been awaiting the arrival of transport, but did at last move northwards, driving back the advanced Russian cavalry scouts. Soon the Japanese were close enough to the main Russian position to bring up their artillery. The Russian guns had been positioned on a spur of the low hills which formed the backbone of the Russian line.

In the ensuing artillery duel, most of the Russian guns were used, thus revealing their positions, and as they were in exposed sites they suffered heavily. By this time Oku was convinced that the Russian force was only small, even though Stakelberg was continuously receiving reinforcements by train. The Japanese therefore decided to mount a general attack on the following day, 14 June.

Stakelberg's intention for 14 June was to attack on his left, and he issued orders to his commander in that sector, General Gerngross, to attack in the night, supported by the reserve. This reserve would be replaced by a fresh reserve, composed of men arriving by train. As was often the case with Russian orders, Stakelberg's messages to Gerngross were courteous and vague. Gerngross was not ordered to attack at a certain hour; he was asked if he would be so kind as to attack, before dawn at least. The orders sent to the commander of the reserve were similarly vague, and the latter was subsequently troubled by receiving conflicting requests from Stakelberg and Gerngross. Because orders were sent individually to each commander, rather than a general order being sent to all, none of the subordinates quite understood what was going on. This made it impossible for officers to respond to unforeseen circumstances in the spirit of the general plan, for the general plan was known only to Stakelberg.

In the event, Gerngross did not begin his attack until well after daybreak. There had been misunderstandings, and in the end he went forward without the reserve. Meanwhile Oku had been preparing his own attack. This was going to be a frontal assault to hold the Russians down, accompanied by enveloping movements on both flanks. Under cover of the night fog he had brought his attacking troops close to the Russian line. When it was light, the Japanese artillery opened fire on the Russian guns and, having learned their positions from the previous day's artillery duel, soon silenced them. Thus just as Gerngross's troops began their advance, the Japanese guns were free to devote themselves to the Russian infantry. Despite casualties from this gunfire, the Russian attack was pressed vigorously, and soon the Russians were within 600 yards of the shelter trenches in which the Japanese infantry had been assembling for their own attack. Fierce fighting took place here and lasted all morning.

At the same time, Russian officers became aware of Japanese forces on their right. Cavalry scouts had sent in a report about these figures soon after dawn, but it did not reach Stakelberg until shortly before noon. Since the Japanese had not been expected to attack from this direction, no telephone lines had been laid. The Japanese forces in this sector were comparatively weak, but because the direction of their advance was unexpected they produced disastrous results for the Russians. Stakelberg went in person to repair the damage, having two horses shot under him in the process. But the Russian line was clearly outflanked and Stakelberg ordered a general retreat. In their withdrawal Gerngross's troops suffered grievously from gunfire, but in general the retreat was orderly. Trains arrived up to early afternoon with fresh troops, and these were thrown into the holding operation while the wounded and the more weary troops were entrained. The main Russian forces later withdrew, covered by a force of cavalry commanded by Samsonov. The Japanese did not pursue; they were tired, there was heavy rain, and the Chinese carters and coolies on whom they relied for transport had mostly fled and those who stayed refused to work because it was a Chinese holiday.

By this time, Western correspondents and military attachés were with the contending armies. While those who were with the Russians complained the loudest about censorship and suspicion, in reality it was the Japanese who controlled the news most closely. Many Western correspondents did not realise that the Japanese showed them only what was considered suitable for foreign eyes (the Russian authorities had the same intention, but carried it out less efficiently and less politely). At one point the *Times* correspondent did make a protest to the Japanese; this was courteously received but achieved little result. Military attachés were usually more perceptive than the journalists. One of them, Ian Hamilton, later described in *A Staff Officer's Scrapbook* his experiences with the Japanese army. This is one of the few first-person accounts by foreigners which have much value, as its author had the knowledge to enable him to penetrate the wool which his hosts so politely placed before his eyes. British correspondents wrote many words to mock the German military writers and their theories, with whom they had been locked in verbal battle ever since the animosities of the Boer War. The enormous casualties incurred by the Japanese as they followed the Prussian precept of mass frontal attack gave the British plenty of ammunition for their assault on the spokesmen of German military doctrine. 'No German has taken part in serious war for the last thirty-three years,' observed *The Times*, 'and the writings of Germans of the younger generation are those of men entirely devoid of practical knowledge of war.'[4] The aged von Meckel, who received a telegram from his grateful Japanese pupils after the Battle of the Yalu, was almost the only German expert who predicted a Japanese victory in the war; the majority of German writers contrived to praise simultaneously the costly Japanese frontal attacks while predicting successive Russian victories.

Many Western visitors were conducted around Japanese field hospitals, and sent home rosy accounts of Japanese efficiency, compassion and hygiene. Significantly, one of the truly professional observers (an officer of the Royal Army Medical Corps) reported that Japanese hospitals were typically inhabited by masses of flies, which thrived on the filth that the hospitals dumped almost on their own doorsteps. But then it was not always possible, it seemed, to site hospitals ideally, although the front-line post described by one Japanese surgeon seems unnecessarily hazardous:

> We found our hospital the target of many missiles. One man, just as I raised him in my arms for the purpose of dressing his wounds, had his leg shattered by a shell which came through the mud wall of the house and grazed my tunic as it passed out.[5]

It was not until late July that the next major battle was fought. This was at Tashihchiao, where the Russian positions had been chosen personally by Kuropatkin, and General Zarubaev left in charge of the defence. The battle commenced at daybreak on 24 July. The previous night the Russian infantry had not occupied the defence trenches but had been allowed to rest in comfort behind the hill. The Japanese began with an artillery barrage, but were unable to silence the Russian guns. At 0900 the Japanese infantry advanced but, lacking artillery supremacy, did not push their attack very vigorously. Stakelberg, commanding the Russian infantry in this sector, did not even consider it necessary to bring his troops out from their shelter. But after four hours, feeling that eventually he might be compelled to order his troops into the firing line, he advised Zarubaev to retreat. This advice, given by a subordinate general whose troops had not yet gone into action, caused considerable adverse comment by military observers later. Stakelberg's recommendation to retreat was, however, couched in such terms as to make it clear that the advice was based on Kuropatkin's general plan of campaign. That is, Stakelberg was warning that if his men were sent to the trenches they would be drawn into a battle from which they would extricate themselves only with considerable loss. Zarubaev replied that he was unable to retreat in daylight, but that he might retreat during the night.

During the rest of the day the Japanese pressed their attacks, but in all sectors their gains were small and their losses high. Coordination between the different Russian formations was good; on one occasion the artillery of one corps was willingly turned to assist the infantry of another corps, with good effect. However, a planned Russian counterattack came to nothing because of a failure to agree among the Russian commanders; there was still a lack of clear-cut authority in the relationships between the higher officers. This counterattack, intended to throw back one of the Japanese divisions, was proposed by one general, who needed to 'arrange the cooperation' of the cavalry. The cavalry commander graciously 'consented' to the proposals, but an infantry commander whose cooperation was required simply refused to contribute any of his men.

The Russian artillery won great credit in this battle. Its guns were fewer than the Japanese, but were of longer range, and rapid-firing. They had been positioned with some care, the experience of Telissu having been heeded. Before the Battle of Telissu, Stakelberg had inspected the artillery positions and pointed out the need to site weapons under cover (that is, to use indirect fire). But the majority of the artillery officers, especially the senior officers, disagreed, saying that indirect fire could be used only against stationary targets. Those battery commanders who disagreed with them seem to have been overruled; with the exception of one battery all the Russian guns at Telissu had been sited for direct fire, and were thereby exposed disastrously to Japanese gunfire. At Tashihchiao it was quite different. The guns were positioned behind rising ground in fields amid six-feet tall kao-liang. The Japanese located few Russian guns and suffered the additional disadvantage that they had to move their own rather short-range guns during the battle so as to follow behind as the infantry advanced. Thus although the Japanese had about 250 guns compared with the Russians' 112, the gun battle was plainly won by the latter. This allowed that portion of the Russian infantry which was actually brought into action to withstand Japanese infantry attacks for 15 hours.

However, although Zarubaev had inflicted great loss on the Japanese without employing his full strength, and although Oku had very little in reserve, the Russian general decided to retreat in the night. He later reported that this was because his guns were almost at the end of their ammunition, but it seems more likely that the main influence in his decision was Stakelberg's earlier advice to retreat. Whatever the reason, the Russians withdrew. A night assault by the

Japanese met only slight resistance from the departing Russian rearguard. Both at the time and in retrospect, it would seem that a great opportunity had been lost by the Russians. Even with little support from their guns, an infantry counterattack would almost certainly have been victorious. Instead, there was a retreat which was one more blow against the morale of the ordinary Russian soldier.

Tashihchiao, which Oku's 2nd Army occupied the following day, was the railway junction for the port of Yinkou. With the Japanese in control of this rail line, the Russians decided to abandon Yinkou and the adjacent town of Newchuang. Soon Yinkou became the supply port for Oku's army, with ships sailing directly from Japan. The Battle of Tashihchiao also opened the way northwards, enabling the 2nd Army to capture the road junction at Haicheng and thereby join up with the 4th Army, which had been marching northwards from Takushan.

The other Japanese army, Kuroki's 1st, was similarly fighting its way northwards. It was opposed by the Russian 'Eastern Force' under Count Keller, whose three infantry divisions were supported by a cavalry division under General Rennenkampf. After the Battle of the Yalu, Kuroki's advance had been delayed by an excursion of the Russian battleships from Port Arthur on 23 June. This naval renaissance had persuaded Togo that he could not guarantee a totally secure supply route for the army's transports. The Japanese command accordingly postponed until the rainy season the battles which it anticipated would take place when the three armies converged on the Russian stronghold at Liaoyang. Meanwhile Kuroki slowly advanced through the mountains, capturing successive passes from the poorly coordinated Russian defenders. Russian mountain artillery was outclassed by the Japanese, and the infantry suffered badly in consequence. One Russian battalion, advancing in close order, was caught by shellfire and lost 300 men in a few minutes. In general, the Russian forces on this sector were poorly led, and old-fashioned in their methods. The artillery was rarely brought into battle in full force; infantry officers exposed themselves to fire with the sole object, it seemed, of showing how brave they were; the men were placed in close order, with scant reference to cover; and infantry firing was by section volleys, which were easier to control but less effective.

By the beginning of August the three Japanese armies had all converged to within about 30 miles of Liaoyang. They were ready for what was expected to the first great battle of the war and what, in retrospect, may be seen as the first of the twentieth century's great battles, with masses of troops fighting on unprecedentedly long fronts with unprecedentedly destructive weapons. A month earlier Marshal Oyama had arrived from Japan to take overall control of the armies. With such large forces spread over such wide fronts, some coordination was obviously needed. The practice of leaving individual army commanders to their own initiative had plainly worked better than the Russian system of the commander-in-chief closely supervising his subordinates in detail. But what had worked well when the Japanese armies were geographically separated was likely to be less effective when they fought side by side, as they would in the future.

Foreign newspaper correspondents had·flocked to Manchuria for the expected battle. How well they described reality is doubtful. A British resident of Mukden probably cut close to the truth of twentieth-century journalism when he wrote:

> Military attachés and war correspondents came and went. Some of these lived comfortably in Mukden, picked up what views and tales they could, and sent their despatches promptly. Others risked their lives at the front, saw the realities of the war, and returned to Mukden to find themselves left behind by their less enterprising brethren in the race to supply what passed for news.[6]

By 23 August the Russians had concentrated 135 000 infantrymen, 12 000 cavalrymen and 599 guns at Liaoyang. Against these the Japanese commanders disposed of 115 000 infantry, 4000 cavalry and 470 guns. During the ensuing battle, moreover, reinforcements continued to reach the Russian forces. The terrain varied dramatically; west of the Mandarin Road there was a fertile plain covered with kao-liang, but east of the road it was mountainous. Here the hills were sometimes bare, sometimes covered with trees. Their lower slopes were often terraced for cultivation and kao-liang, thick and ten feet high, was grown in the valleys. The numerous streams were small but liable to be transformed into rapidly flowing torrents after storms. The main river of the locality, the Taitzu, flowed westward to Liaoyang, then bent northward and again westward.

There were few reinforcements forthcoming for the Japanese forces, whereas Kuropatkin was becoming stronger every day, so from the Japanese point of view the battle was better fought sooner than later. Redeployment of divisions to achieve an overwhelming concentration of forces on one or other of the two axes of the advance

was not impracticable, but was certainly difficult because of the
mountains which separated the two Japanese groups. Likewise,
outflanking movements would be difficult to effect rapidly. The more
simple tactic of a direct assault was therefore adopted, but since the
advantages of two attacks converging on one point could only be
obtained where the two routes of advance joined, it was desirable to
force back the Russian forces as far as Liaoyang, where the two roads
met, and stage the decisive stage of the battle at that point.

Until 24 August Kuropatkin's plan was to conduct a strong but
flexible defence with detached forces well to the south of Liaoyang,
while at the same time assembling a strong reserve. The latter, at a
suitable moment, would be launched into a counteroffensive against
the numerically inferior Japanese. The detached forces were expected to fall back slowly to a well-prepared 'advanced position'
where they would hold the enemy until the Russian counteroffensive
was ready. But on 24 August Kuropatkin learned that a fresh
Siberian corps would be arriving in time for the battle. This encourag-
ing news led him to change his plan; it was now decided that the
detached forces would hold their ground and not retire to the
'advanced position', and that the counteroffensive would be mounted
sooner than originally intended.

Serious fighting began on 26 August. The Russian artillery in many
sectors silenced the Japanese guns, except where the latter were
exceptionally well-hidden in kao-liang. However, Russian shellfire
against Japanese infantry was not outstandingly successful. It seemed
that the quality of the Russian gunfire varied from unit to unit; some
officers made good use of their quickfirers while others were still
unable to cope with these newly-introduced weapons. In the east,
after successive Japanese failures to capture the Hungsha pass, the
attackers resorted to a night operation that was totally successful.
The loss of this pass, together with a storm which threatened to so
enlarge the Tang River as to cut off one of the advanced Russian
formations, persuaded Kuropatkin to once more change his plan.
The Russians would, after all, fall back on the 'advanced position.'
The withdrawal took place during the night of 26–27 August, silently
and without lights. A pontoon bridge was dismantled and its pon-
toons floated down the river for re-use elsewhere. In the east,
withdrawal was aided by fog, while in the southern sector it was only
in the morning, when the Japanese infantry launched another attack
on hitherto impregnable entrenchments, that the Russian departure
was discovered. Not until the afternoon did the Japanese headquar-

ters learn that the Russians had gone; on this occasion at least, Japanese communications were as inadequate as the Russian.

The main battle began on 30 August. Six-and-a-half Japanese divisions made a frontal attack on the Russian 'advanced position' south of Liaoyang, while Kuroki sent his Twelfth Division to ford the hip-high Taitzu about 15 miles east of Liaoyang. The main Japanese attacks of 30 August were unsuccessful, and it seems clear that the Japanese staff had not mastered the technique of controlling such large numbers of men in battle. In many cases, perhaps wisely, units had been instructed to act as they thought best, but this often meant that they took no action at all. Similar results were obtained when units were bidden to act in accord with neighbouring units.

Partly because the guns were placed too far in the rear and were unable to assist the infantry to the planned extent, the Japanese made no headway on this day. Their assaults had been intense, and losses heavy. One Siberian corps, defending 7000 yards of front, was assailed by 45 000 Japanese infantry (six men per yard) with 332 guns and mortars, yet held its ground. In front of their positions the Russians had cut the kao-liang for up to 1000 yards, giving their riflemen an absolutely clear field of fire. It was hardly surprising that some of the Japanese infantrymen seemed unwilling to leave the shelter of the kao-liang and advance the final half-mile against the Russian positions.

However, Kuroki's outflanking move across the Taitzu was completely successful. This not only threatened Kuropatkin's eastern flank, it also threatened his communications along the road to Mukden. For this reason, during the night of 30–31 August Kuropatkin issued an order referring to 'considerable forces' that had crossed the Taitzu; evidently he had an exaggerated impression of Kuroki's strength. He ordered the forces defending the 'advanced position' to fall back on the strong 'main position' which had been prepared at Liaoyang itself. This shortened his front, releasing troops to tackle Kuroki's bridgehead on the Taitzu. This large-scale redeployment was successfully carried out in the night of 31 August–1 September. No sound reached the Japanese, who were concurrently planning a last desperate night assault. When this was launched the Japanese infantry discovered that they were once again attacking empty trenches. But after so many costly failures, this capture of the Russian position raised spirits considerably, even though the Japanese were too exhausted to pursue. It was not until late the next afternoon that their heavy guns were brought up by rail to open the bombardment on the Russian 'main position'.

Meanwhile, using compasses to guide themselves through the thick kao-liang, units of Kuroki's troops encountered various weak Russian forces, and defeated them. Kuropatkin deployed against Kuroki most of the men who had retreated earlier from the 'advanced position'. They were to assemble on 1 September and attack the following day. At this stage and afterwards, both Kuroki and Kuropatkin were misinformed about each other. Kuropatkin was unaware that Kuroki had barely more than a division on the northern side of the Taitzu, while Kuroki, convinced that the Russians were retreating, assumed that the Russian forces assembling for his destruction were merely a strong rearguard.

The Japanese capture of a hill that they called Manjuyama ('Rice Cake Hill') spoiled Kuropatkin's plan. This hill was vital because it projected into the plain and commanded a wide area. So long as the Japanese occupied this hill in force they could threaten the flank of the troops which Kuropatkin intended to send against Kuroki. Manjuyama was lost by the Russians during the night of 1–2 September after some heavy fighting. Attempts to recapture it the next day, despite a heavy pounding by Russian artillery, were unsuccessful. Kuropatkin, having already been forced to postpone his attack, entrusted General Sluchevski with the recapture at any cost of Manjuyama. Sluchevski, however, did not know the ground, and was a man always careful to avoid putting himself in a situation where he might incur blame. Earlier in the battle he had been in charge of a reserve unit, and was asked by a fellow commander to send some reserves to a sector where they could exploit a Russian success; he insisted on writing to Kuropatkin for approval (in writing) of this, and the reserves were never sent. In his new undertaking, the capture of Manjuyama, Sluchevski looked around for the nearest senior officer, found him, and ostentatiously placed himself under his orders. Probably Sluchevski's deficiencies did not directly cause the Russian failure to recapture Manjuyama, but it is quite possible that a more determined officer would have been more successful.

Soon after midnight on 3 September, Kuropatkin received a report from one of his best generals, Stakelberg, saying that the doughty 1st Siberian Corps had fallen back, thus endangering the flank of Kuropatkin's proposed attack on Kuroki. Stakelberg continued his tale of woe with 'Not only am I not attacking with reinforcements, but I cannot attack at all.'[7] At about the same time Kuropatkin heard that the last attack on Manjuyama had failed. As if even this were not enough, the commander of the troops defending the 'main position' at Liaoyang reported that he was running out of reserves of men and ammunition. At this, Kuropatkin gave up. He cancelled the attack on Kuroki envisaged for 3 September, and ordered a retreat. All forces were to retire towards Mukden, the troops at the 'main position' leaving last, and Stakelberg was to provide the rearguard. It was not until about midday on 4 September that the Japanese realised that the Russians were retreating to Mukden. There was a half-hearted pursuit, but the Russians retired in good order, despite a severe thunderstorm.

Japanese casualties in the Battle of Liaoyang were rather more than 20 000, the Russian rather less than 20 000. But it was unquestionably a Japanese victory. Although numerically inferior, the Japanese armies under the direction of Oyama had driven the Russians from prepared positions on a battlefield of the Russians' own choosing. This victory counterbalanced the effect on Japanese and world opinion of the failure of the first Japanese assault on Port Arthur, which occurred at about the same time. All the same, it was a close-run thing, and the Japanese had no cause for complacency. They had failed in their main assault on the Russian prepared position. Their units had not always been well-coordinated. Their infantrymen, contrary to the glowing reports sent home by newspaper correspondents, had not everywhere exhibited that highly-praised fanatical courage. Their artillery had been relatively ineffective, and vulnerable to counterbarrage from the Russian guns. Intelligence had not always been first-class; towards the end of the battle strong Japanese forces were held back unused in the western sector because the arrival of stray Russian reinforcements was believed to presage a strong counterattack in that sector. At the very time Kuropatkin decided to give up, Kuroki was in an unenviable position, being isolated from the main Japanese forces and facing stronger Russian forces.

Kuropatkin's main weakness was his too-frequent change of orders. In particular, in the initial stages the excessive strength of his two detached forces encouraged him to abandon his intention of falling back on prepared positions. When he was compelled to readopt his earlier intention these two large forces began to perform a function which could have been handled better by a small rearguard. Although here, as elsewhere, the Russian commanders showed great skills in retiring, and redeploying large formations in the face of the enemy, such retirements had a crucial effect on morale. Whereas the Japanese attackers, after successive failures, recovered their spirits when they realised that the Russians were retreating, the ordinary Russian soldier, who had been prepared to fight to the last, saw positions that had been sturdily held at some cost suddenly, and for no apparent reason, abandoned to the Japanese. Since the two sides were closely matched, the gradual deterioration of Russian morale may well have been the decisive factor in the result. As for Kuropatkin's morale, it is clear that he was not at his best when he gave the order to retire towards Mukden. If he had been more zestful at that time he would have checked the pessimistic reports which reached him. If he had, he would have discovered that the 'main position' was still resisting Japanese attacks and likely to do so for some time, and that Stakelberg's corps was not in quite as bad a state as had been reported. Evidently other commanders were under as much strain as Kuropatkin. It has to be remembered that these battles of the Russo–Japanese War placed men and officers under fire for days continuously, whereas the battles of earlier wars usually consisted of much manœuvring out of range and then an hour or two of climax.

After the Battle of Liaoyang the Russians retired towards Mukden, taking up position on the north bank of the Sha ho, but leaving their cavalry on the south bank in order to keep the Japanese under observation. Both armies spent the next weeks reorganising and making good the losses of the battle. An organisational change on the Russian side was the formation of the 2nd Army. General Grippenberg was appointed to command this, although it was stressed that he would be under the general direction of Kuropatkin, who stayed with the 1st Army. Losses at Liaoyang had not been especially heavy, and much of the Russian effort in these weeks was devoted to fortification of the new position and to the improvement of communications. Many river bridges were built, as well as a wide military road from Harbin to Mukden. According to Kuropatkin's report to Alekseev, the morale of his men was excellent. They had plenty of bread, he wrote, but would appreciate a little jam.

# 5  The End of the Russian Squadron

While the opposing armies were fighting their first engagement, Admiral Togo's main concern was still the protection of the army's sea communications. Off the Liaotung Peninsula the navy made great efforts to clear the intensive and extensive minefields laid by the Russians at possible landing points; at Dalny, whose port facilities were needed for the siege of Port Arthur, the mines were cleared in three weeks, which was considered admirably fast. Some support was offered by naval guns to the Japanese armies fighting in the Peninsula. Here again there was some risk of loss by mines. Because of this, and because Togo held his best ships in readiness to deal with a possible sortie by the Russian squadron, it was the older and smaller ships that were used in these operations. Prior to the Nanshan operation, gunboats bombarded the railway where it skirted Chinchou Bay; a special train carrying General Stoessel came under fire, and the General had to continue his journey on horseback until the gunboats departed. In the act of retirement one of the gunboats was lost by collision. Later, during the Battle of Nanshan, Japanese naval gunfire took the Russian positions in the rear, creating a critical situation for the defence.

During the same battle, on the other side of the Peninsula the Russian gunboat *Bobr* inflicted serious losses on the Japanese troops. *Bobr* was a small and elderly (1885) vessel, but her armament included a nine-inch and a six-inch gun. She fired only for three hours, returning to Port Arthur when her ammunition was exhausted. Many officers believed that if *Bobr* had been supplemented by other gunboats the Japanese would have been replused, but by this time the Port Arthur squadron was inert. Too many commanders preferred a quiet life.

Makarov had evidently been troubled by such commanders for he had, almost on a daily basis, switched the officers of his destroyers from one ship to another in order to ensure that those craft which put to sea had competent officers. After the death of Makarov this problem, as might be expected, worsened. Some officers virtually refused to put to sea. The army began to show a certain contempt for the navy; wounding hints, and even insults, were passed. A favourite saying in the cafés of Port Arthur was, 'Our navy, of course, is still strictly observing the laws of neutrality.' There was also a riddle; why do Russian squadrons need two admirals? Answer: one to take the ships to sea and one to order them out. Several Russian sources suggest that at the time of the Nanshan operations the *Bobr* was not supported by its sister-ships because their captains refused to lift a finger. As one army officers wrote in his diary:

> The other day the order was given to *Gremyashchi* and *Otvazhny* to put to sea, and both commanders immediately on leaving signalled that one of them had no shells and the other had no fresh water, and they came back. Later in conversation, they cynically justified their conduct, saying they 'could not go to certain destruction.' Both (captains Nikolaev and Lebedev) were relieved of their commands. We would like to see how in similar circumstances army officers would have been treated; clearly they would have been shot on the spot.[1]

And yet, according to another account, Lebedev later died heroically in the land fighting.[2]

Togo kept Port Arthur under close observation. From an advanced base in the Elliott Islands he was able to maintain reconnaissance operations off the Russian base, but he was never able to prevent the Russian destroyers using the port. Often these small ships would creep out at night or in fog to make their own reconnaissance, or to lay mines. The Russians also made use of junks, and neutral ships, mainly Chinese junks, sometimes slipped into the base. To make his task easier, on 26 May Togo declared a total blockade of Port Arthur; neutral ships found in the waters of the Liaotung Peninsula would be intercepted and dealt with according to international law. How far international law would protect the Chinese was doubtful.

Earlier in May Togo had suffered his worst defeat of the war. The commander of the Russian minelayer *Amur* had noticed that the Japanese warships in their frequent patrols past Port Arthur tended to follow a set route. He suggested that mines should be laid, unobserved, across this route. It appears that this suggestion was not received by his superiors with any great enthusiasm, but reluctant assent was finally given. On the morning of 14 May Captain Ivanov took his *Amur* to about ten miles south-east of Port Arthur and laid a line of mines about one mile long, with mines spaced 50–100 feet apart. Low-lying fog prevented the Japanese seeing what was happening; from *Amur* the topmasts of patrolling Japanese ships could be seen above the fog, and the Japanese presumably observed the Russian topmasts but believed them to be Japanese.

The following morning a Japanese detachment, under the command of Admiral Nashiba and including three battleships, passed along the accustomed route. The flagship *Hatsuse* soon struck a mine which lifted the stern several feet into the air and blew a large hole in her side. Nashiba ordered his other ships to retire, but a few minutes later a second battleship, *Yashima*, struck another mine, began to list, and then detonated a second mine. Nashiba ordered his cruisers to take the striken battleships in tow, but no sooner was *Hatsuse* attached to the tow rope than she too struck a second mine, which probably detonated a magazine. A yellow column of smoke and water erupted with a thunderous roar. The funnels were demolished, the mainmast broken, and the ship sank in 12 minutes, taking 492 men with her. *Yashima* was towed away, but despite the efforts of her crew she continued to take water. In the late afternoon she was ceremonially abandoned. She dropped anchor, the 'Sacred Portraits' of Emperor and Empress were reverently transferred to a cruiser, the crew assembled on deck, the national anthem was sung, three 'Banzais' were vociferated, and the flags were lowered for the last time. After these ceremonies the crew was transferred to a cruiser and the ship, still anchored, sank.

The explosions had been heard in Port Arthur and much of the population went to the hills to enjoy the spectacle. Spirits lifted, and in the street passers-by congratulated each other on the event. But apart from sending out 15 destroyers to harry the Japanese, Admiral Witgeft did nothing to take advantage of the situation. In fact he does not appear to have made any preparations in anticipation of the minelaying being successful. The destroyers were easily beaten off by the Japanese cruisers, and the Russians for many months remained unaware that *Yashima* had finally sunk and that Togo in one day had lost one-third of his battleship strength. This was not the end of Togo's misfortunes, for the very same day his cruiser *Yoshino* was sunk by collision in fog with *Kasuga*. Nor had Admiral Nashiba's tribulations ended when his second battleship sank. He had transferred his flag to the despatch vessel *Tatsuta*, which that evening ran on to rocks in fog.

For a few days the Russian navy in Port Arthur regained its popularity, but this did not absolve it from its duty of going to sea. In April, as he departed from Port Arthur for safer quarters in Mukden, the Viceroy had urged his officers to put to sea in order to interfere with the Japanese troop landings. The admirals and captains had duly held a meeting, at which they decided that in the circumstances it was better to do nothing. At the end of May the Viceroy renewed his demand for a more active policy. The Port Arthur admirals had meanwhile held a council of war to decide on policy in view of the imminent return to service of the two best battleships, *Retvizan* and *Tsesarevich*; they had decided that in spite of these reinforcements, the best policy for the navy was to help in the landward defence with men and guns, only putting to sea if the port should fall into Japanese hands. The Viceroy's message induced Witgeft to hold another council, at which the highest army officers were also present. With the possible exception of General Smirnov, the garrison commander, all the officers somewhat naturally preferred their naval colleagues to stay in harbour; already the guns and seamen which had been landed were playing an invaluable part in the defence. It would seem that a few naval officers disagreed with this view, and on the next day a council of captains and admirals continued the discussion. This council decided that a sortie should be made as soon as the two battleships were ready, with a view to fighting a decisive action against Togo. By this time Togo had abandoned the attempt to sink blockships in the entrance of Port Arthur, and instead was sending, almost daily, small craft to lay mines in the waters through which the Russian squadron would pass if it left harbour. Accordingly, when a fast destroyer left for Newchuang with a telegram from Witgeft to the Viceroy, the message stated that the squadron intended to go out, but would first have to find some way of dealing with the Japanese mines. So the intended date for the sortie was postponed, and harbour craft and dredgers were equipped for minesweeping. During this time the destroyers and *Novik* occasionally went out to assist the land forces, or to lay mines.

On 18 June a telegram from the Viceroy ordered the squadron to go to meet the enemy.[3] The ships were immediately coaled and some of the guns that had been put ashore were reinstalled. All ships were ordered to raise steam. Meanwhile Witgeft issued to all ships a stirring hectographed order which referred to the Viceroy's wishes, the exploits of *Bobr*, the successes of Russian minelaying, and which assured his men of the goodwill of God and of St Nicholas the Miracle-Worker (patron saint of Russian mariners). About the same time there appeared an issue of the local newspaper *Novy Krai*, in which the order was already printed as a sensational news item; presumably the editor had been given a copy of the order several hours before the squadron received it. But just before departure time the signal was given to let the fires out. Steam cutters hurried from ship to ship, taking back the order which had only just been distributed. In town, numerous orderlies rushed in all directions as they endeavoured to confiscate all copies of the unfortunate issue of *Novy Krai*. Apparently Witgeft had belatedly realised that the tide on that day did not fit in with his plans.

What precisely his plans were is difficult to discover, partly because they could only be vague in any case; the disposition of Togo's forces would determine how and when an engagement would be fought. Witgeft's intention was to be in the open sea by nightfall so that he would have room for manœuvre and evasion when attacked by torpedo boats. It seems clear, too, that his success would have depended on the degree of surprise he could achieve. Togo, it could be expected, would be at the advanced Japanese base at the Elliott Islands, but it would take him some time to raise steam, organise his battle line, and rally his cruisers and small craft.

The sortie which had been postponed on 20 June was rescheduled for 22 June, but minelaying caused postponement for one more day. To forestall another minelaying expedition by the Japanese, destroyers were sent out on patrol. The Japanese did send in some minelayers escorted by destroyers, and the Russian destroyers hotly engaged the latter without noticing the minelayers. These quietly dropped their mines, observed only by a shore battery. This battery did not open fire because it had not received orders to do so (to avoid disastrous errors, when Russian ships were out the batteries were forbidden to fire without authorisation). When knowledge of these new mines reached Witgeft he decided nevertheless to carry out his plan. Having twice postponed his departure he was probably reluctant to attract the criticism and contempt which yet another postponement would bring. This was not the first or last time in Russian history when war operations were timed more for public relations than for tactical circumstances and, as usual in such cases, there was a price to pay. In this instance the price paid was the dissipation of the surprise factor.

The Russian squadron began to move out of harbour at dawn, and then anchored outside, waiting for a channel to the open sea to be cleared of mines. Already one or two floating mines had come uncomfortably close. While the minesweepers were at work the ships' crews swept for nearby mines and discovered about a dozen actually moored between the anchored ships, a discovery that would have unnerved admirals bolder than Witgeft. It was not until nine hours after the ships had cast off that the squadron began to move into the open sea.

Long before then Togo had completed his dispositions. His destroyers outside Port Arthur had seen *Novik* and some destroyers at dawn, and soon afterwards had noticed smoke rising from the harbour. It became clear that Russian battleships were leaving, so a destroyer was sent to nearby Encounter Rock, where a Japanese cruiser was contacted. This cruiser radioed the news to Togo at the Elliots, and by mid-morning the latter's battleships were ready to leave. Other detachments were recalled to join the main force. During the afternoon Togo's armoured ships cruised up and down about 30 miles from Port Arthur, expecting to cut across the Russian course. Some firing was heard, but this was from Japanese destroyers engaging Russian light craft outside Port Arthur. Togo began to suspect that the Russians had returned to Port Arthur, but at 1800 the two battle fleets sighted each other. Evidently Japanese espionage was not as good as the Russians liked to believe, for it was only at this moment that Togo discovered that the *Retvizan* and *Tsesarevich* had been repaired. The two fleets manœuvred for about an hour, and shortly before dusk the two lines were on gradually converging courses. But there was little daylight left and it seemed that Togo had lost his chance of a decisive action.

In any case, Witgeft refused action, turning away just as it seemed that fire would be opened. Why, having taken his squadron to sea in full strength in order to fight the Japanese, Witgeft should have decided to break away just when action was about to begin remains a mystery. Many explanations have been asserted or suggested, but none is entirely satisfactory. Witgeft himself explained that the appearance of Togo so close to Port Arthur spoiled his plans; a major gun action followed by a night torpedo attack was too risky an undertaking. But when Witgeft turned back towards Port Arthur it was already too late to avoid a night of torpedo attacks. Moreover, even when the ships reached Port Arthur the darkness and the state of the tide compelled them to wait outside the harbour, still a prey for torpedo boats.

What seems to be most likely is that Witgeft, like other Russian admirals and generals, was motivated above all by fear of defeat. He would not initiate a decisive battle unless the circumstances were such that a victory was inevitable. Since he had failed to meet Togo before the latter could gather his full strength, it was better not to fight at all. The explanation of Witgeft's behaviour is not made any easier by the description in many Western accounts of the Russian superior strength on this day. In reality the Russians were not in superior strength either by number or by weight of main armament, even though they had six battleships against Togo's four. The Japanese line of battle had four battleships and two armoured cruisers (16 twelve-inch 1 ten-inch, 6 eight-inch guns) while the Russians had six battleships and one armoured cruiser (16 twelve-inch, 8 ten-inch, 2 eight-inch guns). But in the vicinity Togo also had the old battleship *Chinyen* (4 twelve-inch) and two more armoured cruisers (8 eight-inch). Against the lighter Russian ships, four cruisers and six destroyers, Togo could muster 11 cruisers and at least 30 torpedo craft. This imbalance of torpedo craft, for Witgeft, was probably decisive.

At sunset, with the Russian squadron headed for Port Arthur, and with no chance of catching up with it before night, Togo withdrew his heavy ships, leaving the field clear for his massed torpedo craft. The first wave of attackers moved in on the Russians shortly before 2100, and attacks continued until dawn. By about 2130 the Russians were in the Port Arthur approaches, endeavouring, in the darkness and amid constant torpedo attacks, to find and keep the swept channel through the mines. *Sevastopol* was forced over to port when a consort ahead of her unexpectedly reduced speed and almost immediately there was an explosion on her port side, presumably caused by a mine. During a short-lived panic, two of her sailors jumped overboard. A small fire started in one of her magazines, which was soon mastered by a band of brave men who descended among the fumes. The hole was quite large, but *Sevastopol* continued steaming and was able to anchor in shallow water near the shore.

The other Russian ships also anchored near the shore, and put out their torpedo nets. Japanese torpedo craft continued to attack from several directions but their commanders, distracted by spray and

1a  General Kuropatkin

1b  Lieutenant-General Stoessel

1c  Vice-Admiral Togo

1d  Vice-Admiral Rozhestvensky

2a  A Japanese cavalryman in Manchuria

2b  The Russian cavalry parades for the cinematographer in Manchuria
(from a photograph by N. Rodgers)

3a  Mobilization in Russia, 1904. (BBC Hulton Picture Library)

3b  Quarterdeck of the Japanese battleship *Asahi*

4a  Rifle drill on board Togo's flagship

4b  Japanese infantry landed at Chemulpo

5a The Russian squadron returns to Port Arthur harbour after the Japanese surprise attack; the cruiser *Askold* is nearest camera

5b The Russian cruiser *Varyag* is prepared for scuttling after the Chemulpo engagement. There is a perceptible list, and the third funnel is damaged (courtesy of Foyer des Anciens Officiers de la Marine Russe)

5c & d Two snapshots from the *Sevastopol*, taken as small boats seek survivors of the *Petropavlovsk*. In the background is Golden Hill, with three sunken Japanese blockships beneath it (B. Kamenskii)

6a  Called-up reservists undergo their medicals in St Petersburg

6b  A Russian 6-inch howitzer is brought into position  (BBC Hulton Picture Library)

7a  Japanese field artillery near Telissu

7b  General Zasulich (in white tunic) and his staff at the Battle of the Yalu

8a  The Japanese use captured Russian guns near Port Arthur

8b  Coolie power operates the South Manchuria Railway for the Japanese

9a Soldiers of the 19th Siberian Rifles collect their rations at a field kitchen near Port Arthur

9b Japanese observation balloon, with attendant gas-bag, in Manchuria

10a  Japanese 11-inch howitzer emplaced near Port Arthur (Underwood)

10b  One of Lt Podgurski's naval projectiles is unleashed during the defence of
Port Arthur

11a The last seconds of the cruiser *Rurik* (photographed by a Japanese officer)

11b Shell holes in the stern of the *Rossiya* are examined after the battle of Ulsan

12a A Japanese burial party, plus onlookers, inter a Russian casualty

12b Japanèse infantry in the mid-winter trench warfare of the Sha-ho
(BBC Hulton Picture Library)

13a Officers of the *Suvorov* at Reval. Seated, third from left, is the commander, Captain Ignatius, with Commander Klado fourth from left

13b Officers in the wardroom of the battleship *Aleksandr III* during its first and last commission. Second from left, conspicuously at ease, is Prince Kantakuzen, while fourth and fifth are two brothers of British origin, Ellis 1 and Ellis 2. The ship's doctor is nearest camera on the right

14a The Tsar paces the deck of the cruiser *Svetlana* before the 2nd Squadron's departure. Rozhestvensky is at his left

14b The 2nd Squadron approaches Tsushima the day before the battle. *Suvorov* is leading the first column and *Oslyabia* (nearest camera) the second. Astern of *Suvorov* is *Aleksandr III* (courtesy of Foyer des Anciens Officers de la Marine Russe)

15a The Russian surrender after Tsushima. A boat takes Nebogatov from his
flagship (off picture at right) to Togo's *Mikasa* (off picture at left) for
negotiations. The three-funnelled Japanese battleship *Shikishima* lies
close, and beyond her is a Russian coast defence ship

15b Vladivostok in 1905. The cruiser *Almaz*, escaped from Tsushima, lies in
the Golden Horn

16a A mile of mule carts wait their turn at Dalny (BBC Hulton Picture Library)

16b Official photograph celebrating the Treaty of Portsmouth. President Roosevelt is in the centre, with Witte on the extreme left. Baron Rosen stands between these two, while the small unhappy man with large ears is the Japanese plenipotentiary, Komura

near-misses, dazzled by searchlights, could neither take good aim nor approach very close. Some of the time they could orientate themselves by the Russian searchlights; at other times the shore searchlights, rather uselessly playing on the Russian ships, were also an aid. But Russian gunfire was intense; although none of the attackers was sunk, several were damaged (one by the only torpedo to find a target that night). At dawn the Russian ships, undamaged apart from *Sevastopol*, were able to move into the harbour. *Sevastopol* was soon fitted with the cofferdam previously used to repair *Retvizan*.

For the world's press, this had been a very disappointing engagement; newspaper readers wanted a real battle, not just a skirmish. But, with the Japanese newspapers in the lead, journalists were not slow to avail themselves of that most precious of press freedoms, the freedom to misinform. The *San Francisco Chronicle*, by no means the worst example, had this banner headline for its 26 June edition, 'Prince Uchtomsky among Russians drowned by sinking of Peresviet', followed by the detailed story of this imaginary Trafalgar:

> Tokio is in a frenzy of enthusiasm over the tremendous naval victory won by the Japanese fleet under Admiral Togo at Port Arthur on Thursday ... a naval battle that will live in history was fought in the gathering twilight Thursday night ... A torpedo struck the Peresviet midway in the engagement and five minutes later with a roar like an exploding magazine she sank beneath the waves.

During the following weeks, ships from time to time went out to bombard Japanese troop positions. With the siege of Port Arthur coming ever closer, the ships had shorter distances to move, and shorter ranges for their guns. At times some of the armoured ships accompanied these expeditions. The naval gunfire was very destructive, and if it had been applied more often would have had a serious effect on the Japanese army's progress. But almost always the bombarding ships became engaged with Japanese warships, and retired to harbour. The Russian destroyers continued their reconnaissance; one of them sank a British steamer suspected of supplying the Japanese army, and which refused to stop for inspection. Others from time to time engaged Japanese destroyers and minelayers. Both the Japanese and Russian destroyers seemed quite robust; although Russian destroyers were lost from time to time there were several cases of these ships being mined or torpedoed and yet reaching harbour. One loss felt keenly by the Russians was that of the destroyer *Lieutenant Burakov*, torpedoed in a destroyer action. This vessel, captured from the Chinese a few years previously, was the fastest destroyer in the East, and the favourite for carrying despatches through the Japanese blockade to the telegraph offices at Yinkou and, later, Chifu. The Japanese were also engaged in coastal support operations, despite the danger of Russian mines. The cruiser *Chiyoda* was badly damaged by mining in July, but this was balanced by mine damage to the Russian *Bayan* on the following day.

The failure of the squadron, in its June sortie, to defeat the Japanese, coinciding with the failure of the supposed relief attempt by Kuropatkin's army at Telissu, caused not only despondency but also acrimony in higher spheres. It was not long before Admiral Witgeft received orders of a more than usually peremptory tone from both the Viceroy and the Tsar. He was instructed to keep his ships coaled, armed, and ready to sail, to take back most of the guns that had been landed, and to leave for Vladivostok at the first opportunity, preferably avoiding an encounter with Togo.

Witgeft called a conference of senior officers, which by a large majority agreed that the squadron should stay in Port Arthur. Its contribution to the land defence was great, and the Baltic squadron was expected to arrive in October. If Port Arthur and its squadron could survive until October, therefore, the war might be won, since Togo would at last face overwhelming Russian battleship superiority. Accordingly, Witgeft replied to the Viceroy that a departure of the squadron for Vladivostok would enable the enemy to capture Port Arthur from seaward, and that in any case the squadron would not be able to avoid defeat on leaving Port Arthur. Therefore an escape to Vladivostok was only advisable if the fall of Port Arthur was imminent.

The Viceroy, probably aware that the Baltic squadron could not arrive in October, replied that Witgeft's analysis of the situation was in direct contradiction to his own and the Tsar's orders. He requested that a meeting of flag officers and captains should be held to reconsider the matter immediately, but this council reaffirmed the previous decision to stay in harbour. Before the Viceroy could reply Witgeft sent another telegram, referring to the dangers from mines, torpedoes and fog, and saying that after much prayer and thought the officers maintained their former opinion. This message seems to have reached the Viceroy on 7 August, and he responded with a sharp reminder of how the cruiser *Varyag* had put to sea fearlessly to fight a superior force. If the Port Arthur squadron failed to put to sea despite his orders and the Tsar's wishes, and was destroyed in Port Arthur, it would be a shameful dishonour. Witgeft was further instructed to make known this telegram to all admirals and captains.

This last message made it clear that the courage of the naval officers was in question, although this was rather unjust. While it is true that there was a complete lack of boldness, except on the part of perhaps two captains,[4] there is in retrospect to no reason to doubt the personal courage of the officers. They were more frightened of failure than of death. Moreover, they were able to justify their attitude with real arguments. No doubt they had read Mahan's *The Influence of Sea Power Upon History*, which had been translated into Russian by the Tsar's uncle, the navy's Admiral-General. Mahan's concept of the 'fleet in being' was of direct relevance in this situation. An inert Russian squadron in Port Arthur was of far greater strategic value than a bold squadron at the bottom of the sea. All the same, captains like von Essen were probably right to urge a breakthrough to Vladivostok. Togo's fleet was not all that superior to the Port Arthur squadron. He had, after all, detached four armoured cruisers to deal with the Vladivostok cruisers. Aided by surprise, and with some determination, a proportion at least of the Russian squadron could have broken through to Vladivostok, where it could safely have awaited the arrival of the Baltic squadron.

The Viceroy's recriminative telegram arrived too late to have any effect, because circumstances had already induced Witgeft to change his mind. The Japanese army was close enough to fire into the harbour area enough 4.7-inch shells to produce a few chance hits. Witgeft accordingly decided to accede to the pressure of the Viceroy and the Tsar. Some of the landed guns were reinstalled, and the squadron prepared for sea. Meanwhile *Retvizan* was hit by seven shells and when she put to sea on 10 August she had a hastily stopped hole at the waterline, through which about 400 tons of water had entered.

Shortly before dawn on 10 August, the Russian squadron emerged. Profiting from previous experience, a channel had been swept of mines and the small minesweepers which preceded the squadron could soon return to harbour. But this prompt exit was balanced by Togo's advanced state of readiness; because of the Japanese bombardment of the harbour he had been expecting the Russians to leave, and his main force was quite close to Port Arthur, off Round Island. The Russian force consisted of the battle line, led by the flagship *Tsesarevich* and numbering six battleships, together with four cruisers, eight destroyers and, at a suitable distance, a hospital ship. The damaged armoured cruiser *Bayan* and six destroyers remained at Port Arthur. As with the June encounter of the two fleets, Togo had a numerical superiority, but the Japanese battle line was about equal to the Russian: the Japanese had only four first-class battleships but two armoured cruisers (and later a third) followed the battleships to form a line of six or seven ships. In addition Togo had on call a fourth armoured cruiser and the old battleship *Chinyen*. His cruiser divisions numbered nine ships, and he had 17 destroyers and 29 torpedo boats. This preponderance in torpedo craft promised the Russians, in theory at least, a difficult time after dusk.

At about midday the two fleets sighted each other. The Russians made no attempt to flee, and the stage seemed set for the first pitched battle of the ironclad era. The two fleets were approaching almost at right angles. For the next 40 minutes Togo manœuvred his line into a suitable position. Then the first shots were fired by the heaviest guns. This firing was only slow and intermittent, and had no effect. Soon Togo changed his course so as to bring his line closer to the Russian line, but was temporarily confounded when the Russians turned sharply to starboard. This turn was provoked by the Japanese torpedo boats, which had crossed the path of the Russian squadron. This Japanese manœuvre had caused Witgeft to suspect that mines were being laid in his path, which he turned to avoid. The result of this change of course was that Togo unexpectedly found the Russian line crossing his stern at a distance of about 9000 yards. The shots of both sides were falling close, but there had still been no hits. Togo turned to counter Witgeft's change of course but was once more thwarted by a sharp Russian change of course. Witgeft was now turning back to his original course, having passed the supposed mined area. Again it seemed that the Russians would pass astern of the Japanese line, but this time Togo responded promptly with a change of course which resulted in the two lines steaming towards one another and passing at a distance of about 6000 yards. At this range the secondary armaments of the battleships could be brought into play, as well as the main armaments of the cruisers. There was a lively exchange of fire, but no serious damage was done.

After the two lines had passed each other, Togo found himself in a disadvantageous position, being now astern of the Russian ships as they proceeded in the direction of Vladivostok. Although subsequent accounts fail to make the point, Togo had been out-manœuvred.

Without really trying, but simply by maintaining the most direct course to Vladivostok and with the unexpected diversion to avoid imagined minelaying, Witgeft had secured the best possible position. In the beginning Togo had stood between the Russians and Vladivostok, but now he was trailing behind them. His ships were gradually catching up, but as they did so they came under increasingly heavy Russian fire.

The Japanese battleships were marginally faster than the Russian, and at this time the latter were making about 12 knots, and the Japanese about 14. These speeds were probably the safe maxima for both sides. The slowest Russian battleship (*Poltava*) had a nominal maximum of 16½ knots, and the Japanese battleships were rated at 18 knots, but fears of breakdown and the state of boilers and hulls meant that throughout the whole war the battleships of neither side ever reached their maxima. Of the Japanese battleships only one, and only once, exceeded 15 knots during the war.

Overhauling the Russians at about two knots an hour, Togo could hope to be in a position for a full-scale action well before nightfall but only at the expense, it seemed, of severe damage to his leading ships as the distance closed. Already his two leading ships, which were his best, were beginning to suffer. Although subsequent accounts usually accept that the Russian gunnery was inferior to the Japanese, this may not be true. Captain Pakenham, representing the British Admiralty, stated in a confidential report that at this stage of the battle the Russian gunnery seemed superior to the Japanese, at least at long range.[5] Togo's leading flagship *Mikasa* had already been hit at the mainmast by a Russian shell whose splinters had passed perilously close to Togo who, unwisely, was not under cover at the time. Other ships had also been hit.

Togo therefore decided to change his tactics. Since Port Arthur was virtually uninhabitable for the Russian ships, there seemed little reason to block their return to that port; in fact, to encourage them to do so would be advantageous. On the other hand, their escape to Vladivostok would be disastrous, for once they were there they could hardly be destroyed before the arrival of the Baltic squadron. Togo therefore decided to draw off to a safer distance, to use his superior speed not to overhaul the Russians at close range but to go round them so that before nightfall he could once again block their passage towards Vladivostok.

By mid-afternoon gunfire had ceased and the two fleets had begun to draw away, although their respective masts and funnels remained in view on the horizon. For the next few hours everything, including probably the outcome of the war, depending on whether Togo could maintain his 14 knots without one or other of his battleships overheating its bearings or bursting its boiler tubes. However, a breakdown in the Russian squadron was just as likely. Earlier that day both *Pobieda* and *Tsesarevich* had caused delay while putting right their defects; after so many inactive weeks, mechanical or boiler failures could be expected. But in fact on the afternoon of this day the Russian ships steadily maintained their 12 or 13 knots, although *Poltava* tended to lag.

By 1645 Togo was closing in and the sternmost Russian battleship, *Poltava*, opened fire on the leading Japanese battleship *Mikasa* at a range of 9000 yards. For the next hour there was a general engagement with Togo's and the Russian battle lines on parallel courses. Both sides began to suffer damage, especially the flagships at the head of the respective lines as Russians and Japanese sought to disorganise their opponent's command and coordination. On the Russian side the flagship of the second in command (Admiral Ukhtomski) suffered badly. This ship, *Peresviet*, had her masts damaged and one of her main turrets put out of action. *Poltava*, because of her position at the rear, was also hit hard.

The three leading Japanese battleships received direct hits, especially the flagship *Mikasa*. It was not long before five of Togo's twelve-inch guns were out of action. Not all of these injuries were the result of Russian gunfire, for according to Captain Pakenham a number of Japanese guns were put out of action by their own shells exploding in the breech. Japanese accounts did not admit this, but it is known that after this battle the Japanese-designed fuses of high-explosive shells were replaced by fuses of lesser sensitivity. Hitherto the destructive effect of Japanese high-explosive shells had been compared very favourably with that of the Russian shells; the latter often failed to explode and their charges were less powerful, whereas Japanese shells, filled with the vaunted *Shimose* explosive and detonating on the slightest impact, threw out hundreds of splinters, set fire to paint and decks, flattened structures, and gave off incapacitating and toxic gases. But after this battle some Japanese officers expressed a preference for the older types of shell.

With luck, the Russians might have held their own in this gun battle until nightfall, when they would have had an excellent chance of throwing off the pursuit. But at about 1745 *Tsesarevich*, which had come under heavy fire as the Japanese overhauled the Russian·van, was hit by two twelve-inch shells. One of these killed Admiral Witgeft, who was not under cover at the time, while the other burst at the slit of the conning tower, throwing splinters into the interior which killed or incapacitated all its occupants.[6] Because the wheel was encumbered by bodies, *Tsesarevich* turned sharply to port and made a complete circle, breaking through the line she had been leading. The second ship, *Retvizan*, at first followed the flagship, thinking this was a deliberate change of course, then thought better of it. Togo took advantage of the Russian confusion to shorten the range to 4000 yards, at which distance he was able to pour a devastating fire on the Russian ships with his main and secondary armaments. *Tsesarevich* had meantime hoisted the signal 'Admiral transfers command', so Ukhtomski, as at the time of the *Petropavlovsk* disaster, once more found himself in command of the squadron at a bad moment. On this occasion his troubles were compounded by the discovery that all his signal halliards had been shot away, so his first flags were strung out on the bridge, where few of his consorts could see them. His first signal said merely 'Follow me' as he turned his flagship *Peresviet* back towards Port Arthur. Trailed by the stricken *Tsesarevich*, the confused battleships followed Ukhtomski, pursued until nightfall by Togo's heavy ships. At dusk, with no Russian ship completely crippled, Togo withdrew his armoured ships to allow the torpedo craft a clear field. Throughout the night the Russians were beset by successive flotillas of small craft, but not one torpedo struck a target. At daylight, battered but not destroyed, the bulk of the squadron was safely anchored beneath the shore batteries off Port Arthur. During the night, however, part of the squadron had detached itself with the intention of reaching Vladivostok. *Tsesarevich*, beating off torpedo attacks, succeeded in escaping but because of a badly damaged funnel could not steam efficiently. She went to the German port of Kiaochau (Tsingtao), hoping to coal and make temporary repairs. But she was unable to get ready for sea in time, and under the conventions of neutrality the Germans interned her for the duration of the war. The cruiser *Askold* also broke through, and for identical reasons went to Shanghai, where she too was interned. The cruiser *Diana*, having evaded and beaten off several Japanese torpedo craft, made for Saigon, where the French authorities interned her. According to an unreliable account, her officers had decided that although she had enough coal to take her to Vladivostok there was no margin to cover any bursts of high speed which might be needed if Japanese warships were encountered.[7]

The third Russian cruiser to attempt to reach Vladivostok (*Pallada* returned to Port Arthur), was *Novik*. This fast light cruiser was half the size of *Diana* and carried one-third as much coal. She went first to Kiaochau and succeeded in coaling in ten hours. She then headed around the east coast of Japan, hoping that the considerably longer distance would be justified by the avoidance of the narrow Tsushima Straits, where discovery was most likely. But her endeavour was spoiled by a chance encounter with a Japanese freighter, which reported her position. Since she was obviously headed for Vladivostok and would only steam at her economical speed, it was not difficult to arrange for her interception by cruisers. She was discovered taking coal at the Russian settlement at Korsakov, in Sakhalin, by the cruiser *Tsushima*. After an hour's exchange of gunfire both ships were badly damaged. *Tsushima* was reinforced by a fresh cruiser and *Novik* limped back to Korsakov, where she was scuttled.

Of the other Russian ships, four destroyers were interned at Shanghai and Kiaochau, and one ran ashore, so not one Russian ship reached Vladivostok. But of the larger would-be escapers all except *Novik* had been significantly damaged in the battle, and *Novik* with a little more luck would have reached her destination. It seems, therefore, that criticism of Ukhtomski's decision to return to Port Arthur was wholly justified. Port Arthur could no longer offer a safe haven. Return there meant certain destruction. The only positive advantage of the squadron's return was the contribution of men and guns for the landward defence. But since Port Arthur's importance lay not in itself, but in the ships which it harboured, its defence was of little strategic importance when the besiegers had reached a point where they could drop shells into the harbour. On the other hand, as the break-through of the damaged *Tsesarevich* showed, there was a strong probability that a significant part of the squadron could have reached Vladivostok, especially if it had scattered at nightfall. Even one battleship at Vladivostok would have been a serious embarrassment for Togo when he faced the oncoming Baltic squadron.

The naval battle of 10 August, otherwise known as the Battle of Round Island or the Battle of the Yellow Sea, was not the only naval engagement of that day. The destroyer *Reshitelnyi* had been sent from Port Arthur to Chifu with despatches. Being mechanically defective, this ship was ordered to go into voluntary internment after arrival, rather than return to Port Arthur. After arriving at Chifu, the destroyer commander contacted the local Chinese naval authorities to arrange the disarmament and internment of the vessel. While this was happening, and probably after the breechblocks had been removed, Japanese destroyers entered the port and demanded that the Russian destroyer should come out and fight, or surrender. After some argument the Japanese boarded *Reshitelnyi* and apparently attempted to hoist their flag. The commander threw the Japanese officer overboard and was himself dragged over the side. Shots were fired at him as he tried unsuccessfully to climb back. There was additional struggling between the Russians and Japanese, and it seems that an explosive charge was set off by one of the Russian crew. About half of the crew and half of the Japanese were thrown into the water and eventually swam ashore. Meanwhile the Japanese ships took *Reshitelnyi* in tow as a prize, and she spent the rest of the war as part of the Japanese navy. The Japanese version of this breach of Chinese neutrality was somewhat different, claiming that the Russians had not disarmed and were preparing for sea, that the Japanese were invited to inspect *Reshitelnyi*, where they were insulted, blown up and thrown into the water. However, the accounts of the Chinese local authorities support the Russian version, and even the American press criticised the Japanese action.[8]

After the Battle of Round Island the command of the Port Arthur squadron was entrusted to a relatively junior officer, replacing the much-criticised Admiral Ukhotomski. Captain Wiren had commanded *Bayan*, the one armoured ship which had not taken part in the battle. This fact, and the passing over of the several more senior officers who had commanded battleships in the recent engagement, clearly implied that St Petersburg took a poor view of the squadron's performance. A better choice would have been the captain of *Sevastopol*, who almost alone among the commanders was a bold and intelligent officer; but von Essen's talents were not yet realised (or, more likely, were carefully concealed by less talented superiors). Wiren, in conjunction with the majority of his commanders, decided that the squadron could not go out again, although he subsequently agreed to prepare *Bayan* for service, and started repairs on the two least-damaged battleships. Guns were again made available for the defences, and naval detachments returned to the trenches.[9] Soon all hope of the squadron's revival disappeared when, against the votes of von Essen and one other captain, the remaining supplies of six-inch shells were handed over to the army. Meanwhile, minelaying and destroyer activities continued, with both sides losing ships by mines. By this time drifting mines could be encountered at great distances from Port Arthur. One was struck by Togo's battleship *Asahi*, but damage was slight. The Port Arthur squadron occasionally suffered from 4.7-inch shells, hopefully fired by the Japanese in the direction of the harbour.

In September the harbour became even more perilous when the Japanese introduced their eleven-inch howitzers. These too fired at the harbour and, although most of their shots fell into the water, those which did find a target were very destructive. The Russian battleships were already well-practised in high-trajectory fire from their berths in harbour, but they were unable to damage the well-concealed Japanese howitzers. The first ship to be sunk by the Japanese artillery was a small gunboat, and the second a hospital ship with several hundred wounded on board.

In mid-October Togo learned that the Russian Baltic squadron had just left for the Far East, and might be in Japanese waters in January. Since Togo's ships were in need of repair, with many boilers and worn gun barrels requiring attention, the final destruction of the Port Arthur squadron became urgent. The capture of 203 Metre Hill north of the town was therefore given first priority by the besieging Japanese army. From this hill a view of the entire harbour was obtainable, which meant that observers could direct the fire of the eleven-inch howitzers accurately on to the assembled Russian ships. This was why the struggle for this hill became one of the longest and bloodiest battles of the entire war. Indirect gunfire from the battleships, and courageous fighting by the naval detachments, were the squadron's contribution to the defence of the hill. But after a final ten days of bloody struggle the Japanese captured the hill in mid-December. Immediately after the capture a Japanese artillery observation party established itself on the hill to superintend the destruction of the Russian squadron. *Poltava* had already been sunk by an eleven-inch shell which penetrated a magazine. During the next two days the battleships *Retvizan*, *Pobieda*, *Peresviet* and the cruisers *Pallada* and *Bayan* were shelled until they sank. The water in the harbour was not deep, so the upper parts of the ships remained above the surface. There was little loss of life, for apart from the commanders and a few maintenance men all the crews were fighting in the front line. Meanwhile, Japanese cruisers searching for the Russian destroyers, which were expected to break out towards a neutral port, ran into a minefield and lost *Takasago*.

Captain von Essen of the battleship *Sevastopol* did not relish the destruction of his vessel by the Japanese army, so after the loss of 203 Metre Hill he took her with a skeleton crew to anchor just outside the harbour. Here, by the harbour entry, invisible from 203 Metre Hill and in company with a gunboat and some destroyers, *Sevastopol* prepared to defend herself with her few remaining guns. Net defences were laid out, and torpedo attacks awaited. Togo, plainly worried by the continued existence of this one battleship, sent in torpedo boat attacks on almost a nightly basis. The biggest of these, involving about 30 craft attacking in a snowstorm, was beaten off without any of the 50-odd torpedoes doing significant damage. Later, the battleship was twice damaged underwater and both times the leak was plugged. But the second of these attacks caused such a list that the Japanese concluded that the ship was finished. There were no further torpedo attacks, even though *Sevastopol* began to assist the land defence with her twelve-inch guns. In the attacks two Japanese torpedo boats had been sunk, and others damaged.

When it was decided to surrender Port Arthur, preparations were hastily made to blow up the ships resting on the harbour bottom, to prevent their salvage by the Japanese. But the hurried signing of the surrender document meant that not all the charges were fired. Many of the ships were eventually salvaged, and joined the Japanese navy. In the First World War Japan sold some of them back to Russia and one of them, *Peresviet*, was sunk for a second and final time by a mine in the Mediterranean. As for *Sevastopol*, her redoubtable captain took her into deep water and scuttled her where she could not be salvaged. The surviving destroyers went to Kiaochao and Chifu, where they were interned.

The final unsuccessful sortie from Port Arthur in August had coincided with the last cruise of the three Russian armoured cruisers based at Vladivostok, *Gromoboi*, *Rossiya* and the older *Rurik*. These three ships had been originally designed with a view to commerce raiding against British shipping (Britain being Russia's most likely enemy at the time) and were high-sided vessels with a very large coal capacity. During the first months of the war their activities caused the Japanese much worry, for they were a very potent threat to the shipping that plied between Japan and the mainland. Table 5.1 summarises their operations.[10]

It will be noted that although these three ships, aided at times by some smaller vessels, caused more damage to Japanese communications than the much stronger Port Arthur force, their utilisation was not as effective as it might have been. Of their 190 days of war service, only 53 were spent actively at sea. Apart from the one Pacific cruise, their cruises did not exceed a week, even though they were

TABLE 5.1  *The Vladivostok cruisers in 1904: a chronology*

| Date | Events |
|---|---|
| 9–14 February | Cruise towards Japan. One steamer sunk. |
| 24 February – 1 March | Cruise towards Korea. No results. |
| 23–27 April | Attack on Gensan (Korea). Japanese transport intercepted; its troops refuse to surrender and go down with it. |
| 12–19 June | Cruise to Tsushima Strait. Two transports sunk, one damaged. British *Allanton* captured. |
| 28 June – 3 July | Cruise towards Tsushima Strait. Escape pursuing Japanese cruisers and destroyers. Capture British *Cheltenham*. |
| 17 July – 1 August | Pacific cruise. One British and one German steamer sunk, one British and one German steamer captured. |
| 12–16 August | Cruise to meet Port Arthur squadron. Latter never appears. Japanese cruisers sink *Rurik* and damage *Gromoboi* and *Rossiya* at Battle of Ulsan. |

capable of steaming 4000 miles without coaling. Port activities and coaling seemed to take an unusually long time; no coaling took less than a week, and *Rossiya* once needed 13 days for this task.

The most successful of the forays was that to Tsushima in June. The Russians were shadowed by the Japanese cruiser *Tsushima*, but because of fog and radio interference the Japanese armoured cruisers under Admiral Kamimura were unable to make contact. Thus the Russian interception of three transports, and the long formalities before they were sunk (in those days commerce raiders behaved scrupulously towards the crews of intercepted non-combatant ships), took place almost literally under the eyes of the Japanese navy. One of the intercepted transports, the *Hitachi Maru*, was carrying more than 1000 troops as well as military equipment. According to the Japanese official history the commander of these troops bravely upheld the traditions of Japanese militarism. He made a short speech about not letting the flag fall into Russian hands. Then, bidding any survivors to tell the folks back home about his exploit, he tore up the flag and 'with a smile on his face' committed suicide in the approved style. Other officers followed his example, and while they were busily disembowelling themselves the soldiers obeyed orders and jumped into the sea to avoid the disgrace of capture. During these ceremonies the *Hitachi Maru* was still endeavouring to escape, but Russian shellfire had already made this impossible. Her captain and the first and second engineers (all British) were killed in this action. Japanese soldiers in the water were also killed by the shellfire, and only 152 survivors were later picked up by fishing boats.

A second Russian incursion in these waters failed when the Russians were met by Kamimura's cruisers and torpedo craft. However, the Russians successfully evaded the Japanese who, after nightfall, fired on their own ships and suffered a collision. Because of the continued failure to catch the Russians, Kamimura was bitterly attacked in the Japanese press, and a mob broke the windows of his house. Earlier, he had taken his cruisers to bombard Vladivostok, but had caused no damage to the Russian cruisers anchored there out of sight.

The climax of the Russian cruisers' career was their Pacific cruise. They successfully negotiated the Japanese-dominated Tsugaru Strait and moved down the east coast of Japan. Although they had only four major successes (intercepting neutral ships carrying strategic cargoes for Japan), their appearance in waters off Yokohama forced the Japanese to suspend all sailings for a few days. Despite thick fog, their navigators succeeded brilliantly in taking them back unscathed through the Tsugaru Strait.

Russian luck changed in August. When the news of the Port Arthur squadron's sortie reached Vladivostok, the three cruisers hurried south so fast that a torpedo boat sent after them, to tell them that the squadron had been driven back, never caught up with them. Because of this, just as Kamimura was scouring the sea in search of the Russian ships which had broken through from Port Arthur individually, the Russian Vladivostok cruisers were seeking the Port Arthur squadron in the same waters. When Kamimura, who had four armoured cruisers and six smaller cruisers at his disposal, sighted the three Russian ships he immediately pursued them. The older and slower *Rurik*'s steering was damaged by shellfire, and after a heroic fight she burned and sank. Of her crew, 625 were picked up by the Japanese.

*Gromoboi* and *Rossiya*, which Admiral Kamimura decided not to pursue, had been seriously damaged while trying to shield the stricken *Rurik*. *Rossiya* had lost most of her guns and was additionally the victim of an ammunition fire:

a terrible shock made the ship tremble. Two 8 in shells exploded at the same time under the bridge, spreading yellow fumes from which spurted jets of white smoke. A fire started below the bridge, which grew ever more fierce and reached the deck. It took us twenty minutes to put it out. We could not get near the lower bridge. It was so hot that the water boiled, and the deck resembled an ankle-deep swamp, with charred bodies everywhere.[11]

Apart from the 170 men lost from *Rurik*, there were 47 deaths on *Rossiya* and 93 on *Gromoboi*. Total Japanese casualties were 103, of which most were suffered by the armoured cruiser *Iwate*. Kamimura's flagship *Idzumo*, which fired off almost all her ammunition supply (the Japanese gunnery was evidently not as good as was claimed) had her radio cabin shot away. After this, the Battle of Ulsan, *Gromoboi* and *Rossiya* were under repair until October. On a trial run after this repair *Gromoboi* struck a rock and took no further part in the war. *Rossiya* remained serviceable, but was not used; apparently the Russian command did not wish to put her at risk as she was the only armoured ship still available in the Far East. In a last-minute attempt to restore Vladivostok's fortunes, a number of submarines were sent there by train, and also some torpedo boats in sections. The latter do not appear to have been assembled, but the submarines did put to sea, although without results.

Russian commerce raiding was not limited to the waters of the Far East. In June 1904, two Russian steamers left the Black Sea and passed through the Suez Canal. On emerging into the Red Sea, they brought up guns from below and mounted them. They then hoisted the Russian naval ensign and began to intercept neutral shipping, making prizes of those found carrying contraband to Japan. When they boarded the P & O liner *Malacca*, carrying passengers to the Far East (as well as a quantity of ammunition said to be destined for Hong Kong), there was an immediate uproar in Britain. Since some of the passengers were women, great play was made in the British press with images of English gentlewomen fallen into the hands of dastardly Russians. There being no lack of anti-Russian feeling in Britain, nor of anti-British feeling in Russia, the affair soon caused an international crisis. The inevitable question was raised in the British press and Parliament, 'What is the Navy doing?' In St Petersburg the Tsar's cousin, Alexander Mikhailovich, was among those advocating a tough line against the British who were, after all, making no secret of their active sympathy for the Japanese. But eventually the Russian government, thinking perhaps that conflict with Britain was best avoided, and perhaps having a shrewd idea that the navy ministry's claims about *Malacca's* cargo might be as ill-informed as other statements by that ministry, decided to yield. *Malacca*, whose prize crew was taking her to the Baltic, was released at Algiers, and the Russian government agreed that its two commerce raiders would cease their activities in the Red Sea. But by this time the Russian 'privateers' had left the Red Sea and were at large in the Indian Ocean. They could not be contacted for some time, and it was a British cruiser which finally found them at Zanzibar and transmitted their Tsar's instructions. This intervention caused great satisfaction to admirers of the Royal Navy.[12]

# 6   The Siege of Port Arthur

Of all the phases of the war, it was the siege of Port Arthur which most gripped the imagination of the world. Indeed, towards the end its emotional significance clearly exceeded its strategic significance. For the Japanese, Port Arthur was the base which had been 'stolen' from them by the Russians, and symbolised what the war was all about. For the Russians, Port Arthur revived proud memories of the defence of Sevastopol in the Crimean War and was confidently expected to bring forth new acts of heroism to embellish their military tradition.

Between Dalny and Port Arthur the Russians had prepared two lines of outer defences. The first line was about 15 miles long, stretching across the Peninsula about 12 miles north of Port Arthur. This was attacked by Nogi at the end of July. For one day the outnumbered Russians held their positions, but towards evening the Japanese, after taking heavy losses all day, managed to break through at one point. General Fock thereupon decided to withdraw to his second line, about six miles from Port Arthur. Here the Russians were attacked at dawn on 30 July, and by mid-morning Fock had ordered his troops to withdraw to Port Arthur. That date can therefore be regarded as the start of the close siege of the town.

The apparently premature abandonment of positions, first at Nanshan and then the first and second lines, had a depressing effect on officers and men. Fock had certainly extricated his forces with very small loss while inflicting severe casualties on the attackers, but he had quite failed to gain time.

By July many high officers were aware that their superiors were at loggerheads. In particular, the garrison commandant, Smirnov, who was nominally responsible for the defence of Port Arthur, resented the interference of Stoessel, the commander of the Port Arthur fortified zone:

Stoessel is at daggers-drawn with Smirnov, whom he wanted to completely dismiss from his post but decided not to because

Smirnov had been appointed to it by the Tsar's order. General Smirnov became angry with General Kondratenko, because the latter considers it quite necessary to carry out any suggestion thought up by some junior officer and thereby sets into motion all kinds of fantasies. Finally, General Fock has gone out of his mind and curses everybody and everything. In brief, unbelievable nonsense reigns and there are no officers, let alone soldiers, who regard our leaders with trust and respect.[1]

The immediate approaches to Port Arthur, the terrain on which the battles would be fought, were mainly hilly. Only in the centre, north of the town, was there a valley through which passed the road and railway line. During the months following the outbreak of war there had been intensive work on the defences, but they were still far from perfect. There had been a shortage of key materials like barbed wire.

The pre-war plan for the fortification of Port Arthur had not been everywhere well thought-out. The engineers in 1904 often had to choose between beginning entirely new constructions and completing already-started works in less than perfect locations. The most fortified part of the defences was the eastern sector, although even here the fortifications were not always placed so as to give each other the maximum support, and there was a good deal of dead ground. The batteries which were emplaced between the forts were on hilltops, and poorly concealed. In the northern sector there were some substantial works, but the western sector was defended by works of lighter construction. The ministry of war had been somewhat tardy in carrying out the plan for fortifying Port Arthur; when war broke out most of the seaward-facing guns were in position, but many of the guns planned for the landward defence were not ready. In part this was because in the preceding years the navy's construction programme had made great demands on the Obukhov armaments works; few heavy guns could be delivered to the army, and placing orders abroad was not permitted. When the close siege began the fortress was defended by 646 guns, of which some were old Chinese weapons. There were also 62 machine guns, while during the course of the siege a number of naval guns were landed by the squadron; towards the end of 1904 these naval guns amounted to almost half the total. The garrison was of about 40 000 men, supplemented later by 17 000 sailors.

The defence works ranged from trenches and barbed wire entanglements to redoubts and forts. The forts, which were usually located on commanding heights, were enclosed areas surrounded by a ditch and earthen scarp. Inside the protection afforded by the scarp were built concrete or earthen 'bombproofs' where troops could shelter from the artillery bombardments which preceded infantry assaults. On the far side of the ditch, extending in front of the fort, was usually a buried concrete gallery reached by a tunnel. Part of this gallery provided covered protection, part projected into the ditch to form a 'caponier' from where rifle and machine gun fire could sweep the ditch. To capture a fort, the attackers had somehow to negotiate this ditch and it was in the caponiers, the ditches, and the galleries that the closest fighting took place.

In front of the forts and redoubts were barbed wire entanglements. Such entanglements were often placed over rows of man-traps. The latter were holes of at least the height of a man, taking the form of inverted cones. At the bottom, or apex, a sharpened stake would be fixed in order to impale any unfortunate who, in negotiating the barbed wire under fire, would be sufficiently distracted to take a false step. Sometimes 'fougasses' would be laid in likely areas of advance. These were explosive charges detonated electrically under the advancing enemy; they were not very destructive but had a useful demoralising effect. Between the entanglements and the strongpoints one or more lines of trenches would be dug, with communication trenches leading to the rear. Filled with riflemen, and provided with a clear field of fire, these trenches could hold back all assaults so long as they remained intact.

Some officers criticised the design of the Russian trenches. They were rather narrow, so that officers or stretcher parties had great difficulty in pushing their way through, and it was not easy to send reinforcements to places where the enemy had broken in. To give protection against overhead shrapnel bursts, timber and earthen roofing covered the trenches. A number of officers considered that this had an undesirable effect; habituating the soldiers to protection, it made them reluctant to leave the trench to make counterattacks. According to one Japanese infantry officer, the Russians never left their trenches, even for the most pressing sanitary reasons; on occupying some captured Russian trenches, wrote Captain Sakurai, 'we found them full of nastiness.'[2]

At the beginning of the siege General Nogi had three divisions and two reserve brigades. These were continually being replenished. Of his 400 guns, the heaviest were six-inch and 4.7-inch weapons. Those firing shrapnel shells timed to explode over the Russian positions were quite effective, but were of little use against the thick concrete of the stronger fortifications.

In mid-August, after a series of unsuccessful assaults on individual strongpoints, Nogi undertook a general assault of the eastern sector. After two days of artillery preparation, which inflicted serious losses on the defenders, one Japanese division began its attack, using the broken terrain and kao-liang as cover. The Japanese guns had put out of action most of the Russian artillery in this sector, and the attacking infantry was able to approach quite close to the defences. However, as soon as the Japanese came within effective range of the Russian small arms, they began to take heavy losses and their attacks petered out. Nevertheless, Nogi repeated these costly attacks for several days. Not until his casualties reached 20 000, the equivalent of a division, did he give up.

Why Nogi should have persisted so long and so vainly was fairly clear. Japanese public opinion, and hence the Japanese government, was demanding the joy of a spectacular victory, and no victory would have been so spectacular as the capture of Port Arthur. Second, Nogi, like many Japanese officers, was on familiar ground, having taken part in the capture of Port Arthur in the war against China a decade earlier. On that occasion a general assault had indeed captured the fortress, and for only a handful of casualties. It took some time for the Japanese commander and his government to realise that the Russian Port Arthur was not the same as the Chinese Port Arthur.

Having failed by direct assault, the Japanese had recourse to bombardment, sapping and mining. With artillery superiority and a plentiful supply of ammunition, they had a great advantage. For while the Russian defence works seemed able to hold the Japanese infantry, this only remained true so long as they were substantially undamaged. Prolonged bombardment could gradually kill off the defenders in their trenches, could break down parapets and make the trenches unusable. The Japanese guns soon put out of action that majority of Russian guns which had been placed in exposed positions on hilltops. The larger Japanese guns were usually located for indirect fire; controlled by forward observers they remained hidden from the Russians. The principal defect of the Japanese artillery, the lack of really big guns, was remedied by the transfer from Japanese coastal defences of eleven-inch howitzers. These huge weapons, firing a 500 lb shell, could penetrate most of the Russian concrete structures and were perhaps the decisive element in the outcome of the siege.

While the bombardment continued, the Japanese in September busied themselves with sapping and mining. Perhaps because of a natural dislike of this kind of work or perhaps because of the rocky nature of the ground, they preferred to approach quite close to their objectives before beginning the spadework. Sapping involved the digging of trenches, usually in a zigzag alignment, towards the Russian positions. Sandbags or metal shields were used to protect the diggers. These trenches served as a covered approach to another series of works, the parallel trenches. The latter were dug parallel to the Russian line of defence to provide shelter for Japanese infantry awaiting the signal to attack. By such means the Japanese could get very close to the Russians, sometimes within talking distance.

Mining involved the digging of tunnels directly towards the Russian fortifications, in order to blast out breaches in them. Ideally, a series of mines would be detonated, followed by an infantry assault from the parallel trenches to take advantage of Russian confusion and penetrate the breaches. In practice, the ideal was rarely achieved. What often happened was that the Japanese would capture part of a fortification damaged by gunfire or mining, and there would follow desperate fighting as the Russians tried to dislodge them. Sometimes a caponier or gallery would be partly captured, with a sandbag wall dividing the Russian and Japanese sectors.

All kinds of weapons were used in this close fighting. The Russians made hand grenades to throw down on the Japanese, and the latter made bombs from shellcases filled with explosive and detonated by wadding soaked in kerosene. These were thrown by mechanical means into the air, whence they were intended to drop into the Russian defences. The Japanese also used two kinds of trench mortar, made of wood. A Russian naval officer, Lieutenant Podgurski, devised several methods of using naval mines against the Japanese. He also had considerable success with the eight-inch torpedo-shaped missiles fired from tubes and originally designed for close-range use by ships' steam cutters.

Russian countermining was rarely successful. Tunnels were dug out towards the Japanese, with the aim of discovering their approaching mining galleries. Both sides listened very carefully and did what they could to muffle the sound of their own picks and shovels. The Russian efforts would have been more successful if they had had more sappers available, and more officers experienced in this sort of work. Skill and experience were required to judge, from the faint sounds which came through the earth and rock separating the two sets of tunnels, the direction and the distance of the enemy tunnel. Occasionally it happened that the Russians, listening quietly in their own underground passage, could detect the approach of the Japanese diggers, and then listen as they passed. In such a case a chamber would be dug and a charge would be calculated sufficient to destroy the enemy's work. The charge would then be tamped up and detonated through electric wires. All the preparations would be made with a sense of urgency and in silence; it was essential not to alarm the enemy, and to explode the charges before his own charges were laid and detonated.

Although spectacular results were once or twice achieved with countermining, nocturnal sorties on the surface by infantry were more effective. These had the object of wrecking the entrances to the enemy's mining tunnels, and disrupting his approach and parallel trenches. At first quite large bodies of infantry were sent out on these surprise attacks, but they were often observed by the Japanese in time for a hot reception to be prepared. Because of the consequent heavy losses, Stoessel ordered that only small parties should be sent out. He was criticised for this decision, but in fact the smaller groups were more successful because they achieved surprise more easily, blowing up the Japanese advanced works and escaping back before the Japanese realised what was happening.

Partly because civilians had been evacuated before the town was cut off, partly because of sporadic Japanese shelling, the streets of Port Arthur were deserted at most times. Because reliable information was so scarce, all kinds of rumours from time to time swept through the town and its defences: Kuropatkin was winning great victories, the Japanese were about to lift the siege, the Russian Baltic squadron was expected to arrive in a few days. In December, following a rumour that Kuropatkin's forces were marching to the relief of Port Arthur, a heliograph was set up with the object of communicating with the 'relief force' at Nanshan. When such rumours were found to be false, and especially when the news of Kuropatkin's defeats came through, the garrison tended to go into a state a depression for a few days. According to one Soviet historian, it was the disappointing performance of Kuropatkin which later led General Stoessel into depression and the decision to surrender the fortress.

The Japanese naval blockade was not absolute. Despatches passed periodically between Kuropatkin and Port Arthur, carried by officers who hid themselves on blockade-running junks. Sometimes, too, a destroyer would make a dash for the nearby Chinese port of Chifu, where the Russian consul was in telegraphic touch with St Petersburg. Some carrier pigeons were also taken to Chifu, with the aim of establishing a pigeon post, but this project failed when the pigeons showed no interest in returning .to Port Arthur. Junks, and on occasion chartered steamships, sometimes reached Port Arthur with supplies. For the Chinese junk crews, carrying food into the fortress brought high profits, but also mortal peril.

In mid-September General Nogi again went into the attack, assaulting the fortifications of the western and central sectors. In the west, 203 Metre Hill was a main target. From this hill the harbour of Port Arthur was fully visible, which meant that the warships of the Russian squadron could be accurately bombarded if the summit fell into Japanese hands. Hitherto, the Japanese guns had from time to time dropped shells into the harbour, and scored one or two damaging hits on Russian ships, but without observation of fire such shooting was only haphazard. Both sides realised the crucial significance of this hill, and were prepared to make great sacrifices for its possession. For five days the Japanese stormed this objective and for a time, after hard and destructive fighting, they managed to occupy part of it. But not for long:

> Before the Japanese were driven off 203 Metre Hill, Lieutenant Podgurski prepared some 18 lb guncotton mines, which had not previously been used on this hill. About midnight on September 10 the Lieutenant, together with infantry who had been previously defending the hill, began to play with the Japanese, throwing stones at them. The Japanese replied in kind. Then our side began to throw large rocks, and Lieutenant Podgurski rolled his mine on to them, which produced a tremendous effect. The explosion was so powerful that the trench immediately collapsed on them. Gigantic flames enveloped the men close to the trench, whose clothing instantly caught fire. They began to run away like madmen, jostling each other and thereby passing on the flames. Some ran down the hill, but forgot about the barbed wire there; they got entangled, dropped down one by one, forming human campfires. At the same time our riflemen, supported by newly-arrived reserves, opened up with a hellish, withering, fire. Japanese regiments arrived to support those who had been attacked and were met by the same destructive riflefire, and by guncotton cubes and mines. They strode, ran, crawled and scrambled up the slope, fell to the ground, and burned. Others moved up the hill

like flaming torches ... by 0400 all the trenches had been cleared and the surviving clump of Japanese had withdrawn ... their bodies literally lay in heaps on the slopes and the foot of 203 Metre Hill.[3]

In the central sector the Japanese did capture two redoubts but that was all they achieved in these five days of sacrificial activity. After the fifth day they once more settled down to bombardment, sapping and mining. Having had some success with these less spectacular activities, and especially with their eleven-inch howitzers, the Japanese renewed their infantry attacks at the end of October, this time with a two-day struggle for the fortifications of the eastern sector. Their assaults were mainly repulsed, but they were able to consolidate themselves in the ditches of a few of the defence works.

In the west, at 203 Metre Hill, the Japanese continued their mining operations and at the end of November once more launched their infantry against it. As a preliminary, the hill was subjected to an intense artillery fire, making it resemble, according to one observer, a volcano in eruption. Most of its defenders were in shelter behind the hill; the local commander had entrusted the hill mainly to men suffering from scurvy, and since trench life aggravated this disease they were allowed to go into the sunshine in the rear, being called back only when the enemy could be seen approaching. The summit of the hill was defended by two redoubts linked by trenches and protected by breastworks. Gunfire wrecked most of these works, but during the nights the Russians mended the breaches as best they could with timber and sandbags. The Japanese infantry assault on the hill lasted five days; on a number of occasions the Japanese captured part of the Russian positions but were driven back by desperate counterattacks made by whatever few men the Russian officers could assemble.

Other sectors of the Russian line were also being attacked. In one sector there were so many Japanese corpses littering the hill sides that the two sides agreed on a ceasefire while the dead were collected:

On Redoubt No 1 at about this time the Japanese raised the Red Cross flag alongside their own national flag, and then a white flag in addition. Both we and they began to show ourselves hesitantly from behind our breastworks, but then we emerged completely and came together in the centre ground between the redoubt and our defensive wall. Two Japanese officers and an interpreter came out and asked permission to carry away their dead up to 1600. Knowing that in principle this was permitted, we simply asked them to wait until we had checked the duration of the ceasefire with the commander of our unit. While waiting, we had a talk with the Japanese. As usual, they were extremely polite, conveying their best wishes and hoping that they would meet us again, safe and sound, under different circumstances. They brought out *sake*, their national drink, and the officer hastened to drink some in order, he explained, to demonstrate that it was not poisoned. The Japanese did not stop us looking at their nearest works, and even allowed me to take some photographs. On parting they insisted that we should take with us a cask of *sake*, saying that a refusal would offend them. We took the *sake* and gave it to our soldiers in the nearest sector ... At 1500 we again met the Japanese in front of Redoubt No. 1. This time both we and they came out in large numbers, both officers and men. So as not to be in their debt, we took several bottles of vodka and wine, and also sweets and cakes. As time was short the work had to be hurried, with our own men helping the Japanese remove their bodies to their line. By arrangement, we did not allow the Japanese to get very close to our positions. The bodies were horribly mutilated ... The Russian soldier has a great talent for expressing himself in some sort of international lingo and our men energetically chatted and gesticulated with the Japanese. Despite the large number of corpses, they were soon all carried to the Japanese trenches. Our bugler sounded the Retreat, and both sides quickly went off to their positions. Another few minutes, and the bullets began to whistle again.[4]

Finally, after eight days, in which the Japanese suffered 8000 casualties, 203 Metre Hill was finally captured. Observers on the hill then began to direct the fire of the eleven-inch howitzers on to the ships of the Russian squadron, which were sunk within a few days.

With this destruction of the Russian squadron in December, the strategic need to capture Port Arthur disappeared. Nogi's men could have been sent northwards to join in the fight against Kuropatkin's forces. But Port Arthur had great symbolic significance. Public opinion in Japan demanded its capture; after all, plans to celebrate its capture had been long ready. Almost every family had bought flags and lanterns in anticipation. In the outside world the capture of Port

Arthur would quieten continuing doubts about Japan's chances of winning the war, and thus make it easier to raise loans.

The garrison by this time was in a bad state. Lack of fresh vegetables had caused widespread scurvy. Meat other than horsemeat was virtually unavailable. The commander of the land defences, Kondratenko, together with several of his staff, was killed in December by an eleven-inch shell which penetrated a casemate. Kondratenko had been the most intelligent and energetic of the generals, and had enjoyed the confidence of his subordinates, so his death had a dispiriting effect on the garrison. His replacement by General Fock, in whom few had any confidence, made things worse.

Although scurvy only appeared in September, there had been health problems before then. In July, 8 per cent of the men were ill, in August 10 per cent, and this grew steadily, reaching 22 per cent in November. Lack of proper rest was one cause. Most men probably became habituated to continuous bombardment, and could sleep through all but the closest near misses, but there were few comfortable resting places on the hills around Port Arthur. In the 'bomb-proofs' intended for resting troops the men were surrounded by stores, damp laundry, and wounded men. At times the smell of corpses was added to their trials; Order No. 563, issued for the whole fortified area in September, advised sentries in such conditions to stuff their nostrils with wads soaked in diluted turpentine.

By August the meat ration was down to half-a-pound of horsemeat four times weekly. When scurvy appeared there were suggestions that more horses should be killed, as it was believed that extra meat would help to reduce this disease. However, this was not done. From September, medical supplies began to run short, and all kinds of materials (curtains, old clothes) were henceforth used for bandaging. Hospital space had been scarce from the beginning. Hospital ships were used, but this was an alleviation rather than a solution. By the time the siege ended there were 39 buildings used as hospitals, few of which had hospital equipment. More than half the garrison was sick or injured. About 14 000 lay in the hospitals but probably 6000 more with scurvy were serving in the front line. Shortage of men and shortage of hospital space meant that even soldiers with their teeth dropping out might be sent into action. The death rate from scurvy was quite high, as in the given conditions it was almost impossible to cure this disease.

Morale fluctuated. There had been a severe drop after the Battle of Nanshan; five officers and nine men committed suicide in May and

June. But the unsuccessful Japanese general attack in August boosted morale. As the siege continued, with nerves at extreme tension for long periods and with hopes of relief repeatedly disappointed, there were nervous breakdowns of one sort or another. Most common, apparently, were hallucinations; on one occasion two batteries claimed to have heard over 100 shots from 'Kuropatkin's advanced artillery'. In her *Diary of a War Nurse* O. A. von Baumgarten wrote of Port Arthur morale thus:

> Extreme tension gives rise to phlegmatism, and only then is it realised that the best philosophy is silence. We have now a complete atrophy of sensitivity, i.e. of pity. It is immaterial whether one dies today or tomorrow; one will die anyway. You get up in the morning and somehow can't believe you're alive. Our present existence is like those of people condemned to death. Death itself does not frighten us, but waiting for it is hard. If only the end would come soon, if only we could be killed.[5]

Another medical observer wrote:

> Walking with difficulty among the wounded lying in the corridors, I could not help noticing the unusual silence and tranquillity with which they waited their turn for bandaging. Opening the greatcoat of one or other to select those most needing urgent help, I came to the conclusion that all the wounded, even those who had just been brought in, had fallen into a deep dream. Their wearied and weakened organisms were completely prostrated.[6]

After the capture of 203 Metre Hill, Nogi transferred his main thrust to the central sector, north of the town. By this time he had about 100 000 men, and despite the rocky ground his mining operations were making good progress. Russian countermining was ineffective, largely because there were not enough sappers left to dig the necessary tunnels. The only effective delay to the Japanese underground advance was obtained by filling the counterscarp galleries of the forts with boulders and concrete. This made it difficult for the Japanese to burrow under the walls, although it only delayed, rather than prevented, the mining of the fortification. It was sometimes possible to listen to the Japanese and divine where and when their charges would be exploded. In such a case the defenders would be evacuated, apart from one or two sentries. When the charges had been fired, the defenders would rush back to defend the breaches against the advancing Japanese infantry. One of the Russian forts was destroyed when its own precautionary demolition charges exploded prematurely; the whole structure collapsed, killing most of its garrison. In the view of many officers some of the mined defences were abandoned prematurely. The breaches could have been defended longer, although at the price of perhaps 100 casualties a day. But it was fairly clear to the senior officers that Port Arthur could only be defended for a few more weeks. Hope of relief by Kuropatkin, or of a transformation of the strategic situation by the arrival of the Baltic squadron, had long since evaporated. It was a question now of how long the stocks of food, ammunition and men would last.

On 29 December Stoessel called a council of war to discuss continuation of the siege. At this council, attended by the senior officers, a majority held the view that it was still premature to discuss surrender. Stoessel and Fock, apparently, had another opinion and on 2 January two officers were seen riding out of Port Arthur, carrying a white flag. They carried a letter from Stoessel to Nogi, suggesting that negotiations should begin. The commandant of the fortress, Smirnov, had not been informed of this decision, nor had most of the leading officers. It later transpired that after the meeting of 29 December, Stoessel had sent a message to the Tsar, in which he reported that supplies were running out, that the men were exhausted, and that the fall of the fortress was imminent.

Having received Stoessel's letter, Nogi agreed to begin talks at a village outside Port Arthur. A group of Russian officers, with a student as interpreter, went there and were presented by the Japanese with the proposed text of a surrender agreement, written in English. After one small alteration had been made, the document was signed. Port Arthur was to be surrendered intact. The soldiers would become prisoners of war. The officers could choose to return to Russia on parole. Already, before the document was signed, the Russians had lost their bargaining strength. Some key positions had been abandoned, opening the way into the town; apparently Fock had ordered these withdrawals despite the misgivings of other officers. As news of the negotiations spread, the soldiers, none of whom relished the prospect of becoming the final casualty of the siege, began to abandon their positions to roam around Port Arthur, break into vodka stores, get drunk, rob passers-by, and riot.

After the signing, Russian and Japanese officers sat down together to consummate the surrender with a group photograph. Stoessel offered Nogi a white horse, which was politely refused. Soon after, from Germany, Kaiser Wilhelm awarded Iron Crosses to both Stoessel and Nogi, in recognition of their military prowess.

The Japanese placed guards at water supply points, took 30 000 Russians as prisoners, and then staged a ceremonial goose-step through the captured town. Some Russian officials stayed on for a few months. One of the first acts of the Japanese was to put the dustbins out; perhaps the German education of the new commandant explains this priority given to cleanliness. Private property was respected (for the Russians at least; the Chinese were steadily pushed out). Strelkovaya and Artillery streets were respectively renamed Nogi Street and Mikasa Street. The fort where Kondratenko met his end was converted to a museum and tea-room.

In their operations against Port Arthur the Japanese had suffered about 60 000 casualties, almost the equivalent of an army. Nogi's two sons had died during the fighting in the Peninsula. Russian casualties (killed and wounded) were about 30 000. The close siege had been endured for 240 days, as against the 346 days of the celebrated defence of Sevastopol in the Crimean War. But Sevastopol had never been cut off, and received reinforcements during its ordeal. The Russian casualties equalled 70 per cent of the officers and 64 per cent of the soldiers. The 5th East Siberian Rifle Regiment had suffered most; with wounded men returning to service and becoming casualties again, in statistical terms over 100 per cent of the officers and 92 per cent of the men were killed or wounded. The defenders had suffered especially from artillery fire. Whereas in the Manchurian field armies only about 5 per cent of losses were caused by artillery fire, at Port Arthur this proportion was about 50 per cent.

The fall of Port Arthur had its expected repercussions. The foreign credit of Japan rose and that of Russia fell. The citizens of Japan could at last bring out their celebratory lanterns. Russian revolutionaries could welcome one more nail in the coffin of the tsarist autocracy. Lenin wrote that the capitulation of Port Arthur 'is the prologue to the capitulation of Tsardom.'

General Stoessel, with his wife, returned to Russia by sea, enjoying a warm welcome at Odessa. On arrival at St Petersburg he received a hero's ovation. Among other honours, the Starocherkass Cossacks made him an honorary member, and the St Petersburg Mutual Charitable Society held a special session to honour his wife. Somewhat to the surprise of foreign observers, however, Stoessel was due to be court-martialled. According to Russian regulations, the commander of any fortress captured by the enemy was automatically court-martialled, irrespective of how gallant or intelligent the defence had been. But the commission that was convened after the war was considerably more than a formality, because there had accumulated a great variety of charges against Stoessel and his associates.

Most of the higher officers during the siege had been aware of the animosity between Smirnov, the nominal commandant of the fortress, and Stoessel. Stoessel had himself been commandant before the war, but had then been appointed to command an army corps. Smirnov was his replacement, and an officer reputed to be of firm and honest character. Contrary to later statements, the replacement of Stoessel by Smirnov was not welcomed by all officers; many regretted that a general who was familiar with the local situation should be replaced at that critical stage by one brought in from outside. But Stoessel's army corps never moved out of the Peninsula. As a result Stoessel remained in Port Arthur as commander of the 'fortified region' and, being senior in rank to Smirnov, insisted on supervising the latter's arrangements. Thus the commandant of the fortress was subject to constant interference, with Stoessel frequently disagreeing with his proposals and sometimes countermanding his orders. Undoubtedly Smirnov was seriously hampered by this interference, especially as Stoessel was not an intelligent man. Perhaps more important, in the situation of a close siege the discord led to nervous tension not only on the part of Smirnov, but of his subordinates who, after all, were more capable of organising the defence than Stoessel. Inevitably, senior officers took sides or, if they did not take sides, spent much of their energy smoothing over the hatreds and animosities of others. When the siege was over, the anti-Stoessel faction lost no time in making known its grievances. The result was the long list of charges brought against Stoessel and his associate Fock at the commission of enquiry. Logically enough, the same commission heard a charge against Smirnov which, in essence, suggested that if Stoessel were as bad as Smirnov had alleged, then Smirnov had neglected his plain duty of putting him under arrest.

The evidence placed before the commission was wide-ranging.[7] Perhaps never before had so much dirty military linen been washed in public. But the charges against Stoessel were narrowly defined, even if numerous. The most serious of the charges was that Stoessel's surrender of the fortress had been in breach of regulations; not only was the surrender undertaken without the agreement of the senior officers, as regulations stipulated, but it had taken place before the resources of the defenders were exhausted. Fock was also involved in this accusation, and in the associated charge that Fort No. 2 had been surrendered prematurely. Stoessel was further charged with refusal to obey Kuropatkin's instruction to leave Port Arthur, instructions that had been sent when it became known that he was having a bad influence on the defence. Among other charges were the general one that he had interfered in the defence, imposing certain harmful decisions, and specific accusations that he had sent in inaccurate reports and been over-generous in awarding decorations to his friends and associates. He had also permitted Fock to distribute inside Port Arthur certain 'Observations', in which Fock criticised, sometimes cruelly, the actions of his colleagues.

The most complete and readable account of the allegations believed by Stoessel's enemies is Nozhin's *The Truth about Port Arthur*. Like other books with that kind of title, it is unreliable, but it has served nevertheless as a major source for accounts of the siege of Port Arthur. It appeared almost simultaneously with the convening of the commission of enquiry, achieved high sales, and was translated into several languages. Nozhin was the editor of the Port Arthur newspaper *Novy Krai*, and contrived to continue publication during the siege, until Stoessel ordered him to close down. Nozhin was a strong supporter of the Smirnov faction and his book tends to given all credit for the various successes of the defence to Stoessel's enemies, while blaming Stoessel for all the failures. However, he provided little hard evidence for any of his allegations, and there were many cases of self-contradiction in the book. Nozhin and his newspaper were discussed before the commission and it was evident that many officers approved of the paper's supression.

On the question of Stoessel's refusal to quit Port Arthur when ordered to do so, the evidence left no doubt that he had indeed refused, but there was some difference of opinion about the circumstances. According to the Smirnov faction, Smirnov had twice sent oral complaints to Kuropatkin through officers carrying official despatches out of Port Arthur. Kuropatkin had then sent a message to Stoessel, requesting him to leave the fortress by the first available blockade-runner and proceed to headquarters, where he would in due course receive a new field command. At the same time Kuropatkin had sent a message to Smirnov informing him of the action taken. Stoessel had refused to act on Kuropatkin's instruction and had, moreoever, intercepted the message destined for Smirnov and ensured that it was never delivered.

In his evidence Kuropatkin produced a somewhat different story. He said that he had begun to have misgivings about Stoessel when reading the latter's reports, which alternated between extreme optimism and desperate demands for reinforcements. Kuropatkin had then asked for Admiral Witgeft's private opinion of Stoessel, and received a highly critical report. In June, therefore, he sent a message to Stoessel requesting him to join the forces in Manchuria, and a message to Smirnov informing him of this decision. The message to Stoessel was twice repeated, and eventually a reply was received. In this reply, Stoessel wrote that the spirit of the defenders would fail if he left: 'my departure would cause a general sadness ... Smirnov is perhaps an excellent man, but is rather a professor. If it was Kondratenko it would be a different matter.' Stoessel concluded by saying that if Kuropatkin, despite all this, still wanted him to leave, then he would do so. Kuropatkin discussed the matter with Alekseev, and they decided to let Stoessel stay. Kuropatkin admitted that he had received oral messages from Smirnov via blockade-running officers, but said he regarded these as in bad taste. He concluded, not without wisdom, that 'if the place had not capitulated, but had been forcibly taken by the Japanese, the question of Stoessel's decision to stay would certainly not have been raised and everyone would have said that he had acted for the honour and glory of Russia.' This evidence by Kuropatkin, while perhaps giving a poor impression of Stoessel, did not really confirm that particular charge against him. As for the question of whether it was Stoessel himself, one of his staff, or a bureaucratic error which prevented the delivery of Kuropatkin's message to Smirnov, this was never really settled by the commission.

The main witness to support the charge of unwarranted interference in the organisation of the defence was, of course, Smirnov. He had, after all, been the immediate victim of Stoessel's conduct. But although Smirnov seems to have been an honest and competent officer placed in a difficult situation, his detailed accusations against Stoessel seem sometimes to be most damaging to his own reputation. For example, with controlled indignation he told the commission that Stoessel had issued an order that when several enemy batteries concentrated their fire on one Russian battery, the latter should cease fire and its gunners take cover; 'This order is certainly not in agreement with our regulations, which insist that even when a battery has exhausted its ammunition it stays in position.' Such an accusation, and the way it was expressed, seems to suggest that Stoessel was capable of modifying a regulation in the light of experience and commonsense, whereas Smirnov was not.

Nor does Smirnov emerge very creditably in a passage of Lieutenant Colonel Rashevski's diary, describing how a Japanese mine was countermined by the Russians. After the Russian chamber had been excavated, the charge laid and tamped in, it was essential to act quickly so that the Japanese would be blown up before they had time to lay their own charge. Rashevski wrote that the charge was ready at 1100 and that Smirnov had expressed the wish to explode it himself. 'Towards noon the commandant arrived, and as he insisted on seeing the effect of the explosion we hastily ran wires and batteries to a protected part of the forward rampart. At 1230 the commandant personally detonated the charge.' In other words, the urgent detonation was delayed for 90 minutes to satisfy the whim of Smirnov. Such situations are not unknown at other times and places, or in other armies, but these parallel cases hardly excuse Smirnov. Smirnov's champion, the wily journalist Nozhin, seems to have realised this, for in his *The Truth about Port Arthur* he wrote that Smirnov arrived in time to fire the charge at 1100.

Other accusations against Stoessel at this stage of the enquiry concerned his responsibility for the food shortage. He had made no arrangements to grow vegetables, it was claimed. Stoessel defended himself, rather weakly, by saying that the ground was too rocky. An accusation which had made a great impression on public opinion was that Stoessel, before the siege closed in, had overruled Smirnov and permitted the export of tinned food from Port Arthur. It transpired, however, that most of this food had been 'exported' to the army in Manchuria, in response to an urgent request; unwise, perhaps, but hardly a criminal folly. More substantial was the allegation, apparently true, that Stoessel in the later stages of the siege had ordered the cessation of work on the second and third lines of defence. But his explanation, that these fortifications demanded the services of scarce manpower for work which could not be satisfactorily completed in the time available, is not implausible.

The affair of the *Novy Krai* was well-aired. This threw more light on the intrigues and insubordination of various officers than it did on Stoessel's failings. It seems true, however, that Stoessel from the very start was suspicious of this newspaper and its editor. Like others brought up in the Russian bureaucratic tradition, he felt that information and its distribution was too important to be left in non-official hands. Many officers found the newspaper useful; they were told so little by their superiors that they relied on it for information not only of the outside world but also of the siege itself. But several officers testified that the newspaper gave useful information to the enemy. For example, it gave the heights of certain batteries and the disposition of certain units. It was not difficult for the Japanese to obtain copies via the local Chinese, and they could extract useful information from it. But since each issue was subject to a three-stage military censorship, the editor could hardly bear all the blame for this. A captain who had served in Fort No. 2, which was so closely beset by the besiegers that Russians and Japanese could talk to each other, produced an interesting piece of evidence:

> There was a rumour amongst us that a prince was visiting the Japanese troops. I questioned the Japanese about this and they said it was not a prince but the army commander who was visiting the positions. In their turn they asked the following question, 'Is General Stoessel wounded?' I was astonished and asked, 'How did you find out about that?' They replied that they had learned it from the *Novy Krai*.

Nozhin, contrary to Stoessel's wishes, had left Port Arthur during the siege. Stoessel probably suspected that the editor would publicise complaints and criticisms about him. In this he was correct, although the court did not go very deeply into what information Nozhin had divulged to Russian and foreign journalists when he arrived in China. What is certainly true is that Nozhin's departure was with the connivance of Smirnov and Smirnov's associates. An interesting sidelight on the state of the Russian navy was cast when it was revealed that, when arrangements were being surreptitiously made to ship Nozhin out of Port Arthur, at least two destroyer captains refused to take him when requested to do so by Admiral Loshchinsky. Perhaps this was because Loshchinsky had added to his request 'Don't let Stoessel find out', but it is a sad navy whose destroyer captains refuse to obey their admirals. Eventually a new set of officers was appointed to one of the destroyers, and it was this vessel which took Nozhin to Chifu. Nozhin subsequently repaid Loshchinsky, for in his book he singles out that admiral for high praise, giving him the credit, among other things, for mining the two Japanese battleships. In other accounts of the war Loshchinsky is hardly mentioned.

The officer who had commanded the sector of the defences in which the controversial Fort No. 2 had been located expressed the opinion of many officers when he told the commission that it was Fock who had been the 'evil genius' of the defence. Both Smirnov and Stoessel, he said, had good qualities; the former had the confidence of the officers and men, while the latter had been very far-seeing in his anticipations of where the enemy would strike next. But Stoessel had been very much under the influence of Fock, whom he regarded as almost infallible. As a co-accused, Fock was at a disadvantage at the enquiry; unlike Stoessel, he had few friends to defend him, for he seems to have been disliked by everyone except Stoessel. Moreover, his actions were not easily explained away. At Nanshan, where he had been in command, he had withdrawn without using more than a quarter of his troops. He had ordered the allegedly premature evacuation of Fort No. 2, the first permanent work to be abandoned, and during the surrender negotiations with the Japanese he had ordered an end to resistance in a vital part of the defence, thus weakening the Russian bargaining position. In addition, his 'Observations' had damaged the morale of his colleagues.

The essential fact about Fock, which explains much of his behaviour, is that he was a theorist: not only a theorist, but a poor theorist, the intensity of his devotion to a theory being in inverse proportion to its applicability. A second aspect of Fock's character was almost certainly what others might have described as soft-heartedness, but which might also be described as sensitivity. In particular, he did not glory in the deaths of his soldiers, but rather considered their lives to be precious. One of his theories was that defences should not be held to the last man.

Defences, said Fock, were intended to delay the enemy's advance while inflicting as many casualties as possible. There comes a time in the life of every defence work when continued resistance is wasteful, when one's own forces begin to suffer more than the enemy. It is precisely at this stage, according to Fock, that the position should be abandoned. Morever, any attempt to recapture the position from the enemy is most likely to produce excessive casualties and has small hope of success. This theory seems intelligent, but Fock spoiled its presentation by his obviously weak analogy between a siege and a gangrenous body; as soon as a doctor sees that the gangrene has spread to a new part of the body, said Fock, he cuts it off in order to save what is left. Also, in practice Fock seems to have given his theory undue preference over practical factors. While in retrospect his decision to abandon certain positions may seem wise, the abandonment of positions absolutely vital to the continuing defence quite justifiably aroused the anger of his fellow-officers. There were times and places when a position did demand 'excessive' sacrifices. At Nanshan there seems little doubt that Fock's intention to withdraw

sooner rather than later meant that he was psychologically unpre-
pared to make a strong defensive effort.

When the siege began, Fock had few official duties. Ostensibly he
was commender of the Reserve, but there was no Reserve. However,
he advised Stoessel, and wrote his 'Observations' on the conduct of
the defence. When Kontratenko, commander of the landward defence, was killed, Smirnov feared that Stoessel would wish to appoint
Fock to replace him. To avoid this, which Smirnov regarded as a
potential disaster, Smirnov arranged to split the command and
entrust Fock with the least critical sector. However, on seeking to
acquaint Stoessel with this intention, he was told that Stoessel was
'unavailable'. When he did eventually find Stoessel it was only to be
told that the latter had already appointed Fock to Kondratenko's
position. As Smirnov anticipated, although Fock was his junior he
did not carry out his orders, preferring to make his own decisions and
getting them approved by Stoessel. When Fock ordered the abandonment of Fort No. 2, Smirnov was indignant; having impressed on
everybody the need to defend positions to the last, he could foresee
the effect on morale of abandoning a key position while it was still
capable of defending itself. At the commission of enquiry, however,
the former commander of that locality admitted that at the time of its
abandonment the fort could have held out for only a few more hours.
In other words, while Fock's decision to withdraw may have had a
bad moral effect, it did represent a refusal to spend men's lives on
short-term objects.

Fock was described by his accusers as visiting the positions,
compiling his 'Observations', and thus 'trying to show how superior
he was.' Some witnesses, however, said that his comments on the
conduct of the siege were helpful. Even Kondratenko, it was said,
had admitted that Fock's 'Observations' would have been useful if
they had not been expressed so offensively (Stoessel acknowledged
that Fock's wording was 'too severe'). Kondratenko had been
especially offended by a passage which said 'the generals have dug
like pigs into Flat Mountain, but have not been able to defend it.'
Using such language, it is hardly surprising that in the circumstances
of a nerve-wracking siege Fock should have made enemies. It has to
be remembered, too, that he had intellectual pretensions, and that
intellectualism was disliked by most tsarist army officers. One officer
also alleged that in conversation with soldiers Fock had gloried in the
fact that he was not a Slav, but a Teuton.

Some of the allegations about Fock's tactlessness and pride might be regarded as the kind of innuendo and solidified rumour which such enquiries typically bring forth. However, Fock himself sometimes revealed the defects of his character. For example, when hard pressed on one point, his counsel suggested that the court might allow junior officers to testify in Fock's favour, men who had actually fought in the trenches as opposed to those who had merely supervised the fighting. But Fock objected to this: 'it is not fitting that I should get testimonials from lieutenants.'

There seems little doubt that it was Fock who persuaded Stoessel that Port Arthur should be surrendered, even though a majority of the officers were in favour of continuing the fight. Fock's decision to abandon certain key forts, before the surrender negotiations were concluded, could only have been a deliberate move aimed at making a surrender inevitable whether the other officers liked it or not: for the relinquishing of these strongpoints made it almost impossible to continue a successful defence. Fock's motivations were probably in accord with his 'gangrene' theory, but also owed much to human considerations. Everyone acknowledged that the defence had to end soon in any case, and Fock probably saw no reason why hundreds if not thousands of Russian soldiers should die just to postpone the inevitable for a few days. Also he was very conscious of the likelihood of a general massacre if the Japanese should break into the town by force. This possibility did not appear to be taken very seriously by his fellow-officers, but Fock was presumably aware that when the Japanese had captured Port Arthur from the Chinese there had been a bloody massacre. As for Stoessel, his behaviour at the time of the surrender is difficult to defend. Being in effective command, and the senior officer, the responsibility was his, and he had undoubtedly acted in breach of regulations by entering into negotiations without first obtaining the approval of a council of his senior officers.

Smirnov was accused of not taking energetic measures against Stoessel at the time of the surrender; of accepting, as it were, a *fait accompli*. Earlier, it transpired, Smirnov had asked for the opinion of the lieutenant colonel who presided over the Port Arthur military tribunal as to whether he, Smirnov, had the right to arrest Stoessel. He was told that he could only do so if Stoessel had clearly infringed the regulations or the law. Evidently, at the time (October and November), Smirnov did not feel that he could prove that Stoessel had violated the regulations, and he appears to have given no further thought to the question.

After hearing the evidence, the commission of enquiry, which consisted mainly of elderly army officers, found Smirnov not guilty. Fock was convicted of a 'disciplinary fault' and reprimanded. The majority of the charges against Stoessel were found to be unsustained, or relating to acts which could be justified, or of no legal force. But Stoessel was found guilty on the charges of prematurely surrendering the fortress. For this he was sentenced to be shot, but the Tsar commuted this to imprisonment and Stoessel spent only a short time in prison.

At the time there were many who thought that the commission had been too soft; the humiliations of the Russo–Japanese War could be made bearable only by the sacrifice of scapegoats. But probably, although the enquiry did not get to the bottom of many questions, its conclusions were sound. After all, the defence of Port Arthur had been an achievement even though it perhaps ended a few days too early. However, resentment against Stoessel and Fock persisted. Seven decades later, Russian historians still presented the siege of Port Arthur as the story of brave soldiers and competent officers betrayed by the 'treachery' of Stoessel.[8] This seems a rather simple-minded view, deserving reconsideration.

# 7   The Road to Mukden

Towards the end of September 1904 Kuropatkin's staff at Mukden began to prepare plans for an offensive. The staff said that this should be undertaken as soon as possible, in order to relieve the pressure on Port Arthur and to anticipate the arrival of Japanese reinforcements. Both these reasons lack substance. Although it is true that a great Russian victory would have relieved Port Arthur, the ever-pessimistic Kuropatkin probably had little hope of such a victory at this stage. As for reinforcements, the Russians would gain more than the Japanese by waiting, and knew it. Kuropatkin had other reasons for an offensive, and his staff officers merely brought forward the question of reinforcements and Port Arthur because the real reasons were less easily stated.

Kuropatkin probably needed a successful offensive action at this time to boost the morale of his troops and to strengthen his own position as commander. After all, he had not been outstandingly successful hitherto, and even though there seemed to be no general who could have done better than he, the imminent arrival of Grippenberg to take over the recently-formed 2nd Army suggested that his replacement was not unthinkable.

The direction of Kuropatkin's thought was indicated by his general order to the troops on 2 October. This took the form of a proclamation in which Kuropatkin explained why the previous succession of withdrawals had been justified, and declared that the Russians could now look forward to a victorious advance. The publication of this order must in due course have attracted the attention of Oyama, whose expectations of a Russians move would thereby have been confirmed.

Kuropatkin's plan was that General Bilderling would move southwards parallel to the Mukden-Liaoyang road to pin down the Japanese forces in the west, while Stakelberg would operate with a stronger force in the mountainous east. A characteristic weakness of the battle orders was the instruction to the advancing units to dig themselves in if the Japanese should be encountered in what seemed to be superior force or in an offensive attitude. This stress on the desirability of creating a 'position' was inconsistent with Kuropatkin's other remarks on the importance of a sustained rapidity of advance. It appeared that all the Japanese needed to do if they lost the initiative (as they were likely to do when the Russians attacked) was to prepare an offensive. In essence, this is what actually happened in this encounter, which became known as the Battle of the Sha ho.

The Russians began their advance on 4 October, and for three days threw the Japanese back. By 7 October the Japanese situation was perilous, but it was precisely at this crucial stage that Kuropatkin ordered his troops to dig in. In the west, three lines of entrenchments were started, while in the east, where the rocky and broken terrain hardly justified much trench-digging, the day was passed in reconnaissance. Nor did the Russian forces move forward on 8 October. All this gave time for a beleaguered Japanese brigade in the east to withdraw quietly and, more important, for Oyama to concentrate his troops for his own offensive. Kuropatkin, as ever, was fearful of a Japanese attack and had halted his successful advance to prepare for it, while Oyama, knowing that he was being attacked, had responded with a counteroffensive intended to gain the initiative. Thus Kuropatkin's fears were to a large extent self-fulfilling and the Russians, not for the first or last time, had sacrificed the initiative in favour of their predilection for defensive tactics.

On 9 October the Russians again moved forward but, because the Japanese were already concentrating, were unable to get very far. On the next day the Russians halted again, providing the Japanese with the chance to make final preparations for the counteroffensive. This began the following day, and after a week of heavy fighting the Russians were beaten back to the north bank of the Sha ho, and it was there that they passed the winter. Russian casualties at the Battle of the Sha ho were about 41 000, and Japanese 16 000.

Irrespective of the casualty lists, the battle represented a great Russian defeat. Not only had an opportunity been lost to defeat the Japanese, but the morale of the Russian troops had received one more blow. Encouraged to hope for a victory, the Russian soldiers had fought hard for two weeks over a 40-mile front, only to see their efforts once again ending in retreat. Retreat certainly brought out the best in the Russian army, but withdrawals which seemed brilliant and well-organised on the generals' maps did not always look quite the same on the ground. A reserve officer later wrote:

I saw officers who had shouted themselves hoarse and yet had been able to do nothing. What can you do when men can't hear your voice or your whistle? Not everyone is within earshot of the officer, and there is constant interruption by the din of gun and rifle fire.

'To the wood!' the company comander shouts hoarsely, pointing in that direction with his bared sword. The men closest to him hear, understand, and hurry in the indicated direction. But those who are more than fifty paces away do not hear and continue on their way. The company straggles and its commander becomes desperate.

'Where are you going, you fools?' he orates, at the end of his tether. The confused men become even more disorganised. And each second *Shimose* and shrapnel are exploding, and there is a continuous hum of bullets, like bumble bees.

'Company halt!' wails the officer, quite desperate. Some men halt but others don't hear and move on. The officer is beside himself. Already soaked, he no longer talks, just croaks. He swears furiously at those who ordered this accursed retreat, but there is nothing he can do; the company is retreating in disorder. The only praiseworthy thing about these retreats is that our men never run. They always walk. Phlegmatically walk. . . .

To keep up his men's strength the commander ordered them to be issued a nip of vodka, which was brought up under cover of night with the kitchens. But later there was much repentance about this, because thanks to this ill-starred vodka, taken on empty stomachs, half the regiment became drunk.[1]

The battle of the Sha ho marks the end of the first period of the land war; both sides could congratulate themselves on achieving their strategic aims, but neither could feel entirely satisfied. Kuropatkin's strategy had been to withdraw slowly northwards until he had accumulated preponderant strength. He had succeeded in his withdrawal, but not without getting involved in some damaging battles whose effect was to lower morale and to postpone the day when he could be sure of overwhelming the Japanese. As for the Japanese, they had planned to advance rapidly, gain key territory such as Port Arthur, and defeat the Russians before the latter could bring their full potential to bear. They had certainly advanced, and they had convincingly although not finally defeated the Russians in battle, but they had not captured Port Arthur before winter, nor scored that spectacular victory which would force the Russians to capitulate. It seemed that the Russians might retain enough stamina to enable them to fight on until the last Japanese reserves had been exhausted.

The strategy of both sides had been hampered by transport difficulties. For the Japanese, there had been anxiety about the sea communications between Japan and the mainland, and the difficulty of bringing up supplies from the coast to the armies as they penetrated northwards. For the Russians, the basic problem had been the movement of supplies and reinforcements over the single-track Trans-Siberian Railway.

By 1904 Japan had built up a considerable merchant fleet, and most ships were put at the disposal of the army and navy, leaving foreign vessels to fill the resulting gaps in commercial services. The Japanese coast was well-provided with ports where transports could assemble and await their cargoes and then slip down the coast to begin the 100-mile crossing from Japan to the nearest point of Korea. This nearest point was the Korean port of Fusan which, however, lacked a rail outlet. Most ships therefore passed Fusan to creep up the west coast of Korea, initially to Chemulpo and Chinampo, and later to ports in southern Manchuria. The lethargy of the Russian squadron enabled these supply and transport operations to proceed with remarkably little loss. Only the cruisers from Vladivostok operated against them, and not often.

During its march from Chemulpo to the Yalu, Kuroki's 1st Army was supplied from the sea; as its route was along the coast its lines of communication from successive base depots could be short. After the Battle of the Yalu the port of Antung became available, and a light railway (narrow-gauge) was laid from Antung northwards to the road junction of Fenghuangcheng, which became the initial base for the 1st Army's advance towards Liaoyang. This railway was later extended and was a valuable supplement to the hundreds of transport carts serving the army. Its wagonettes, hand-propelled, could each carry 1000 lb.

Although Kuroki sent out detachments far and wide to recruit Chinese carts, horses and carters, these remained insufficient. At this stage of the war good daily rates were offered, but were not enough. Even when the Japanese offered to pay half-value compensation for horses which died in these operations the locals were unenthusiastic. It soon became necessary to use various kinds of compulsions, but this did not prevent coolies and carters disappearing at any favourable opportunity. In June, heavy rains washed away bridges and made roads impassable for vehicles for a week. The army had to be put on half-rations and the exceptional measure was taken of using the combatant troops on coolie duties, carrying sacks of rice.

Kuroki also had the services of the transport corps (conscripts rejected for health reasons and given brief training as military coolies, carters and drivers). Despite this, and despite the use of a very convenient base port, the 1st Army was the worst-placed for supplies. Unlike the other armies, it was far from the main railway, its advance was along mountain roads that were impassable at certain periods, and the surroundings were poorly endowed with horses, carts, forage and grain. It was not until the railway was reached at Liaoyang that these problems were solved. Until then, each advance was followed by a long pause during which supplies were laboriously brought up to the latest advanced base.

Further to the west of the 1st Army was the 4th. This, to the strength of one division, had landed at Takushan and pushed northwards. The road was quite serviceable, being only disrupted occasionally by rain, and the locality was populated enough to provide forage, meat and vegetables. This relative ease of supply was one reason why the First Division was followed by others, to create a complete army. This army was able to abandon its original supply line when it reached the main railway at Haicheng.

The 3rd Army, besieging Port Arthur, had the fewest worries about transport. The port of Dalny was cleared of mines in July and the railway branch thereto was reopened at about the same time. For the supply of forces distant from the railway, a number of narrow-gauge tramways were laid. In addition, junks were used along the coast, and there were Chinese coolies, carts and packhorses for difficult areas. The eleven-inch howitzers were served by tramways.

When the 2nd Army landed in the Peninsula, reliance was placed on native carts and coolies. Up to the capture of Dalny this army lived on a hand-to-mouth basis, sometimes having only two or three days' supply in hand. For the advance northwards to Liaoyang there were two usable roads, and the railway. In their retreat the Russians had taken away all the locomotives, and some of the rolling stock, but had done little damage to the track. Soon man-powered trains were organised. Standard Russian freight cars of 20-ton capacity were used (but loaded only up to about 5 tons), each being powered by 16 coolies (eight pulling on ropes and eight pushing). Trains of up to 40 cars were run at first, but after some spectacular runaways (due to absence of braking), a 10-car limit seems to have been imposed, with single-car formations on the down grades. From July, Japanese rolling stock and locomotives began to arrive in Dalny, and the line was progressively changed from the Russian 5ft to the Japanese 3ft 6 in. gauge. By October the conversion had been made as far as Liaoyang, which became the main supply base for all the armies, and was served by regular steam trains from Dalny and Newchuang.[2]

Supplementing the railway was the road service, which at its peak (just before the Battle of Liaoyang) was employing thousands of carts, both native and army. The road was divided into stages of about 12 miles and over each stage 300 or 400 carts made an out-and-back trip each day. Pack donkeys and sometimes even native wheelbarrows were also pressed into service. The 2nd Army's problems had been greatest in June and July, before the railway was operating properly. At one stage it was proposed to send transports to the west side of the Peninsula, where they could unload close to the army at ports such as Kaiping. But the emergence of the Russian squadron in full strength in June caused the cancellation of this project, as Togo was no longer willing to provide escorts. However, after the Battle of Round Island and the capture of Newchuang, transports were able to serve Newchuang, where a depot was established. From this port supplies could be forwarded either by rail or by river. Thus by the beginning of September the 2nd Army's various supply routes were ample, and could be shared with the other armies.

Like the Japanese, the Russians found it difficult to find enough Chinese carts and carters. Just as the Japanese were crippled after the Battle of Telissu by the flight of their carters, so did the Russians discover after the Battle of Mukden that hundreds of carts and their contents had disappeared. Like the Japanese army, the Russian army could not rely entirely on its own transport services. It did have limited resources, based on a standard four-wheeled cart (which on the Manchurian roads was less manageable than the two-wheel push-carts favoured by the Japanese), but without local help it could hardly move. Even with local carters it was still tied rather too closely to the line of railway.

There was one Russian piece of equipment that was the envy of foreign military observers. This was the mobile field kitchen, virtually a boiler on wheels which could cook food on the march. This raised morale with the promise of regular hot food, and the prolonged boiling contributed to the mastery of intestinal diseases. Apart from the few days after the Battle of Mukden, all Russian troops except the advanced cavalry detachments were very well fed. There was a surprisingly small reliance on tinned food; meat and vegetables were readily available in the Russian-held part of the Manchuria.

While the supply situation was satisfactory so long as the Russians were stationary or slowly retreating, however, it is doubtful whether long advances could have been sustained by the carts and pack animals. In anticipation of such advances in 1905, Decauville portable light railways were laid behind the front. These narrow-gauge lines could be laid at the rate of two or three miles each day, and could be taken up at twice that speed. The longest of them was 30 miles, and its horse-drawn wagonettes covered that distance in about six hours. The wagonettes carried a 1.75 ton load, and many were equipped to carry eight stretchers, this form of transport being the most comfortable for the wounded.

The Trans-Siberian line from Europe as far as Harbin, and the line southwards from Harbin towards Mukden and Liaoyang, formed the vital Russian link. On their carrying capacity depended the success of Kuropatkin's policy of accumulating an overwhelming preponderance over the Japanese. At the beginning of the war the Trans-Siberian carrying capacity was very limited. The line was broken at Lake Baikal, and although in summer train ferries were able to handle all the traffic that was offered, in winter men and supplies had to cross the ice of the lake without benefit of mechanical power. Even when a track was laid across the ice, enabling freight cars to be drawn over by horses, this break was the weak link in the line of communication. However, the railway around the Lake was completed in September 1904. At the beginning of the war the Russians expected to run only three pairs of trains daily (that is, Kuropatkin would receive three loaded trains and return three empties each day). But thanks largely to an unusually competent minister of transport, Prince Khilkov, this meagre total was progressively increased.

By the end of the war no fewer than 16 pairs of trains were handled daily by the Trans-Siberian line. Kuropatkin's misfortune was that by the time the railway capacity had been built up to his requirements, important battles had been fought and lost. Increased capacity was achieved by careful traffic control, with trains moving at a uniform but rather slow speed; by increasing the number of passing loops; by placing the eastern part of the line under martial law (which meant that railwaymen might be required to work for days without a break and could be court-martialled for desertion if they refused); by the transfer of equipment from other railways; and by the upgrading of the track at critical points. Because Kuropatkin's troops could be fed mainly on local supplies, most of the trains were devoted to the carriage of troops and ammunition. A typical troop train consisted of two engines hauling 28 freight cars adapted for troop transport (that is, provided with windows, a stove, and sleeping shelves), six other freight cars for kit and ammunition, and a conventional passenger car for the officers. Such a train could carry 1064 men and 36 officers. Transit time from Europe was occasionally as long as 50 days, and the prolonged separation of the officers from the men was later said to have helped the spread of anti-war and subversive propaganda among reservists moving to Manchuria.

During the war, both belligerents found that their manpower plans needed modification. The Japanese war ministry had always realised that its army could never match the size of Russia's. It had relied on the war being short, but the profligacy with which the generals sacrificed their men's lives meant that by summer 1904 Japan already faced a shortage of trained men. Men of the Second Reserve (the *Kobi*, men who had completed their seven years in the active army and First Reserve) had already been mobilised. In September 1904 the length of service in the *Kobi* was doubled from five to ten years. As this change was retrospective, men who had passed out of the *Kobi* up to five years previously found themselves mobilised for active service. This call-up of the 1888–92 intakes increased the army by about 120 000 men which, with the intake of new conscripts, enabled losses to be made good and the army's divisions to be increased from 13 to 17 in 1905. Training the new men, and retraining the old, was a serious problem because experienced officers and NCOs were required at the front. Eventually the training period was reduced to six months, after which the trainees went straight into battle. Unsurprisingly, the reinforcements sent to Manchuria in 1905 were inferior to those of 1904.

Japan having gained command of the sea early in the war, transport of troops to the front line was simple, and the full strength of the army could be brought to bear. With the Russians it was very different. At the beginning of 1904, of Russia's 29 army corps, only two were east of the Urals, and they were considerably below their nominal strength. These two Siberian corps, at the beginning of the war, had great difficulty in reaching their full complement because their reservists were widely scattered and had to travel long distances to join their units. Moreover the population of the region was so small that it could not provide enough reservists in any case. Reservists from European Russia had therefore to be sent.

During the war the Russians assembled almost 1 000 000 men in the Far East. Of five army corps sent east, three were composed of reserve divisions. Crack troops like the guards divisions were not sent. From the beginning, the Russo–Japanese War was regarded by the Russian war ministry as a minor war which did not justify general mobilisation. At the same time, becuase of the need to guard the western frontiers and anticipated internal disorder (especially in Poland), it was accepted that the best troops should be kept in the western borderlands. Raising new troops without wrecking the existing plan for general mobilisation was achieved by successive partial mobilisations. Whereas general mobilisation envisaged the call-up of the highest categories of reservists from all parts of the Empire, partial mobilisation entailed call-up of all categories from just a few selected areas. This caused much resentment, in one area family men who had been in civilian life for ten years or more found themselves sent to the distant Manchurian front, while younger men in adjacent areas were untouched. Local military authorities, who were entrusted with medical examinations and call-up formalities, were often unreasonable and unsympathetic. An army doctor, present at the re-examination of men claiming exemption on medical grounds, later wrote:

> Reservists of the older categories were also mobilised. Before us processed an endless line of rheumatics, emphysematics, the toothless and the varicose. The committee chairman, a brave cavalry colonel, frowned and complained that there were so many 'protesters'. But what astonished me was the number of the clearly unhealthy who were not 'protested' by the army doctors.[3]

At the same time as older men were being drafted to Manchuria, young men who had completed their four years of active service in the standing army were released into the reserve, and unless their reserve unit was in one of the areas chosen for mobilisation they escaped war service. Kuropatkin later complained that the reservists sent to him as reinforcements were of low morale, vulnerable to seditious propaganda, and liable to suffer heart attacks in mountain operations. As for the cavalry reinforcements, the Transbaikal and Siberian Cossacks whom he received 'consisted of old men mounted on small horses'. For these reasons, call-up of family men and Second Category reservists was stopped in 1905, and some of the men finishing their four years' active service were held in the army and sent east, but by that time the decisive battles had already been fought.[4]

Foreign observers, just as in previous and subsequent wars, agreed that the Russian soldier was stolid, submissive and of great endurance, but because of his limited education and peasant origin was not capable of much initiative even though he was ready to die for his Tsar. This description is very much a stereotype, and possibly many of those who saw these qualities in the Russian soldier did so because that is what they expected to see. Not all Russian soldiers were peasants; many of the reservists were from the urban classes. Nor were all Russian soldiers submissive; Kuropatkin complained of occasions when reservists came to blows with regulars, whose attitude to the war was different from their own. By no means all Russian soldiers were ready to die for their Tsar in a war which by no stretch of imagination could be regarded as defence of the Motherland. One general wrote in one of his orders:

In the rear hospitals there have appeared a large number of Other Ranks with wounded fingers. Of these, 1,200 have only the index finger injured. The absence of the right-hand index finger means release from military service. Therefore, bearing in mind that in action the fingers are well protected by the trigger guard, there are grounds for presuming deliberate self-injury. In view of the foregoing, the commander-in-chief has ordered that measures be taken to impose legal responsibility on those who are guilty.[5]

Kuropatkin claimed that as early as February 1904 there had been cases of reservists plundering railway stations, and later in the war he was horrified to observe reservists escaping the battlefield by acting as stretcher-bearers, sometimes with ten or more men carrying one stretcher to the rear.

Just as commentators had their stereotype of the Russian soldier, so did they unanimously report the spirit of self-sacrifice that moved the Japanese soldier, 'that wonderful spirit of sacrifice', in the words of the British *Official History*, 'which animates the heart of every man – soldier or sailor – and makes him feel it is a privilege to give his life, if by that means the welfare of the nation may be advanced.' There was a touch of envy in such accounts; in Western eyes the Japanese warrior was a model to be emulated. After the war a Japanese infantry officer, Sakurai, in a book called *Human Bullets* gave an idealised picture of the Japanese martial spirit. The book became a bestseller in Japan, was translated into several languages, and made a great impression on martial if unperceptive readers abroad. Its author described how impatiently the soldiers of Japan waited for that sweet-sounding, heart-gladdening word 'mobilisation', how the soldiers of Japan 'all felt our bones crackle and our blood boil up' when the long-awaited word came in the month of cherry blossoms, 'emblematic of the spirit of Japan's warriors', and how the hearts of the soldiers of Japan were fired by the war songs sung by groups of innocent nursery-school children who came to send off the embarking units.[6]

This idealised picture of the Japanese soldier was not entirely accurate. Towards the end of the war the Russians encountered Japanese troops who did not seem at all keen on fighting, whose bones all-too-obviously failed to crackle and whose blood failed to boil up. But in the earlier period of the war the Japanese infantry did indeed seem willing to take enormous casualties. The soldiers who fought in the first months of the war were very fit, and were trained in offensive action so that, for example, privates would take over from killed NCOs, and NCOs from killed officers. But towards the end of the war there were signs that the Japanese army, like the Russian, had absorbed older reservists from the towns who were somewhat more resistant to patriotic indoctrination.

By the end of the 1904 campaign, both sides had modified their tactics in the light of experience. These modifications were not always applied generally, for on both sides there were officers who could not un-learn what they had been taught in their training schools. For both sides the Battle of Telissu seems to have been a turning point, probably because it confirmed some of the ideas which had been born in the preceding engagements. After Telissu, for example, the Japanese began to abandon their concept of the 'decisive' (that is, dense) infantry assault. After Telissu the Russians usually preferred to employ their artillery in indirect firing from concealed positions.

At the Yalu, at Nanshan, and at Telissu the Japanese infantry had attacked en masse, following the German doctrine of 'momentum'. In doing so they had suffered great and unnecessary losses, so they began to attack in extended lines or in groups, using all available cover and digging themselves in wherever they halted. During the second half of the war the standard Japanese attack began with the infantry removing their packs (to be picked up later) and going forward carrying only water, two or three days' rations, about 300 rifle rounds, and a blanket. In the daytime their scouts would reconnoitre the line of advance, and the infantry would follow up at night. Before dawn broke they would have dug themselves into cover, waiting to move forward the following night. After these first trenches were vacated, they would be occupied by the second wave of attackers. In this way the attacking infantry could get close to the Russian defences without being caught in the open by artillery fire.

Cutting the Russian barbed wire was usually entrusted to volunteers; in the early part of the war few of these had survived unscathed, for at night the defenders used searchlights to illuminate the approaches. But the introduction of one-man steel shields reduced the casualties, and the same shields were used to protect diggers of approach trenches. When the barbed wire was cut, the Russian entrenchments would be assaulted, often at night.

Many of the Russian officers strove to bring their infantry tactics up to date, but many others did not. Throughout the war some infantry companies continued to fire by volleys directed by an officer rather than individually; firing by numbers in this way dated from the earliest days of firearms, but was hardly suited to modern conditions, for although it gave officers better control it prevented the individual soldier shooting at his own speed at a target of his own choice. The Russians also packed too many men into their trenches. This too dated from early days but was absurd in 1904, when the magazine rifle enabled fewer men to protect a given frontage. Densely packed trenches meant that fewer men were available for the reserve, and that too many were exposed to shrapnel. Over-reliance on the bayonet persisted among Russian officers; on several occasions Russian troops who were successfully defending their trenches were sent into a bayonet counterattack, only to be flattened by artillery and small arms fire.

By the end of 1904 the Russians had a superiority in artillery. Gunner officers seemed more willing than their infantry colleagues to learn from experience. At the Battle of Tashihchiao the Russians for the first time used indirect fire on a large scale, and reaped the reward. When the Japanese guns were brought closer to the front, thus revealing their positions, they were badly damaged by Russian guns firing from behind cover. The Japanese infantry also felt the effect of Russian shrapnel in this battle. Both sides realised that it was dangerous to change the position of the guns in battle, and for the

Japanese this was a serious problem. Their guns were of relatively short range and could not properly support the infantry as the latter advanced. Typically the opposing guns taking part in artillery duels were only about two miles apart, and until they had been silenced the intervening ground was impassable to infantry in daylight. Quick-firing guns rarely fired quickly, because it was difficult to secure a satisfactory flow of ammunition; a battery, because it was liable to bombardment, found it safer to leave its horses and ammunition carts as much as half a mile in the rear. Horses were especially vulnerable in retreat, and this was why many Russian guns were lost during withdrawals. Although the Russians had an advantage in field guns, they did not have any good howitzers (valuable for placing heavy shells over short distances), and it was not until 1905 that they had true mountain guns at their disposal.

The biggest disappointment for the Russians was the performance of their cavalry. Hitherto the Cossacks had a high reputation both at home and abroad, but during the war they achieved little. It is true that the first shots of the land war were fired by Cossacks reconnoitring Japanese movements in Korea. It is true also that the Cossacks provided effective screens in rearguard actions, yet there was no occasion when a dashing cavalry operation affected the course of the war, or even of a battle. Cavalry's main role, reconnaissance, proved almost impossible to fulfil, for the Russian horsemen found that they could hardly penetrate the combined infantry and cavalry screens with which the Japanese covered their main bodies. Only by fighting its way through could the cavalry obtain information, and even then it would almost certainly be blocked on the way back. Eventually the Russians tried sending groups of two or three men on reconnaissance and these had a little success. But throughout the war information about Japanese movements was scarce, and in several battles (notably Telissu and Mukden), this was fatal. The Japanese did not rely so heavily on their cavalry for information; to some extent (exaggerated by the Russians), they used the spy network which had been established before the war.

The second main function of cavalry, attacks on supply lines, was equally beyond the capacity of the Russians. In their one big operation behind the enemy lines, a seven-day excursion to Yinkou they succeeded both in reaching their objective and in escaping back to their own lines, but without inflicting much damage. The 5000-man force which carried out this raid may have inspired stirring headlines in the Russian newspapers, but with its thousand-odd bullock carts it hardly fitted the traditional image of dashing Cossack raiders. As for the Cossacks' performance in the big battles, this was insignificant. It was usual to place cavalry detachments, acting independently, on the flanks of the Russian positions, but they rarely found, or even sought, useful employment except in retreat. In general, the cavalry would have done better if it had been better prepared for actions on foot. In this war there was little occasion for sabre charges. In most actions the cavalry fought dismounted and the Cossacks, with their carbines, without much training in marksmanship or infantry tactics, were at a disadvantage. The horse artillery was likewise ineffective, mainly because the guns were too small to deal with earthworks and buildings.

The Japanese cavalry was technically inferior to the Russian, but obtained better results. At the final big battle of the war, Mukden, it was Japanese cavalry that threatened to cut the railway north of Mukden, and which rushed in to exploit a gap which appeared between two Russian armies. The Japanese cavalryman was a less expert horseman than the Russian, and his mount was smaller (Japanese breeds were inferior, and horses ordered from Australia were no match for the Russian horses). But the Japanese cavalry, perhaps because it was conscious of being second-best, attempted only those functions for which it was suited. In its screening function, combined with infantry and artillery detachments, it effectively blocked all possible routes leading to the main forces and in this way prevented the Russian cavalry discovering troop movements and dispositions. In action it usually dismounted; the Japanese were quicker than the Russians to understand that cavalry was essentially mobile infantry.

Foreign observers criticised the Russian addiction to positional warfare. The Russian officer seemed to regard a battle as a contest for 'positions', rather than as an opportunity to destroy the enemy's army. In their training, Russian officers learned how to select and fortify a good position, and this was the foundation on which they planned their battles. A foreign military attaché during the war heard two Russian officers discussing a battle in which both sides had planned to advance; they regarded it as fortunate that the Japanese had attacked first because otherwise the two attacks would have met head-on, in which case the Russians would have been compelled 'to fight without positions'. The Russians did not favour more dynamic types of operation, apart from the classic bayonet charge which more often than not merely put them under damaging fire.

Possibly 1812 and *War and Peace* were the origin of the Russian addiction to defensive tactics and strategy. Kuropatkin's aide, Khar-kevich, was something of a specialist on the 1812 campaigns, and gave lectures about them on the train taking the men eastwards.[7] Kuropatkin's general strategy of retreating before the Japanese, stretching their lines of communication while his own forces built up, was a sound one. But whether the same philosophy was valid for the individual battle, as distinct from the campaign, is doubtful. In battle the Russian idea was to stand on the defensive and then, having weakened the enemy, to make a victorious counterattack. In practice the Russians never found it possible to move from a defensive to an offensive stance. In the big battles of the campaign massive counter-attacks were indeed planned, but they were invariably either cancel-led or carried out half-heartedly. It is an open question whether, if the campaign had continued, the Russians would ever have been able to change to an offensive attitude. Indeed 1812 is no sure guide here, for Napoleon's retreat from Moscow was voluntary, more or less forcing the Russians to turn their retreat into an advance. But the Japanese were also over-cautious at times. There were times when the Japanese could have turned Russian defeats into routs, but did not do so. Moreover, towards the end of the campaign the Japanese also became addicted to positional warfare. The first stage of the Battle of Mukden was essentially a fight for position.

'Positions' developed into long fronts. Just as the time-scale of battles lengthened so that the nineteenth-century concept of the one-day battle changed into battles which lasted a week or more, so did the line of front grow from two or three miles into scores of miles. With entrenched infantry armed with machine guns and magazine rifles, observers concluded that direct assaults were no longer practic-al. Only outflanking movements promised any success against such fronts, which is why the length of front grew, with each side stretching itself outwards so as to extend its flanks.

Many of the older generation of officers in the West considered that fronts would henceforth be impregnable, but many younger officers (those who would hold senior positions in the First World War) thought that persistent and intelligent attacks could eventually break any front, especially if the attackers enjoyed artillery superior-ity. This was a question whose solution was left to controversialists in the military journals. The First World War showed that both sides of the argument were right; it all depended on what scale of slaughter was acceptable. So far as the Russo–Japanese War is concerned, the

Japanese did not flinch from repeated frontal attacks on strong positions, but by 1905 they had realised that willingness to die is not everything, especially when the casualty rate exceeds the recruiting rate.

At the beginning of 1905 the two armies faced each other near the Sha ho, south of Mukden. The Japanese line was a flat semi-circle facing the Russians, who were occupying the right bank of the river. Both sides, in places separated by only a few hundred yards, had fortified their positions. On 19 January Kuropatkin issued orders for an attack, orders so lengthy and complex that one observer commented that Kuropatkin had arranged his battle as though it were a ballet. The immediate object of the attack was to gain ground, including the small town of Sandepu. Going over to the offensive was evidently not easy for the Russians, long habituated to defensive actions. General Linievich wrote in his diary before the battle:

> the 2nd and 3rd army commanders, Grippenberg and Kaulbars, did not come out in favour of a frontal attack. Both, like myself, favoured a long outflanking movement. That is, we must manœuvre so as to force the Japanese themselves to go into the attack ... Today I visited the 2nd Army commander General Grippenberg and the 3rd Army commander General Kaulbars. Both are sighing over the imminent difficult changeover to the offensive; Grippenberg is especially fearful, and has little expectation of success.[8]

The Japanese, despite the rather slow Russian deployment, were at first rather surprised by the offensive, and part of Sandepu was occupied by the attackers. Japanese reinforcements were sent, but although the Russian advance was thereby blocked, the situation was still finely-balanced. Much of the fighting took place in a snowstorm, with gale-force winds and temperatures 28 degrees below freezing. If Kuropatkin had committed his reserves at this stage, when the Japanese were nervous, vulnerable and half-frozen, he might have won a great victory. Instead, he ordered his troops to withdraw, and the ground they had gained was progressively lost to Japanese counterattacks. The Russians lost about 14 000 men, and the Japanese about 10 000, in this operation. Only one of the Russian armies participated, and of that only a part was committed to the battle. As a German commentator later wrote, it is useless to comment on the Battle of Sandepu because it was conceived and executed without determination or unity, and so was naturally foredoomed to failure.

The commander of the Russian army involved, General Grippenberg, was later blamed by Kuropatkin for starting the attack too early, against orders. On his part, Grippenberg blamed Kuropatkin for ordering a retreat when victory was in sight. After the battle Grippenberg obtained the Tsar's permission to return to St Petersburg on grounds of ill-health, and supporters of Kuropatkin believed that he intended to intrigue against Kuropatkin in the capital, hoping to take the latter's place. There may have been grounds for this suspicion, but there was also reason to relieve Grippenberg for health reasons (among other things, he was too deaf to use a telephone). The robust, risen-from-the-bottom General Liníevich commented, with his usual animosity towards Baltic Germans: 'In my opinion, Grippenberg saw from the battle ... that this was not the same as fighting the Turks or Bokharans, and he simply fled from the battlefield. In spirit he is a German, not a Russian.'[9] Stakelberg also relinquished his command after Sandepu. Kuropatkin dismissed him as a corps commander because during the battle he had captured a village without first obtaining permission to do so.

A reserve officer later described how he felt during the Battle of Sandepu:

You go into the attack beneath a hail of shells and bullets, every second liable to be killed or wounded. All around you scores of men, dressed in clumsy grey greatcoats and with shapeless bags hanging at their sides, drop down in heaps, silently or not so silently. Drop down without a murmur, with not a curse against man or nature, but remembering in the difficult moment of death only God and their poor distant homeland. At such a time you don't pay any attention to the place you have been ordered to go to. But when this place is reached, when you don't need to go any further, then your spirit is quite crushed. It is then that this cruel festival of death hits you in the eye. Somehow you don't want to believe that men can carry out this slaughter, this terrible bloodletting, and cause so much suffering to their fellow-men. But however much your brain works on this question, all the facts are clear, and make you conclude that mankind is far from maturing to an understanding and to an application in life of the words of our Saviour ... I don't know, but it seems to me that here on earth there can be no moral suffering, no affliction, greater than that which overwhelms a man on the field of battle. When he begins to realise what is happening, and what is going to go on happening.[10]

The last major battle of the land war took place at Mukden, with a front that was as long as 100 miles at the beginning, contracting to about 75 miles later. The battle lasted for three weeks, and ended in defeat, though not disaster, for the Russians. By this time the Japanese armies had been reinforced from the south. Nogi's 3rd Army, released by the fall of Port Arthur, had already joined the three other armies facing Kuropatkin and a new army, General Kawamura's 5th, was marching from the south-east towards Mukden. Thus the forces that the Japanese brought into action at Mukden represented their maximum effort; although new divisions were being raised in Japan their quality was not expected to be high. The Russians, too, were now much stronger, although for them further expansion was easy.

On 19 February Kuropatkin, feeling that his forces were stronger than the Japanese, gave orders for an offensive movement. At about the same time Oyama, realising that his own strength was at a peak, decided that he too would go into the attack and win a great victory, his own Sedan, before it was too late. His plan was to attack all along the line, make an outflanking move with Kawamura's troops in the east and then, having drawn the Russian reserves towards Kawamura, send in Nogi's army on the western wing to envelop the Russian flank and cut the line of retreat northwards. With his centre strongly fortified, Oyama felt able to divide his main effort between the two wings.

The Russian plan was to attack the western wing of the Japanese line, push it back, and thereby outflank the Japanese. Kuropatkin had scheduled his attack for 25 February, but by 24 February it was clear that the situation was changing. Japanese troop movements made it evident that his plan could no longer be carried out, so on the evening of 24 February he cancelled his offensive. On the same day Kawamura, advancing from the south-east, had captured a pass and pushed back the Russian outposts. Two days later he seemed to be threatening to outflank the Russian line in the east. To meet this threat, Kuropatkin sent one corps as reinforcement. This corps had to march 50 miles, but almost as soon as it arrived it was recalled to meet a threat in the west; it reached Mukden on 3 March, having covered a total of 125 miles, and so wearied itself that it took hardly any further part in the battle.

Meanwhile, on 26 February the Japanese armies had attacked all along the line. As usual, the frontal attacks were costly and failed to capture the Russian positions. They did, however, occupy the Russian defenders and prevent their despatch to the flanks. On 27 February, Japanese cavalry moved out from the western end of the line and pushed back the Russian cavalry detachments facing them. Behind, and screened by the Japanese cavalry, came Nogi's 3rd Army which had hitherto been hidden behind the Japanese lines. By 3 March Nogi was moving towards Mukden, less than 10 miles distant. Until 6 March Kuropatkin was unaware of this danger. Unable to penetrate the Japanese cavalry screen, he had no knowledge of Nogi's emergence.

By the evening of 6 March it was clear that the Russian line was in danger. The westernmost of Kuropatkin's three armies was forced to change its front from south to west, a difficult operation which it achieved with little loss of cohesion. This army held up the Japanese advance, and was intended to mount a strong counterattack. But an early failure caused Kuropatkin to call off this offensive. If he had persisted he would probably have won the battle, for Nogi's 3rd Army was awkwardly placed at the time. With the abandonment of the counteroffensive came orders to withdraw, and by 8 March the withdrawal had developed into a general retreat after Kuropatkin had been further unnerved by Japanese cavalry attacks on the railway line north of Mukden. The Russian rearguards secured the retreat, but at one stage a gap formed between two of the armies. Into this gap rushed Japanese cavalry and artillery, cutting off part of the Russian forces. This resulted in heavy losses, including about 12 000 men taken prisoner. However, the Japanese intention of cutting the line of retreat north of Mukden was not achieved; Oyama, after all, had been denied his Sedan. In the three-week battle Russian casualties were about 65 000, with another 20 000 taken prisoner, compared to Japanese casualties of about 41 000.

General Bilderling, the army commander regarded as responsible for the losses of the retreat, was presented after that battle with 38 questions which he was required to answer. In this way it was hoped to discover precisely what had gone wrong. After the war, however, Kuropatkin admitted that he had ordered the retreat a day too late. At the same time he complained that he had been ill-served by his cavalry; the four regiments of cavalry which should have discovered Nogi's advance in good time suffered only 22 casualties in three weeks of fighting, which hardly suggested that they had tried very hard.

In retrospect the fatal mistake made by Kuropatkin was the despatch of his reserves to the eastern sector just as the Japanese were about to launch their strong outflanking movement in the west. He had been led into this trap partly by his own prejudices; the Russian staff had often claimed that although the Japanese were strong fighters in the mountains, they could be beaten on the plains. This convenient explanation for their defeats, that the Russians unlike the Japanese had not been trained for mountain warfare, convinced them that the Japanese would never choose to attack over the plains if they had the alternative of a hilly battleground. Thus whereas foreign military commentators had forecast before the battle that Oyama would attack in the flat western sector, because only there could he manœuvre his masses of troops, Kuropatkin and his staff held to their theory of the Japanese preference for the mountainous east. Second, Japanese deception helped the Russians maintain their opinion until it was too late. Nogi's army was held concealed behind another army, and one of its divisions was sent east to join Kawamura. Russian intelligence soon became aware of 3rd Army men operating in the east, and drew the conclusion that all of Nogi's 3rd Army was there, as well as Kawamura's 5th Army (which, unknown to the Russians, was considerably smaller than an army).

The Japanese, who were short of ammunition, did not pursue the Russians after the battle. Because of their losses the Japanese were actually in a poorer strategic position after their victory than they were before it. Unlike the Russians, their losses could not be replaced easily. This improvement in the Russian strategic position was unnoticed by Russian public opinion, and Kuropatkin was replaced by one of his army commanders, Linievich. This was not the end for Kuropatkin, however, as he stayed to command one of the three Manchurian armies. After the war he wrote his memoirs, and other books too.[11] He was always ready to draw instructive conclusions from the most distasteful experiences. Of the 1905 civil disturbances he wrote, 'The enormous effect of bombs thrown by revolutionaries and anarchists should be utilised for the purpose of war.' In the First World War he commanded an army against the Germans, and displayed the same qualities of bureaucratic caution.

One of Kuropatkin's subordinates in Manchuria, Rennenkampf, also commanded an army in 1914. He was intended to support the army of another Manchurian veteran, Samsonov, who had advanced into East Prussia in order to take the pressure off the French. Because Rennenkampf failed to come to his rescue, Samsonov was disastrously defeated at the Battle of Tannenberg. In view of this, it is interesting to note that in 1905 General Linievich wrote in his diary about the Mukden defeat, 'Despite my entreaties, Rennenkampf flatly refused to help and sent only four troops of the Nerchinsk Regiment.'[12] Samsonov, also a cavalry officer, whose conduct in the war was less spectacular but more competent than Rennenkampf's, had a noisy argument with the latter on Mukden railway station. According to some accounts, this confrontation between a full-blooded Russian and a full-blooded Baltic German ended in blows.

# 8  Tsushima

By the summer of 1904 enough new and refitted warships had accumulated in the Baltic to swing the balance of naval power in Russia's favour, if only some way could be found to move them to Port Arthur. The nucleus of this fleet was five battleships, of which four (*Suvorov*, *Aleksandr III*, *Borodino*, and *Orel*) were similar to *Tsesarevich* and almost ready for service. Five modern cruisers were ready or almost ready. These included two fast light cruisers of the *Novik* type (*Izumrud* and *Zhemchug*); another *Novik*-type vessel, *Almaz*, was also available but, having been redesigned as a viceregal yacht for Alekseev, had little fighting value. Until the death of Makarov, only leisurely steps had been taken to prepare these ships for service, but work was then accelerated and by autumn most of them were ready; those which were not could follow the main force, it was decided.

Press opinion in St Petersburg was strongly in favour of sending out the '2nd Pacific Squadron' as soon as possible, and influential right-wing papers sharply criticised what it called the apathy of the navy ministry. Among them was *Novoye Vremiya*, to which Commander Klado, subsequent historian of the naval campaign, contributed.[1] But sending a fleet half-way round the world in wartime, with intermediate ports restricted by the rules of neutrality, was no small endeavour in the days of coal-burning boilers and temperamental reciprocating engines. At the end of August, a conference was held to decide finally whether the 2nd Pacific Squadron should be despatched. It was realised that Port Arthur might fall before the new squadron could arrive, and that in such an event it was likely that the existing Pacific squadron would be destroyed. Thus the 2nd Squadron might well be obliged to make for Vladivostok, which could only be reached by passing through narrow Japanese-controlled waters.

Whether the enterprise would have been abandoned had not the commander-designate of the 2nd Squadron, Admiral Rozhestvensky, declared he was willing to face the Japanese in an uncertain battle is not clear. Indeed, Rozhestvensky's attitude is itself uncertain. Grand Duke Alexander Mikhailovich, who attended conferences on the subject, in his 1932 *Once a Grand Duke* described Rozhestvensky's readiness as 'ludicrous' and 'quasi-Nelsonic', and quoted him as admitting that he would have no chance against the Japanese but nevertheless public opinion had to be satisfied. Fleet-General V. A. Shtenger, who helped Rozhestvensky prepare the 2nd Squadron, wrote many years later in emigration that the Admiral was against the despatch of the Squadron but did not express open opposition in meetings:

> With Admiral Rozhestvensky I could have only a short conversa-tion about this. He simply said that he had not wished to convince the participants of the uselessness of sending such a squadron as it was, because they would all have thought that Admiral Rozhest-vensky feared the imminent difficulties, even more so because there were among them those who were ready to replace him and themselves take on the responsible task.[2]

In public Rozhestvensky took the attitude that:

> We are now doing what needs to be done still, defending the honour of the flag. It was at a previous stage that another course ought to have been taken ... Sacrifice the fleet if need be, but at the same time deliver a mortal blow to Japanese naval power.[3]

Evidently Rozhestvensky had a strong feeling for the 'honour of the flag'. But to send the 2nd Squadron on such a risky expedition was a great strategic mistake. So long as this squadron existed, even in the Baltic, it was a bargaining counter, an argument that one day might help to persuade the Japanese to accept a tolerable peace settlement. At the bottom of the sea the 2nd Squadron might, or might not, symbolise the honour of the navy's flag, but that was not the purpose for which the ships had been built.

Rozhestvensky was a strange character, but descriptions of him vary widely. He certainly was rude to his subordinates, a man who preferred to shout rather than explain, and a man whose fighting spirit outweighed his perception. Indeed, this was why he comman-ded the squadron; other more eminent admirals had been offered the command but had agilely refused, not wishing to risk their reputa-tions in a doubtful enterprise. McCully, the US assistant naval attaché in St Petersburg, reported that he met Rozhestvensky at this period and 'ventured to hope that I might have the pleasure of meeting him again in the Far East. He did not answer but not very politely grunted and turned away.'[4]

The navy ministry, planning the route of the 2nd Squadron, was faced with the total absence of Russian bases between Libau on the Baltic and Port Arthur in the east. Moreover it could be expected that Britain would make things as difficult as possible for the Russians. Russia had an alliance with France, but the French had no wish to be dragged into war; they could therefore be expected to make only marginal compromises with the laws of neutrality. France did quietly make available some colonial anchorages, but refused to supply coal en route.

Neutral powers seemed uncertain whether colliers supplying the Russians should be regarded as belligerent or non-belligerent. In Britain, Admiral Fisher declared (quite ineffectively) that neutral colliers should not be loaded with British coal if it was destined for Rozhestvensky. But the German government, and especially Kaiser Wilhelm, had reason to value Russian goodwill at this time, and it was on German colliers that Rozhestvensky mainly relied. The Hamburg Amerika line agreed to supply 340 000 tons of coal at agreed points between Denmark and Korea. Welsh coal was preferred, being more calorific and less smoky, and it seems that the bulk of the 'German' coal came from Cardiff.[5]

To deal with breakdowns en route, a repair ship was included in the Squadron, and each of the large ships carried a naval architect. With its colliers and supply ships, and its repair ship, the 2nd Squadron could perhaps be regarded as the forerunner of the self-contained 'task force'.

The Squadron was delayed by various failures in the new ships, which revealed themselves in hasty sea trials. There was also sabotage aboard the battleship *Orel*; an engineroom artificer, not relishing the prospect of a watery grave in the Pacific, put metal shavings in the vessel's main bearing. But in October the Tsar was able to hold the farewell Imperial review, making a short speech on each battleship.

The Squadron, when it left Libau, included the four new battleships, comprising the First Division led by Rozhestvensky in *Suvorov*. A quite modern battleship, *Oslyabia*, led the Second Division, which contained the elderly battleships *Navarin* and *Sisoi Veliky* and the equally venerable armoured cruiser *Nakhimov*. Four

modern and one old cruiser accompanied the battleships, together
with eight destroyers, the repair ship *Kamchatka*, and six supply
ships. A few more cruisers, including auxiliary cruisers from the
Volunteer Fleet, and a few destroyers were to join the Squadron as
soon as they could be got ready.

For some weeks previously an extensive and expensive Russian
intelligence system had been operating in Scandinavia and Western
Europe, watching for any signs of Japanese activity. Apparently the
possibility of Japanese torpedo boat attacks in the North Sea seemed
very real to officials of the navy ministry, still shaken by the surprise
attack on Port Arthur. Hekkelman, head of the Russian intelligence
agency in Berlin, moved to Copenhagen. Here, carrying a false
British passport in the name of Arnold, he organised about 100
observers and hired nine boats to patrol the Narrows. Of the 300 000
roubles and 540 000 francs allocated to the 2nd Squadron's protective
intelligence, he received at least 150 000 roubles. He gave good value
for money by sending in fanciful reports of Japanese torpedo boats.
How seriously Rozhestvensky took these warnings is uncertain, but
as commander he was bound to take precautions against surprise
attack. He decided to leave Skagen a day early so as to confuse
potential attackers.[6]

Soon after leaving Denmark, the repair ship *Kamchatka*, which
had lagged behind the other ships and whose captain was drunk,
began to fire on various foreign commercial ships that passed in the
night, and radioed that she was being attacked by torpedo boats.
From these messages Rozhestvensky calculated that if the torpedo
boats were pursuing his ships they would catch up at about midnight.
Sure enough, at about that time an unidentified warship appeared on
the beam, while a rocket was sighted ahead, and a number of small
ships could be seen approaching. The alarm signal for repelling
torpedo attacks was given, and the ships opened fire. For some
minutes there was noise and confusion as half-trained gunners sought
to fire as many shots as possible into targets which were only vague,
or even imaginary. The result of this ten-minute battle was the
sinking of one Hull trawler, damage to two others, and damage to the
Russian cruiser *Avrora*. What had happened was that the Russians
had sighted *Avrora* and mistaken her for a Japanese torpedo boat,
and at the very same time they had come upon British trawlers fishing
the Dogger Bank and coordinating their movements with rocket
signals.

Although the Russians realised that some trawlers had been involved, the majority of the officers believed that torpedo boats had been lurking among those trawlers. Fearing torpedoes, the Russian ships did not stop to pick up survivors. Rozhestvensky sent a message to St Petersburg which virtually accused the Hull trawlers of obstructing the flight of his shells: 'Our ships did not help the trawlers because of their apparent complicity, which they showed by their persistence in trying to pass through our line.'

The British press and many members of the Parliament did what they could to stampede the British government into declaring war against Russia. For several days the newspapers wrote of Russian barbarity and of the 'Russian mad-dog fleet'. Papers quoted each others' most aggressive fulminations to support their own: 'The true explanation of the North Sea outrage, says the Outlook, lies in the natural barbarity and insolence of the Russian ruling class, combined with no effective realisation that condign punishment awaited its expression. Respect for others can only be inculcated in such a character by force.'[7]

Russia took a conciliatory line (in Russia the occurrence was referred to as the 'Hull incident' whereas British newspapers usually termed it to the 'Dogger Bank outrage'). The British government at this time was more interested in building a triple alliance of Britain, France and Russia than in making war to avenge the deaths of a few fishermen. So when St Petersburg agreed to submit the dispute to international arbitration, and to pay compensation, tension was allowed to subside. The international commission eventually decided that Rozhestvensky had made an understandable mistake, and in the circumstances could not be blamed for continuing on his way without stopping. Russia continued to aver that there had been torpedo boats present, but paid the compensation assessed by the commission.

After the Dogger Bank incident the battleships went to Vigo. In this Spanish port Western newspaper correspondents were lying in wait for them. Among the pressmen was Edgar Wallace, the *Daily Mail's* special correspondent. Not yet world-famous, Wallace found newspaper reporting a satisfying outlet for his powers of fiction. He wrote that in Vigo he approached two Russian petty officers in a brothel, plied them with drink, and wheedled the truth (exclusive, all rights reserved) out of them. This truth, he wired, was that Rozhestvensky had had a vision of Japanese torpedo boats, and gave the order to fire under its influence. The 2nd Squadron later assembled at

Tangier, where the indefatigable Wallace again awaited it. This time he reported that his two petty officers had been 'ferretted out and buried at sea'.

From Tangier the bigger ships proceeded round the Cape of Good Hope, while the other part of the Squadron used the Suez Canal. Madagascar was to be the rendez-vous for the two sections and also for the detachment which had left the Baltic after the main force. Soon after leaving Tangier it became clear that Rozhestvensky was not only concerned, but was obsessed, with the coal question. He was uncomfortable with his dependence on German colliers. If the captains of these chartered vessels should withdraw their cooperation, Rozhestvensky would be stranded. Also, the Admiral felt that he should be ready for battle at any point along his route. Since full speed and damage to funnels implied high fuel consumption, it was essential that his ships should have a good coal stock at all times. This meant that coaling was carried out every week, well before the bunkers were empty. Moreover, Rozhestvensky insisted that ships should carry 50 per cent more than their normal bunker capacity. Coal was stacked in all available space, including the mess decks. The men, unable to keep themselves or their ships clean, were quite debilitated by the frequent coalings in tropical climates. They had little energy left for anything else, which is one reason why training was slow. Normally a new battleship needed at least a year to shake down; Rozhestvensky's new battleships had never properly completed their trials and their crews, largely fresh conscripts and old reservists, had little opportunity to learn how to work together.

At the year's end, having successfully taken his battleships around the Cape (an unprecedented exploit, given the lack of bases), Rozhestvensky anchored off Madagascar. A few days later his ships were joined with those which had been routed via Suez. One of the latter, the battleship *Navarin*, had mutinied while lying off Crete.[8] News from St Petersburg was received. Copies of *Novoye Vremiya* arrived with articles showing how the 2nd Squadron, if unreinforced, was no match for the Japanese. Such articles caused a further drop in morale. The news that Port Arthur had fallen, and that the Pacific squadron no longer existed, was also a heavy blow even though not unexpected. It meant that the ostensible purpose of the 2nd Squadron's mission was no longer valid. Strategically, the navy ministry at this point would have been better advised to order the Squadron home, but the resulting loss of prestige was evidently felt to be unacceptable. Rozhestvensky presumably realised that if the Squadron was to go forward to Vladivostok it should resume its voyage as soon as possible, so as to arrive in Japanese waters before Togo had refitted all his ships after the Port Arthur campaign. However, the end result of the flow of telegrams[9] passing between Rozhestvensky and St Petersburg was that the Squadron remained off Madagascar for two months, enjoying the benevolent neutrality of the French colonial authorities.

During this time the men developed all kinds of psychological and physical ailments. Cooped up in their steel ships in a hot, moist and thundery climate, their morale further deterioriated. Training sessions did little to relieve the monotony. There were frequent anti-torpedo exercises, and a few gunnery practices at sea. Due to the lack of suitable ammunition, such practices were quite inadequate for training the inexperienced guncrews. Few hits were scored by the battleships on the targets, although one stray shell did hit an accompanying cruiser. Ships' commanders showed themselves incapable of manœuvring their vessels together, and there was a gentle side-on collision between two of the battleships. Meanwhile, in the warm waters of Madagascar a thick growth of flora and fauna sprouted from the ships' bottoms.

Finally in March the Squadron set off across the Indian Ocean. Here there were no friendly colonial anchorages whose officials would turn a blind eye on the Russian ships. For three weeks the Russian armada was lost to view. It coaled in the open sea, and kept well away from shipping routes. The world's press exhausted itself in speculations about the route Rozhestvensky had chosen. In Britain the Russians were believed to be planning a circumnavigation of Australia, while in the East Indies the Dutch navy was put on the alert. Eventually the Russian ships were sighted off Singapore beneath a sky blackened by their smoke; they had taken the shortest route. They steamed past the island in four columns at 8 knots, taking one hour to pass and picking up despatches from a cutter hired by the Russian consul.

Back in St Petersburg, the press had been agitating for the despatch of reinforcements for Rozhestvensky. The latter, who realised that the barrel had already been scraped in fitting out and manning the 2nd Squadron, did not welcome the possibility of waiting to be joined by a 3rd Squadron. But despite his lack of enthusiasm such a squadron was prepared. Its nucleus was the old battleship *Nikolai I*, the even older cruiser *Monomakh*, and three coast defence ships (*Ushakov*, *Seniavin* and *Apraksin*). The latter boasted long nine-inch or ten-inch guns, tall funnels and small hulls. Never intended for ocean service, they became known as 'flatirons' and 'self-sinkers'. Commanding this ill-assorted squadron was Admiral Nebogatov, a man of sound commonsense but hardly a great leader.

Virtually any kind of sailor was accepted to man these ships; the Black Sea fleet and the commercial fleet's engineering side had already been plundered to man the 2nd Squadron. The officer position also seemed desperate, but appearance here did not quite match reality. Rozhestvensky, never a good judge of men, had not chosen the best subordinate officers. Thus there was a pool of reasonably competent officers available to serve Nebogatov. These officers were certainly not hopeless, although not all were complete masters of their profession. One of them, while his ship was bound for the English Channel, wrote in his diary: 'suddenly we heard the ring of the engineroom telegraph, and the engines stopped. It appeared that the Staff Navigator had made another of his mistakes, and that we were proceeding up the Thames.'[10]

Nebogatov's ships, which had left the Baltic in February, were only three weeks behind the main force at Singapore. Their passage out had been quite rapid, partly because Nebogatov had not been obsessed by coal stocks, but mainly because there had been no delays. En route, some training had been given, and it seems probable that Nebogatov's unpromising crews were already better-prepared than those of the 2nd Squadron. They had practised, for example, night navigation without lights, in the process almost colliding with a liner off Gibraltar.[11]

Nebogatov caught up with Rozhestvensky off Indo-China. The 2nd Squadron had spent some weeks here, anchored comfortably in Camranh Bay and elsewhere, visited occasionally by a French cruiser which would courteously invite the Squadron to move on (Tokyo at this time was threatening Paris with serious consequences if French complacency about Rozhestvensky's use of neutral waters should continue). Although Rozhestvensky and most of his officers had had a low opinion of the fighting qualities of Nebogatov's ships, when the latter finally arrived there was a lifting of morale, and Rozhestvensky could write in a general fleet order that he now had a superiority in heavy ships over the Japanese. 'The Japanese have more fast ships than we, but we are not planning to run away from them.'[12]

The 2nd Squadron, now including Nebogatov's ships, went to sea for the last time in mid-May, and course was set for Vladivostok via the Korean Strait. Rozhestvensky moved northwards very slowly.

His slowest vessel (a supply ship) had a speed of only 9 knots. Moreover he spent a day on manœuvres, which gave Nebogatov's ships their first and last chance of practising evolutions with the Squadron. Thus it was not until the end of May that the Russians approached the Korean Strait, by which time Togo was wondering whether, after all, Rozhestvensky had decided to take the longer route around the east coast of Japan.

The 2nd Squadron entered the Strait at night, in misty conditions. With lights dimmed it evaded the observation of the Japanese cruisers. But its hospital ship, following well astern, was fully illuminated in accordance with international convention. A Japanese auxiliary cruiser spotted this hospital ship and moved ahead to where it presumed the Russian squadron would be. Its presumption proved correct, and in the small hours the Russian radio receivers picked up a Japanese message: 'Sighted Square 203 enemy squadron apparently bearing eastern passage'. At Togo's base at Mosampo, all hands were on deck by 0500, and clouds of black smoke began to float upwards from the Japanese funnels. Soon the Japanese fleet was at sea. On the battleship *Asahi* the officers gathered round the tobacco tray near the after turret, where an observer found them quite confident of victory, smoking cigars and listening to a gramophone.

The 2nd Squadron was meanwhile being shadowed by a light cruiser, which radioed its composition, bearing and deployment. By 1900 the Russians could see that they were being shadowed by about a dozen cruisers. Morale among the Russians seems to have been fairly high. The previous night few had slept, because torpedo attacks had been anticipated, and in their gloomy nocturnal conversations the men had talked of their fears, of how their families would manage if they were killed, what it was like to be drowned or blown to pieces. But in the morning the mood changed. One sailor wrote:

The mood of the crew was excellent, above normal. You could hear cheerful conversation. There were some who almost up to the opening of the battle played a balalaika, or played draughts. A stranger seeing them would not, I think, have guessed that these were people who this very day were going into battle, a battle in which many perhaps were fated to die. On purpose, it seemed, everybody was behaving as though indifferent to any danger.[13]

At midday the 2nd Squadron was still proceeding slowly through the Korean Strait, with its 12 armoured ships in line ahead. The First Division was leading, consisting of the four *Suvorov* battleships; then came the Second Division of four older vessels, and finally the Third Division of Nebogatov's *Nikolai I* and three 'self-sinkers.' Soon after midday the line redeployed. The First Division turned in succession 90 degrees to starboard and then 90 degrees to port. There was some confusion during this manœuvre, and it has never been established whether or not the strange formation which resulted was really what Rozhestvensky had intended. The armoured ships were now in two columns. The port column was somewhat astern of the starboard column and consisted of the eight older vessels.[14]

At 1320, not far from Tsushima Island, the smoke of Togo's ironclads was sighted through the mist. It was a grey day, and the Russian ships' smoke hung low over the moderate swell. Togo was somewhat to starboard and ahead of the Russians, but was moving across to port as he approached. At about 1325 Rozhestvensky signalled his four leading battleships (the starboard column) to increase speed, incline to port, and thereby place themselves once more at the head of a single line of 12 ships. By 1345 Togo's ships were sufficiently close for identification. Heading his line were the four surviving modern battleships, led by the flagship *Mikasa*. The two Italian-built armoured cruisers *Nisshin* and *Kasuga* followed, forming a six-ship division. Directly astern, and likewise in line ahead, came Kamimura's division of six armoured cruisers. Thus Togo, like Rozhestvensky, had a line of 12 armoured ships. But the Japanese line comprised only modern ships, easily capable of working together.

When Togo approached and crossed the path of the Russians it seemed that he either intended to concentrate his strength against the older battleships of the port column, or to exploit his superior speed to attack the rear of the Russian line. But at about 1345 he surprised his opponents by ordering an in-sucession turn which would result in his ships reversing course while still maintaining a line-ahead formation with the battleships in the van. This change of direction meant that Togo could move across the head of the Russian line (that is, cross the Russian 'T'); he would be able to fire all his broadsides at the leading Russian ships while only the nearest Russian ships would be able to make effective reply. However, making an in-succession turn was dangerous because each ship would turn on the same point, whose range and bearing the Russian guns would soon establish.

As the battle was eventually won by Togo, his mistakes have been regarded as calculated risks, but it seems likely that this unexpected turn, far from being a Nelsonian stroke of genius, was a result of an earlier mistake. In the mist and the smoke it is unlikely that Togo had a clear impression of the Russian deployment. He probably was unaware that the Russian starboard column was not abreast of, but in advance of, the port column. This misapprehension would have led to his initial approach being designed to enable him to attack the weaker port column first. At some point he would have realised that Rozhestvensky's unorthodox deployment permitted a faster return to a single line than he had anticipated, and that if he continued his initial approach his rear (that is, his armoured cruisers) would find themselves under the fire of the most powerful Russian battleships. To avoid this situation he could have continued on his course until he was out of range of the Russians, and then turned to make a second approach. But the mist would have deterred him from this course of action; remembering his experience before the battle of Round Island, when Witgeft almost evaded him, he must have been very conscious of the risk of losing contact. Such a loss of contact would have resulted in the Russians reaching Vladivostok and thereby transforming the strategic situation in Russia's favour. So the perilous in-succession turn was probably adopted as the best way out of an unexpected situation.

Fortunately for Togo, the prospect of each of his ships coming under the concentrated fire of the Russian battleships was more frightening in theory than in practice. Rozhestvensky's line was in considerable confusion when the gunfire began. This was because the First Division, in placing itself at the head of the line once more, had squeezed out its fourth ship and obliged the following ships to reduce speed or even stop engines to avoid collisions. Thus when fire was opened at about 1350 the Russian line, in Nebogatov's words, 'was nothing but a heap'.

The range when *Suvorov* opened fire at the leading Japanese battleship *Mikesa* as it made its turn was about 7000 yards, but both the light and the sea were against the Russian gunners. According to a British naval attaché with the Japanese fleet, Togo's battleships were surrounded by falling shells, but there were remarkably few hits. Moreover, many of the Russian shells failed to explode.

The Japanese opened fire a few minutes after the Russians. After they had completed their turn they pressed against the head of the Russian line, concentrating their fire on *Suvorov* (leading the First Division) and *Oslyabia* (leading the Second). With their well-trained and battle-tried gun crews, they were soon able to confuse the Russian gunners and rangetakers with a steady stream of accurately directed high-explosive shells. Without penetrating the Russian armour, the Japanese shells reduced *Suvorov* and *Oslyabia* to chaos and confusion. They had a shattering effect on unarmoured structures because their shellcases broke into hundreds of splinters, they set fire to paint and wood, and they emitted toxic fumes.

In this kind of bombardment, where armour penetration was less important than fire and blast, the guns of the Japanese armoured cruisers, and the secondary six-inch guns, were as effective as the battleship's twelve-inch weapons; the latter might fire a heavier shell but they fired more slowly. It was probably the armoured cruisers which sank *Oslyabia*. This battleship was hit by several shells on its waterline armour and the shock broke off the thick steel plates, leaving an unprotected skin in which a subsequent shell blew a hole 'big enough to drive a troika through'. The stricken battleship soon capsized, taking with her the entire engineroom complement: these men had been locked into their compartments at the beginning of the battle, and nobody troubled to release them. This was the first ship to go down; the crews of some of the Russian ships were told that this was a Japanese battleship going to the bottom, and cheered dutifully. Among those drowned was Midshipman Trouveller, an Englishman reputed to have been the best officer of the ship. When the abandon-ship order was given, he went below, saying he wanted to study the damage, and was not seen again.[15]

*Oslyabia* sank at 1450, having dropped out of the line at 1425. *Suvorov* and the other battleships continued to suffer. The Russian battleships tended to turn away from the Japanese, which remained to port. With the Russians making about 9 knots and the Japanese about 14, the two lines described concentric arcs, with the Russians on the inside. At about 1430 splinters had entered the slit of *Suvorov*'s conning tower, killing or wounding all its occupants. The battleship's helm jammed and from this time neither *Suvorov* nor Rozhestvensky took any leading role in the battle. *Aleksandr III* took *Suvorov*'s position at the head of the line. Soon she too had to drop out, and was succeeded by *Borodino*. But at 1500 fog patches caused Togo to lose contact. The battered Russian line turned south-east for ten minutes, then resumed its course towards Vladivostok. *Aleksandr III* had rejoined the line. At about 1540 the Russian line approached *Suvorov* which, isolated and wrecked, was under the fire of Kamimura's armoured cruisers. Coming under heavy fire once more, the Russian line withdrew to the south and with the help of mist patches succeeded once more in breaking contact.

During these confused deployments the Russian cruisers had been fighting the Japanese cruisers and, despite the handicap of the supply ships that they were escorting, gave a good account of themselves. The Russian battle line unintentionally approached the scene of this cruiser action, and for the first time Nebogatov's ironclads were able to use their guns at an effective range, seriously damaging four Japanese cruisers. *Suvorov* was still afloat in this vicinity:

> Parallel to us, without masts or funnels, with a severe list, moved the wreck of a burning ship. Its side was red-hot. Smoke was pouring directly out of the deck because of the absence of funnels, and was wrapping itself around the dying battleship in a black cloud, giving it a particularly terrible and monstrous appearance. But nevertheless it moved ahead and continued firing.[16]

Although Rozhestvensky was wounded and incapable of any further direction, great efforts were made to save him. A destroyer, in a perilous manœuvre, came alongside the stricken *Suvorov*. Under fire, the Admiral was lowered on to the destroyer's deck. Most of the flag officers, as well as one or two officers and men of the battleship's crew, also jumped down on to the destroyer. At least two officers, however, refused to leave the battleship, explaining that they preferred to remain with their men. Later that evening *Suvorov*, after several torpedo attacks, disappeared beneath the waters in a cloud of steam, taking her crew with her. Apparently she was firing her one intact gun right up to the end. As for Rozhestvensky, he belatedly transferred command of the Squadron to Nebogatov, and was taken from the scene of battle in a semi-conscious state. Subsequently he and his flag officers were transferred to a sister destroyer, *Bedovy*.

Shortly after 1800 the Russian battleships, still grimly plodding towards Vladivostok, once more encountered Togo's battle line. At a range of about 6500 yards, a heavy fire was directed against the leading Russian ships, *Aleksandr III* and *Borodino*. The former was soon forced out of the line:

> After some time another battleship appeared on the starboard side, moving directly towards us. Its masts and funnels were still in place but it moved with a noticeably increasing list. Our own guns, because of the range, were not firing, and our gunners gathered round the embrasures, watching intently, their faces pale and their eyes wide open. I heard someone whisper, 'God help them!' The

battleship was already so close that we could make out individual figures. Its list was still increasing. Its rising side was covered with men while on the bridge stood two officers, majestic and calm, with their hands gripping the rail. At this moment there was a flash and a shot rang out from her starboard side. Immediately afterwards the battleship capsized. Men slid down along the rising side and the giant lay keel-upward, the propellers still turning. A little longer, and everything was hidden beneath the waves. The gunner standing by me crossed himself. 'O Lord, may their souls rest in peace!'[17]

After *Aleksandr III* it was the turn of *Borodino*, which after a short bombardment capsized and sank. *Orel*, the last ship of the First Division, was saved when failing light persuaded Togo to withdraw his armoured ships to leave a clear field for his torpedo craft.

Nebogatov steamed onward with the dejected remnant of the 2nd Squadron. Under his command he had *Orel*, seriously damaged, and seven older ships. During the night there was a succession of torpedo boat attacks, during which *Navarin* was sunk and three other ships damaged. Three Japanese torpedo boats were sunk by Russian gunfire (these were the only Japanese ships sunk during the three-day battle). By choice, Nebogatov's original ships did not use their searchlights, nor did *Orel* (whose searchlights were smashed). It was probably this which saved them, because it was by the Russian searchlights that the Japanese located their targets. In view of the tired state of the Russians, their unwise use of searchlights, and the damage they had already suffered, the results of the night engagement hardly served to restore the reputation of the torpedo boat as a weapon.

At dawn, Nebogatov's flagship was leading *Orel*, *Apraksin* and *Seniavin*, with the cruiser *Izumrud* still keeping company. *Sisoi Veliky*, *Nakhimov*, and *Monomakh* had departed in search of a suitable coast beside which their damaged hulls could be scuttled. The destroyers had scattered in the hope of reaching Vladivostok or China. Three cruisers, including *Avrora*, had fled towards Manila, where they would be interned by the US authorities. Three cruisers were trying to break through to Vladivostok but two of them would be sunk, leaving *Almaz* (the intended viceregal yacht) to bring details of the disaster to Russia. The 'self-sinker' *Ushakov*, unable to keep up with Nebogatov, would soon be sunk after a gallant fight against Japanese cruisers. It was clear that the Squadron had been shattered, although there were still those who believed that the Japanese had suffered as badly as the Russians. What Nebogatov and his officers did not know was the full extent of the disaster, that their little group of ironclads were the only intact Russian ships in the vicinity. Thus when early that morning smoke appeared on the horizon it was at first hoped that it might signal the approach of friendly ships.

However, it soon became clear that Nebogatov was surrounded by the enemy. He had at his disposal only two modern twelve-inch guns (on *Orel*); one of these had only four shells in its magazine and the other had lost its shell-handling elevator. All his other guns could be outranged by the Japanese, whose ships were faster than his. When firing commenced it was evident that the Japanese intended to keep their distance and shell the Russians at leisure. The weather was fine, and they had the whole day before them.

Scorning naval tradition, and regulations, Nebogatov decided to surrender. A white flag and then a Japanese flag were hoisted, and the firing stopped. A Japanese boat was sent to take Nebogatov to Togo, who accepted his surrender. The Russian crews were transferred to Japanese ships and the four prizes were taken over by Japanese crews.

*Izumrud*, a very fast ship, refused to surrender and broke through the Japanese ring. She would have reached Vladivostok had she not been blown up by her crew after exhausting her coal supply; evidently her captain feared she might be captured by the Japanese if he waiting for a collier from Vladivostok. Of the 2nd Squadron only *Almaz* and two destroyers reached Vladivostok. The others were sunk, scuttled, captured or interned. The wounded Rozhestvensky was captured when the destroyer *Bedovy*, carrying him, surrendered to pursuing Japanese destroyers.

News of the defeat caused a great shock in St Petersburg. Exaggerated hopes had been placed in Rozhestvensky's mission, and moreover the families of most of the officers lived in that city. Nebogatov made a convenient scapegoat, and he and other officers who surrendered their ships were court-martialled after the war. Nebogatov was sentenced to death, but this was commuted and in the end he spent a short period in prison. The captain of one of the captured coast defence ships lost his commission, served in the ranks in the First World War, distinguished himself, and was personally recommissioned by the Tsar.

Rozhestvensky maintained a dignified silence after his return to Russia and his side of the story of Tsushima was never properly told.[18]

# 9 Peace and its Sequel

In February 1904, when the news came of the Japanese surprise attack on Port Arthur, there had been shock and indignation among Russians, but in general the war did not arouse great enthusiasm. The country was not in peril, Manchuria was far away, and few shared or even understood the government's ambitions in the Far East. When the war started there had been one or two patriotic demonstrations in the cities, but it is hard to say whether these were spontaneous or arranged by the local police.

Portrayal of the Japanese as 'yellow monkeys' was typical both of the coloured cartoons sold on Russian streets, and of the mildly scurrilous rhymes learned by schoolchildren. The press, which did not have a wide circulation outside the big cities, did what it could to maintain interest, but by no means all of the newspapers were in favour of the war. The right-wing *Novoye Vremiya* of the capital was perhaps the most belligerent, regaling its readers with tales of Russian heroism but at the same time criticising the government for the defeats. In the first week of the war, citizens besieged the newspaper kiosks in search of the latest news, but the spirit of the citizenry was also reflected by the queues at the State Bank, where holders of government bonds hastened to exchange them for cash.

As the war progressed both the right and the left, for different motives, attacked the government's conduct of the war. The population in general, the masses which were hardly considered to be part of 'public opinion', became increasingly resentful of the economic burden of the war, of the call-up, and of its inability to make its voice heard.[1] Revolutionary propaganda became more widely appreciated, and in January 1905 the gulf between rulers and ruled developed into a real crisis. Striking workers in St Petersburg, marching with their families to petition the Tsar, were shot down by troops in the incident known as 'Bloody Sunday'. This ignited violent demonstrations and strikes throughout the Empire. There was a general strike in St Petersburg which, with strikes elsewhere, impeded the war effort and lowered Russia's credit abroad. In Poland resistance was especially widespread and violent. Soon the unrest spread to the countryside, and there were demonstrations when new drafts left for Manchuria. This unrest was not exclusively directed against the war, being primarily a protest against living and working conditions, but it made the continuation of the war difficult and even politically hazardous.

Russia's ability to continue the war seemed to be thrown into even greater doubt by the mutiny of the battleship *Potemkin* in June. The sailors of this vessel took over the control of their ship and cruised around the Black Sea, bombarding Odessa before seeking asylum in Rumania. Russia had already lost the Pacific and Baltic squadrons, and now it seemed that the one remaining squadron was as likely to fight against the government as for it. All in all, even though the Russian army in Manchuria by mid-1905 was sufficiently strong to beat the Japanese, many Russians doubted whether it would have the chance to do so. The French, whose financial help seemed indispensable, were urging Russia to make peace,[2] while at home the social unrest was threatening to achieve what the Japanese army had failed to achieve, a break in the authorities' morale.

The Japanese people's response to the war was very different from that of the Russians, partly because it was misinformed of the reality of the situation. While censorship was strict in Russia, it was directed mainly against subversive ideas and it was possible for the alert newspaper reader to gather a good picture of what was happening in the East, and why. Japanese censorship was more complete and rigid, little significant information being released. Thus the Japanese newspapers, in order to maintain the bellicosity of their readers, regaled them with fanciful tales of great victories and the exploits of real or imagined heroes. No hint was given of the fundamental difficulties facing the Japanese armed forces.

In 1904 the Japanese people were not even informed of the outbreak of war until the evening of 9 February. Foreigners in Tokyo, who knew what had happened, could not understand why everyone seemed so calm. But when the news was released there were demonstrations and processions with drums, trumpets and lanterns, and much singing of slogans and the national anthem. Towards the end of 1904, however, there were signs of doubt among the population. This was partly because everyone was impatiently anticipating the greatest victory of all, and this victory seemed unaccountably delayed. A German doctor wrote that in Tokyo scaffolding and wires had been erected along the streets for flags and lanterns. The Japanese were so sure of the imminent fall of Port

Arthur that all stocks of lanterns had been sold out, according to this German, months before the siege ended.[3] In Yokohama whole warehouses were filled with celebratory materials. So great was public impatience that in some localities triumphant lantern marches were made on the strength of false rumours about the fall of Port Arthur. In October the government felt compelled to ask the Emperor to issue an edict advising his people to spend less time celebrating and more time on the real war effort.

The reality of war was already percolating into the Japanese popular consciousness. Apart from the casualties, and the departure from home of the breadwinners with no government help offered to their families, there was ever-increasing taxation. In total, the war expense of 1904–05 amounted to about seven times the state revenue of 1903. Four-fifths of this was financed by loans, of which half were floated at home and half in London, New York and Berlin. Despite the military victories, foreign purchasers of Japanese bonds needed to be tempted by very favourable terms, which absorbed more than one-eighth of the face value of the bonds. Right up to the end of the war, Russia was regarded by foreign investors as a better risk than Japan.

To fill the gap between what could be raised by Japanese government bonds and the actual expenditure, taxation and duties were increased. Such increases fell proportionately most of all on the poorer classes; there was a land tax, income tax, beer and spirit tax, death duties, and even a one-third tax on streetcar tickets. Prices rose sharply, partly as a consequence of calling up for war service about one-fifth of the male working population.

Port Arthur was eventually captured, and the celebratory lanterns could at last be brought out, and then used again to celebrate the victories at Mukden and Tsushima. Such celebrations, confirming that the Japanese were a great and invincible people, did much to compensate for the privations of war. But by the summer of 1905 there were signs that morale both at home and in the army might one day crumble. The élite of the reserves had already been mobilised, and at the Battle of Mukden the Japanese army included men who were regarded as only second-rate, both in terms of physique and morale.

Throughout the war there had been supply difficulties. Even expensive recourse to foreign munitions suppliers like Krupp had not enabled the Japanese army to follow up its victories. Although after each victory it was the Russian rearguards which were primarily responsible for the Japanese failure to exploit success, lack of ammunition was another important factor. Mukden, in terms of men and material, represented the peak Japanese effort, and the human and material costs of that victory left the Japanese army in a weakened situation relative to the Russians. New victories seemed likely to bring Japan only closer to defeat.

The Japanese people had no inkling of the catastrophe towards which their armed forces were heading. For them, it seemed that victory should follow victory and that the war would inevitably end with a huge Russian indemnity to compensate them for their sufferings, with the Japanese flag hoisted in Siberia perhaps as far west as Lake Baikal. Only the ruling oligarchy and a few staff officers realised the truth. They badly needed peace, but seemed unable to obtain it by military means.

Immediately after the Battle of Mukden both Oyama and the war minister stressed the necessity of making peace promptly. Ever since the summer of 1904, Japanese envoys in neutral capitals had been sounding out the prospects of peace, but Nicholas, assured by his generals that victory was just around the corner, had been in no mood for negotiations. It was not until the shock of Tsushima in May 1905 that he seemed to become more responsive. Accordingly, as the more far-seeing Japanese leaders had anticipated in February 1904, the good offices of the American president, Theodore Roosevelt, were sought. At the beginning of June the Japanese ambassador in Washington was instructed by his government to request the President to invite the two belligerents to start discussions. The invitation was to appear as entirely on the initiative of the President; there was to be no hint that Japan was behind the suggestion.[4]

Roosevelt, a former assistant navy secretary, had taken as much interest in the maritime operations of the war as had the Kaiser in the land operations. Like the American and British public his sympathies had been with the Japanese, but as the war progressed he began to regret the unbroken succession of Japanese victories. It seemed that for the USA the best outcome of the war would be a limited victory for the Japanese, leaving Russia too weak to monopolise Manchuria but strong enough to contain further Japanese expansion. Peace in 1905 would therefore be nicely timed from the American point of view. For this and for reasons of political prestige Roosevelt was quite willing to lend his good offices to the cause of peace; like the world at large, he was unaware that it was Japan, not Russia, which had most to fear from a prolongation of the war. He quietly ascertained that Nicholas would be receptive to his proposals, and then formally offered both emperors his mediation in arranging talks between the two sides. On 10 June Japan accepted his suggestion, and on 12 June Russia also agreed.

That Japan had acceded to Roosevelt's suggestion two days before Russia did so was badly felt by the Japanese public, as it seemed an unnecessary loss of face. In any case, said the newspapers, peace negotiations were premature since Japan had still to win that final crushing victory which would force Russia to accept Japan's minimum demands. This popular opposition to peace made it difficult for the Japanese government to select its plenipotentiaries. The first elder statesman who was invited refused, saying that the Emperor needed his presence in Tokyo; in reality the leadership realised quite well that any plenipotentiary would be risking his political future, since the terms which could be reasonably expected were pitiful compared with the expectations of the Japanese public, its press, and its rank-and-file politicians. Finally the foreign minister, Komura, agreed to go.

Komura, one of the few key leaders who had not gained his position through fortunate birth, had always taken a hard line. As ambassador to Peking, in 1895 he had advised his government to make war on China. He later became an advocate of war against Russia, and his sponsorship of the Anglo-Japanese alliance in his capacity as foreign minister had facilitated Japan's initiation of such a war. As a proponent of successful wars, Komura was therefore one of the architects of Japan's apparent new greatness. During the peace negotiations with Russia he would take a harder line than his government, but nevertheless would be obliged to accept terms which most Japanese regarded as humiliating. Thus it was that Japan's most successful hard-liner would be condemned by his people as treasonably soft.

Russia, too, had some difficulty in finding a plenipotentiary. The foreign minister initially suggested Witte, but the Tsar refused to appoint a man whom he had previously dismissed, and whom he did not like. But others refused the appointment, knowing full well the difficulties of representing a government that had been defeated but refused to admit it. So in the end Nicholas was obliged to accept Witte who, in fact, was the best man; he was very intelligent, had a useful blend of integrity and unscrupulousness, and was respected abroad. Even General Linievich, who had written to the Tsar to express the opposition of his officers to an immediate peace, privately admitted that Witte could be relied upon to uphold manfully Russia's interests. Although Witte was assured that he could ask for fresh instructions if he felt it necessary, Nicholas made it clear that he would not conclude the war on humiliating terms: 'Our army is still intact and I have faith in it.' He would never agree to pay an indemnity or to limit Russian forces in the Far East.

Japan's terms for peace, as given to Komura on the eve of his departure, included three 'absolutely indispensable' conditions: Russia should acknowledge Japan's unlimited freedom of action in Korea; Russia and Japan should both withdraw their troops from Manchuria; Russia should cede to Japan Port Arthur and the Liaotung Peninsula, together with the South Manchurian Railway from Port Arthur northwards. These three conditions were what the government recognised as the essential aims for which the war had been fought. Then there were four 'relatively important' conditions: Russia was to pay an indemnity to cover Japan's war expenses; Russian warships interned in neutral ports were to be handed over to Japan; Russia was to cede Sakhalin to Japan; Russia was to grant fishing rights off the Maritime Province. Finally there were two 'not absolutely indispensable' conditions: Russian naval strength in the Far East was to be limited; Vladivostok was to be demilitarised.

The Japanese leaders, while striving very successfully to maintain the image of negotiating from strength, were well aware that they were in a position of weakness. To remedy this weakness they recognised that it was desirable before concluding peace to achieve four objectives: to win another victory over the Russian army in Manchuria; to float new foreign loans; to drive out Russian forces still in areas of northern Korea untouched by the war; and to occupy Sakhalin. But Japan was only strong enough to achieve two of these objectives; foreign loans were obtained (on rather onerous terms), and in July Japanese troops were landed in Sakhalin and soon overcame the weak Russian forces. The outside world had been expecting a Japanese assault on Vladivostok, but seemed to accept the Japanese explanation that it was only unsuitable weather that had prevented such an attack. However, the capture of Sakhalin had a certain moral effect, for it was the first occasion in the war that the Japanese had occupied Russian territory.

Roosevelt chose Portsmouth, New Hampshire, as the most convenient location for the negotiations. It was pleasantly situated, cool in August, but not likely to be crowded with curious holidaymakers. A conference room in the naval storehouse was the setting for the meetings of the peace conference, which lasted from 9 August to 5 September. In this room Witte and Komura faced each other across a long table, flanked by their advisers. At the first regular meeting of the conference, Komura presented the Japanese peace terms. In reality these were Komura's own conditions rather than those of the Japanese government because Komura, feeling that his instructions were too weak, had decided to include the acquisition of Sakhalin and the payment of an indemnity in the 'absolutely indispensable' category.

Witte's strategy at the talks is fully explained and praised in his memoirs. Starting from Nicholas's insistence that there should be no indemnity and nothing 'undignified', Witte throughout the conference emphasised that Russia was not defeated and was not asking for peace. It was simply that peace was desirable for humane reasons. He also sought to transform the foreign, and especially American, climate of opinion. Realising that if American opinion could be swung towards favouring Russia, Roosevelt might be expected to persuade the Japanese to be more conciliatory, Witte swallowed his distaste and began to play American-style politics. In his relations with the press he put aside the usual attitude of the Russian bureaucrat and sought to ingratiate pressmen by supplying them with the information that they needed for their articles. In the middle of the Atlantic, on his way to the conference, Witte gave an interview to a British journalist. This interview, described as the 'first mid-Atlantic interview', was transmitted by radio, and this new technological marvel attracted a large international audience to Witte's thoughts about the coming negotiations.

At Portsmouth, Witte and Komura privately agreed that the two sides would limit their press releases to statements which both sides approved, but Witte nevertheless met with newspaper correspondents to give his side of the story. These correspondents therefore began to regard the Russian delegation as friendly and frank, and the Japanese as secretive and hostile, and this feeling was reflected in their reports and articles. Since most Japanese newspapers depended on American press agencies for their news of the conference (the Japanese government as usual being highly secretive), Witte's conduct meant that the news reaching the Japanese public was often originated by himself.

Witte also took care to conciliate the American Jewish community, which was influential and could determine the success of any further Russian attempts to raise loans on the American market. Displaying some courage and adaptability, Witte visited the Russian Jewish community where he defended Russian policies in the presence of people who had left Russia to escape the anti-Jewish discrimination and violence of Nicholas's government. As Witte was known to be opposed to governmental anti-semitism, his reception was not un-friendly.

With his copious handshaking, and his carefully cultivated relations with the press, Witte showed that he understood the important factors in political success in the USA. There is no evidence that he ever kissed any babies, but he does appear to have embraced at least the conductor of his private railway car. Probably Witte's conduct had less effect on the outcome of the conference than he claimed, but it was a brave effort.

After several sessions of the conference it was evident that agreement could be reached on Japan's leading role in Korea, on the evacuation by both sides of Manchuria, and on the retrocession of Port Arthur and the Liaotung Peninsula to Japan (what China thought about this last proposal was not considered very important by either Russia or Japan). But Komura's insistence on the transfer of Sakhalin to Japan, and the payment of an indemnity by Russia, brought the conference to a crisis. Nicholas remained adamant that 'not a kopek nor an inch of Russian land' should pass to Japan, while Komura, although willing to make concessions (like replacing the word 'indemnity' by 'reimbursement') would not concede on any important matters. That Komura in these two demands was express-ing his own wishes, and not those of his government (which regarded the two issues as only relatively important), was not known to the Russian delegation. However, this ignorance was of no account since the Russian government, in constant telegraphic touch with Witte, had no intention of yielding.

By late August the conference was approaching a breakdown. Witte ordered a private railway car to be kept ready for him, and Komura made a donation to a local charity in appreciation for Portsmouth's hospitality. Behind the scenes Roosevelt was in touch with both delegations; he wanted the conference to succeed, he wanted to avoid the imminent intervention of Britain, France and Germany in the role of additional mediators and, should the confer-ence fail, he preferred that the blame should fall on Russia.

Witte was willing to let the conference fail over the issue of the indemnity, for the world would surely condemn Japan for continuing the war simply for money. On the other hand, if the conference failed over the issue of Sakhalin, Russia would lose sympathy, because Sakhalin was occupied by Japan, was close to Japan, and controlled the La Perouse Strait which was strategically important for Japan. For this reason, prompted by the American ambassador in St Petersburg, the Russian government decided to offer a compromise: Sakhalin would be partitioned, with the southern half going to Japan. Meanwhile Komura telegraphed his government on 26 August, saying that the conference was about to break down over the indemnity and Sakhalin issues, and recommending that no concessions be made on these two; he argued that Japan's honour would be damaged if, after having continually insisted on these two points, she would finally admit that they were not vital after all.

The receipt of this telegram in Tokyo was followed by a feverish series of long meetings involving the cabinet, the elder statesmen, and the chiefs of staff. At a final meeting, with the Emperor presiding, the war minister declared that because of the officer shortage Japan could not continue the war, and the finance minister said that it would be impossible to raise any additional funds. Finally accepting the inevitable, the government telegraphed Komura: 'our Imperial government is determined to conclude peace during the present negotiations by any means necessary.' Komura was instructed to offer in exchange for Sakhalin the withdrawal of the demand for an indemnity, but not to break off negotiations if this offer was rejected. If the Russians did refuse, Komura was quietly to persuade Roosevelt to appeal publicly to the Japanese government to withdraw the demand for Sakhalin 'for the sake of humanity and peace'. If the President would not agree to do this, Komura was nevertheless to withdraw the demand.

At the time this telegram was despatched, Tokyo was unaware that Russia was willing to cede the southern half of Sakhalin. When this fact became known, a supplementary telegram was hastily sent to amend the final concession, limiting Japan's willingness to forgo Sakhalin to the northern part of that island. On 29 August a disappointed Komura and a contented Witte finally agreed on the peace terms, with no indemnity and a partition of Sakhalin.

The peace treaty was signed on 5 September 1905. Witte went home to a warm welcome, and Nicholas conferred on him the title of count. Komura's welcome was rather less than warm. Although he had done his best to wreck the prospects of peace by his insistence on an indemnity, he was loudly condemned by the Japanese people and press as a 'softie' who had humiliated his nation.

The Japanese press had always regarded the peace talks as premature, and was suspicious of their proceedings. It was, as always, ill-informed. It had sent correspondents to Portsmouth but many of these could only speak their own language, which was of little use because the Japanese delegates did not wish to speak to them. Their few really informed reports were cruelly censored by the government's supervisors of incoming telegrams, so that not even the newspaper editors saw them. The Japanese public had been led to expect great things from the peace talks; everyone counted on an indemnity, and many believed that this indemnity would be shared out among the people. Without an indemnity it seemed impossible to restore the war-ravaged economy and lift the common people out of the privations that war had brought.

First news of the peace, and of the withdrawal of the demand for an indemnity, came with special editions of two Tokyo newspapers. Evidently the editors had been shattered by the news, for they provided no comment, simply printing the bare facts as headlines. Some newspaper offices put out flags bordered with mourning crêpe. In Yokohama only two people were said to have hoisted flags to celebrate the peace, and they were both Frenchmen.

On 5 September, just as the treaty was being signed at Portsmouth, and in a shade temperature of 96 degrees Fahrenheit, crowds gathered for a mass anti-peace rally in Hibiya Park, Tokyo. A firecracker was set off to open the proceedings, a band played, balloons with anti-government and anti-peace slogans were launched, and fiery speeches made. After half an hour a second firecracker was exploded, the national anthem was played, three 'banzais' were shouted, and the meeting finished. The participants then marched towards the Emperor's palace, making use of the traditional if unexercised right of the people to appeal directly to the Emperor. This move took the police by surprise. Fearing that the crowd with its brass band and placards would damage the imperial flowerbeds, the police moved in. The crowd was incensed, swords were drawn, and the Tokyo anti-peace riot began.

Order was not restored until the evening of the following day, by which time most police stations, many churches, a number of newspaper offices and some streetcars had been burned by the mobs. Six police superintendents, 26 inspectors, 422 policemen, and about 40 firemen and soldiers had been injured by the time martial law and heavy rain put an end to the riots. A few days later there was a magazine explosion on board Togo's flagship *Mikasa*, which sank in

shallow water. Many attributed this to sabotage by fanatical opponents of the peace, but the British naval attaché reported that
carelessness was a more likely cause.[5]

When Witte returned triumphantly home to St Petersburg after the
Portsmouth negotiations, he arrived during a strike. The disturbances
which had begun in January 1905 had still not been finally settled. In
the countryside and in the non-Russian parts of the Empire the
situation had worsened. A fresh wave of strikes, including a strike on
the indispensable railways, forced Nicholas on Witte's advice to grant
his people a measure of constitutional government. This concession,
which divided the middle-class opposition from the working-class
opposition, together with the régime's use of troops to suppress
dissent, eventually brought internal peace. But part of the army and
navy joined the rebels. There were minor naval mutinies at Vladivostok, Sevastopol and Kronstadt, and a much more disturbing mutiny
in the Manchurian army as it returned home.

By October 1905 the Russian army in Manchuria exceeded 1 000 000
men, and the railway was not capable of returning these men to
European Russia in less than about ten months. Since the troops were
already discontented, the decision about which troops to send home
first was a painful and perilous one. Despite the opposition of his
colleagues, Linievich decided that the reservists should be separated
from the rest of the army and sent home first. These were the most
troublesome men, and presumably Linievich wished to get rid of them
as soon as possible. He justified the decision on grounds of natural
justice, but Kuropatkin pointed out that the regular troops who had
been in the East since 1904 had an even stronger moral right to go
home first.

Linievich's decision was disastrous. The already disaffected reservists were sent home, unaccompanied by any of the steadier regular
troops, and en route were easily persuaded by agitators to join the
strikers. The railway strike committees had the power to decide
which trains to pass and which to hold up, and they also controlled
the telegraph line. The resulting chaos meant that demobilisation was
held up, causing additional loss of morale among troops still in
Manchuria. The situation was only partially remedied by the charter
of ships to take some of the troops home by sea. In effect, mutinous
troops and strikers controlled the railway, and hence Siberia. It was
not until a trainload of regular troops under Rennenkampf was
despatched westwards from Harbin, and another train eastwards

from the Urals, in order to arrest, hang or shoot the rebels at each station, that order was restored.

Most historians agree that Russia had to accept defeat and end the war because of internal disturbances and the increasing difficulty of obtaining foreign loans on favourable terms. This collective opinion is probably wrong; in view of what happened in Russia after peace was made it seems likely that the Russian government would have been better advised to continue the war, to fight at least one more battle. A victory would almost certainly have been won, thanks to the increased Russian strength and the exhaustion of Japan's resources. Such a victory would immediately have boosted the government's popularity at home and its creditworthiness abroad. The generals had strongly expressed this view, and generals, seeking to restore their reputations, are not always wrong.

# Notes and References

## 1 THE INEVITABLE WAR?

1. A. N. Kuropatkin, *Zapisi*, vol. 1 (Berlin, 1909), pp. 202–3.
2. See Delmer Brown, *Nationalism in Japan* (Berkeley, California, 1955).
3. While not the last word, T. H. von Laue's *Sergei Witte and the Industrialization of Russia* (New York, 1963) is an exhaustive guide to the 'Witte System'.
4. D. W. Treadgold's *The Great Siberian Migration* (New York, 1957) clearly brings out the role of state planning in eastern development.
5. The ideological underpinning of Russia's eastern expansion is one of the topics covered in A. Malozemoff's *Russian Far Eastern Policy 1881–1904* (Berkeley, 1958). See also G. A. Lensen, *The Russian Push Toward Japan* (Princeton, New Jersey, 1959).
6. A good guide to the interaction of Japanese politics, nationalism, and expansionism is S. Okamoto, *The Japanese Oligarchy and the Russo–Japanese War* (New York, 1970).
7. G. A. Lensen's *The Russo–Chinese War* (Tallahassee, Florida, 1967) gives a full description of the Russian part in the Boxer campaign.
8. 'Chinese girls and women of all ages ... raped first and bayonetted afterwards by men whose governments were wrapping themselves up in the soft wool of Mary's little lamb' is how one observer described the behaviour of the foreign troops (quoted in Lensen's *Russo–Chinese War*, p. 259).
9. A useful account, translated from the Russian, is B. A. Romanov, *Russia in Manchuria 1892–1906* (Ann Arbor, Mass., 1952).
10. J. A. White, *The Diplomacy of the Russo–Japanese War* (Princeton, New Jersey, 1964), p. 27.
11. R. R. Rosen, *Forty Years of Diplomacy* (New York, 1922) gives the Russian ambassador's view of these and preceding Russo–Japanese negotiations.

## 2 THE CONTENDERS

1. For details of the CER, see E. K. Nilus, *Istoricheskii obzor Kitaiskoi vostochnoi zheleznoi dorogi 1896–1923* (Harbin, 1923), and G. Sokolskii, *The Story of the Chinese Eastern Railway* (Shanghai, 1929).

2. A. J. Beveridge, *The Russian Advance* (New York, 1903) quoted in G. A. Lensen, *Russia's Eastward Expansion* (Englewood Cliffs, New Jersey, 1964), pp. 135–7.
3. As with most wars, absolutely reliable figures of strengths and losses are scarce. Military statistics given in this book are unlikely to be precise.
4. G. Kerst's *Jacob Meckel* (Gottingen, 1971) covers this phase of Japanese military development.
5. Here, and at certain other points where the nature of the Russian army is discussed, specific sources are not given because the text simply renders the conclusions reached from a study of a mass of memoir material listed in the Bibliography.
6. Much has been written about Kuropatkin, not least by himself. V. A. Apushkin's *Kuropatkin* (St Petersburg, 1907) is fair enough, given that it was written at a time when its subject was highly controversial. See also Chapter 7, note 11.
7. V. I. Nemirovich-Danchenko, *Na voine* (St Petersburg, 1904), p. 134.
8. Technical descriptions of weapons in this book are based largely on their very full treatment in the British *Official History*.
9. According to M. Kostenko, even the Viceroy, Alekseev, had a Japanese barber up to the outbreak of war. Naturally enough, this craftsman was later presumed to have been a spy. For the Mukden situation see D. Christie, *Thirty Years in Mukden 1883–1913* (London, 1914).
10. Frederick T. Jane's *Imperial Japanese Navy* (London, 1904) and *Imperial Russian Navy* (London, 1904) are still good sources, thanks to Jane's cordial relationships with the naval authorities of the two countries. For Britain's contribution to the Japanese Navy, see J. C. Perry, 'Great Britain and the Imperial Japanese Navy 1858–1905 (unpublished 1962 Harvard dissertation).
11. Admiralty Intelligence Dept, *Reports from Naval Attachés* (BR802/413), not dated.

## 3  ADMIRAL TOGO STRIKES

1. *Port Artur: vospominaniya uchastnikov* (New York, 1955), p. 49. This book is a collection of eyewitness memoirs by Russians who subsequently emigrated. It is replete with interesting anecdotes, which have to be digested cautiously since most of the contributors were writing from memory.
2. Kuropatkin, *Zapisi*, p. 224.
3. The diary of E. A. Planson (head of the Viceroy's diplomatic staff in Port Arthur and therefore well-informed) was published in *Krasnii arkhiv* (Moscow, 1930), No. 41/42, pp. 148–204.
4. Ibid, pp. 164–5.
5. Rudnev's account was published in *Russkaya starina* (St Petersburg, 1907), No. 2.
6. For more on Makarov, see B. G. Ostrovskii, *Admiral Makarov* (Mos-

cow, 1954); A. D. Dobrovol'skii, *Admiral S. O. Makarov, puteshest-vennik i okeanograf* (Moscow, 1948); Voenno-morskoye izdatel'stvo, *S. O. Makarov-sbornik dokumentov* (Moscow, 1953); F. F. Vrangel', *Vitse admiral S. O. Makarov* (St Petersburg, 1911–13), two vols.

7. Christie, *Thirty Years*, p. 169.
8. Ostrovskii, *Admiral Makarov*, p. 294.
9. An American naval observer described Witgeft as 'disliking energy or action in both theory and practice', but obstinate once he had made a decision (R. von Doenhoff, *The McCully Report* (Annapolis, 1977), p. 164). McCully's observations cover much of the naval side of this war and his first-hand impressions are useful, but he tended to accept hearsay uncritically, which in Russia was always a dangerous temptation. Thus he informed Washington that Russian warships carried female nurses (p. 139), and that their sunken ships at Port Arthur were merely taking a voluntary rest, and would be raised and sent into action when the Baltic Squadron arrived (p. 258).

# 4 THE WAR IN MANCHURIA

1. From part 5 of Mukerjee's *Poem on the Russo–Japanese War* (Calcutta, 1904–05). Mukerjee's Bengali verse is superior to his English.
2. Tretyakov's account was translated into several languages; for example, N. A. Tretyakov, *Nan Shan and Port Arthur* (London, 1911). It is internally consistent and is in factual accord with the descriptions of foreign attachés.
3. In a letter dated 17 May Kuropatkin urged Stoessel, 'It is most important to get Fock back within the Port Arthur garrison in good time.' See A. I. Sorokin, *Oborona Port Artura* (Moscow, 1954), p. 85.
4. Extracts from the newspaper's military correspondent were reproduced in *The Times*, *The War in the Far East* (London, 1905). Another of his frank comments was, 'German military advice throughout this war has been consistently wrong' (p. 332).
5. Ibid., p. 490.
6. Christie, *Thirty Years*, p. 174.
7. This and the preceding details of this battle are from F. R. Sedgwick's *The Campaign in Manchuria; Second Period* (London, 1912). This contains the best of the shorter descriptions of this engagement.

# 5 THE END OF THE RUSSIAN SQUADRON

1. S. A. Rashevskii, 'Dnevnik polkovnika S. A. Rashevskogo', in *Istoricheskii arkhiv* (Moscow, 1954), No. 10, pp. 122–3. Rashevskii, a sapper officer, is one of the more reliable eyewitnesses of the Port Arthur operations, although not unprejudiced. Unfortunately he was killed by the same shell that killed Kondratenko (see Chapter 6), so posterity was denied his post-war observations.

2. *Port Artur : vospominaniya uchastnikov*, p. 37. In this account Lebedev is described as commander of the *Zabiaka*, so presumably he had been demoted to this gunboat.

3. This chapter is a synthesis of a score of books noted in the Bibliography. One source for the messages exchanged between the Squadron and the Viceroy and St Petersburg is A. Belomor, *Portarturskaya eskadra nakanuniye gibeli*. This was published in *Russkaya starina* (St Petersburg, 1907–08), pp. 67–80.

    Belomor (pseudonym) was a prolific naval writer of this period. Elsewhere he exhibits a certain eccentricity, as when he declares that the Russian battleships should have used their rams, but he seems to be factually reliable.

4. These were von Essen of the *Sevastopol* and Grigorovich, the port director. Both emerged from this war with enhanced reputations and played important roles in the First World War.

5. Captain W. C. Pakenham had by this time replaced Captain E. C. Troubridge as British naval observer with Togo's squadron. Captain T. Jackson and Captain J. de M. Hutchinson were also active. The Japanese command was not enthused to have British representatives aboard, and their presence was not publicised. Partly this was because of a fear that British officers might dilute the glory of Japanese victories (Troubridge and Jackson, at least, did not hesitate to give their advice to Togo). For some months a British naval attaché was also at Vladivostok, but learned little about the Russian side. See P. Towle, 'The Evaluation of the Experience of the Russo–Japanese War', in B. Ranft (ed.), *Technical Change and British Naval Policy 1860–1939* (London, 1977), pp. 65–79. The war took place just as the 'all-big-gun' *Dreadnought* was taking shape. Opponents and proponents of the concept could both find good arguments from the experience of this war, partly because the Battle of Round Island was a big-gun encounter while Tsushima was a short-range engagement with medium guns playing a crucial part. For the lessons believed to have been learned in this conflict by the Royal Navy, see *Mariners Mirror* (Greenwich, Nov. 1974), pp. 383–94.

6. These were fateful shots, perhaps the most fateful of the war. They were also lucky shots, judging from Pakenham's reports (Ranft, *Technical Change*, p. 71). At these long ranges Japanese shot-spotting and aiming procedures failed absolutely, so much so that the captains of most of the Japanese armoured ships claimed, with conviction, that it was their own gunners who had fired the two vital shots.

7. This explanation is from V. Semeonov's *Rasplata* (London, 1909). As first officer of the *Diana* he had good reason to go to some lengths in explaining why that cruiser had turned its bow towards the fleshpots of Saigon in preference to Vladivostok. His account does not really effect a concordance between three facts: the distance from Round Island to Vladivostok is roughly 1000 miles, whereas the distance to Saigon is about double this, and *Diana*'s designed range at economical speed was 3750 miles. Since Semeonov and Klado were the naval authors whose accounts were first translated they strongly influenced subsequent histories of the war (including, regrettably, the British *Official*

*History*). Neither is reliable, although Semeonov had a gift of literary expression which makes his books worthwhile reading. His book describing this phase of the war, *Rasplata*, was published in St Petersburg in 1907, with an English edition of the same title following in 1909. For more on Semeonov, see Chapter 8, note 13.

8. For example, the *Chicago Daily Tribune* editorialised on 14 August 1904 about 'infraction of the sovereignty of China' and added, virtuously, 'When similar cases have occurred in our history we have always returned the ships so acquired.'

9. It would seem that the ships had gone into battle with some of their guns still landed, together with gunners and ammunition. The cruiser *Pallada* landed eight three-inch guns, and other battleships and cruisers had from one to three of their six-inch guns ashore, making a total of 12 six-inch and 14 three-inch. The figures are from P. K. Khudyakov, *Put' k Tsusime* (Moscow, 1907), p. 14, and should be taken with caution.

10. For a fuller account, see V. E. Egorev, *Operatsii vladivostokskikh kreiserov v russko-yaponskuyu voinu 1904–1905gg* (Leningrad, 1939).

11. From a Russian officer's diary, quoted in *Opérations maritimes de la guerre Russo–Japonaise*, vol. 2, (Paris, 1910), p. 228.

12. With the Vladivostok cruisers the Russians had demonstrated the use of a concentrated force against enemy communications, while with their auxiliary cruisers in the Indian Ocean they had shown the feasibility of using lone raiders. The British Admiralty pondered these events and their relationship to ocean trade protection. The wrong conclusion (that the convoy system was inapplicable in the age of steam) was duly drawn. See also the Admiralty papers at the Public Record Office, especially Adm. 116/866B.

## 6 THE SIEGE OF PORT ARTHUR

1. Rashevskii, 'Dnevnik polkovnika S. A. Rashevskogo', pp. 142–3.

2. T. Sakurai, *Human Bullets* (London, 1907), p. 148. To be fair, Captain Sakurai was writing about the end of a 58-hour battle.

3. M. Kostenko, *Osada i sdacha kreposti Port-Artur* (Kiev, 1906), pp. 190–1.

4. Rashevskii, 'Dnevnik polkovnika S. A. Rashevskogo', pp. 288–90.

5. Quoted in Prince Abamalek-Lazar, *Boevaya rabota russkoi armii v voinu 1904–05gg*, vol. 2 (St Petersburg, 1913), p. 403.

6. V. B. Gyubbenet, *V osazhdennom Port Arture* (St Petersburg, 1910), pp. 45 and 119, quoted in Abamelek-Lazar, *Boevaya rabota russkoi armii*, p. 403.

7. Among the considerable number of publications devoted to this hot issue are Smirnov's *Doklad generala Smirnova* (Nagoya, 1905 – evidently Smirnov was quick off the mark); Fock's pamphlet (A. Fok, *Sdacha Portarturskogo forta No. 2*, St Petersburg, 1907); and Stoessel's 'To my enemies' (A. Stessel', *Moim vragam*, St Petersburg, date uncertain). Accounts of the proceedings of the commission of enquiry

are from *Comptes rendus ... de conférences sur la guerre Russo–Japonaise ...* (Paris, 1908–10), and V. A. Apushkin, *Delo o sdache kreposti Port Artura yaponskim voiskam v 1904–05gg* (St Petersburg, 1908).

8. For example, in Rostunov's book, *Istoriya russko-yaponskoi voiny* (Moscow, 1977), V. P. Glukhov writes: 'However, Stoessel, Fock, Reis and similar people betrayed the Port Arthur garrison, the soldiers and officers of which were filled with determination to continue the struggle.' (p.251)

## 7  THE ROAD TO MUKDEN

1. *Russkaya starina* (St Petersburg, 1908), No. 2, pp. 398–400.
2. The British *Official History* provides copious technical detail on Japanese transport arrangements and, to a lesser extent, on Russian. An unseen but presumably thorough treatment is P. A. Belov's 'Zheleznodorozhnii transport v russko-yaponskoi voine 1904–1905gg', in *Trudy Voenno-politicheskoi akademii Krasnoi Armii im. V. I. Lenina* (Moscow, 1940), No. 4, pp. 105–36. For war zone transport see Yu. Lebedev, *Ocherk postroiki i eksploatatsii putei soobshcheniya na teatre voennykh deistvii* (St Petersburg, 1907).
3. V. Veresaev, *Na voine* (St Petersburg, 1908), p. 15. Veresaev was a reservist and hostile to the régime. He later became a Soviet novelist.
4. The current mobilisation plan (No. 18), designed with war against Germany and Austria in mind, was wrecked by the war against Japan, largely because so much rolling stock was in the east. For more than two years, until the introduction of Plan No. 19, Russia was without an achievable mobilisation plan. This is discussed at length in K. Ushakov, *Podgotovka voennykh soobshchenii Rossii k mirovoi voine* (Moscow–Leningrad, 1928).
5. Quoted in Veresaev, *Na voine*, pp. 185–6.
6. Sakurai, *Human Bullets*, pp. 3–4, 20.
7. Source for this snippet is Rerberg, no admirer of Kuropatkin (see note 11).
8. M. N. Pokrovskii (ed.), *Russko-yaponskaya voina iz dnevnikov A. N. Kuropatkina i N. P. Linievicha* (Leningrad, 1925), p. 13.
9. Ibid., p. 28.
10. *Russkaya starina* (St Petersburg, 1908), No. 10, p. 137.
11. F. P. Rerberg, *Istoricheskiye tainy velikikh pobed i neob'yasnimykh porazhenii* (Alexandria, 1925) gives some details about Kuropatkin's literary accomplishments. However, it should be remembered that the author had an intense dislike of Kuropatkin, and was very much a Grippenberg man. (He has an indicative passage – p. 325 – where he describes how he, Bilderling, and Brusilov hid behind a pillar in a St Petersburg theatre so as to avoid the necessity of shaking hands with Kuropatkin who 'after all that had happened under his leadership in Manchuria should have stayed modestly in some dark corner and

never shown himself'.) The official Russian history of the war was divided into chapters, each allocated to a particular officer. The account was written with great speed and Rerberg was 'invited' by the head of the historical commission to amend his draft for greater conformity with Kuropatkin's own version of events. He claims that Kuropatkin's memoirs (*Otchet generala Kuropatkina*) were printed at government expense and were meant to be a source for the authors of the official history. Being classified as secret, they could not be publicly criticised, which prevented those, like Grippenberg, who felt unjustly treated, from making counterattacks. Kuropatkin's *Zapisi generala Kuropatkina o russko-yaponskoi voine* was published in Russia in 1908, but then withdrawn. It was again published (in Russian) in Berlin in 1909, and in other languages soon after. The original was in four volumes, and not all this material was translated.

12. Pokrovskii, *Russko-yaponskaya voina*, p. 87.

## 8   TSUSHIMA

1. N. L. Klado was an instructor at the Nicholas Naval Academy, a prominent navalist, and the carrier to absurd lengths of 'fighting coefficients' (the computation of numerical equivalents for guns, speed and armour with a view to forecasting the performance of ships in battle). In 1904 his articles were a thorn in the side of the navy ministry, and it was partly at his urging, supported by his fighting coefficients, that Nebogatov's detachment was despatched. After the Tsushima catastrophe he wrote a book to show that he could have done it better (this was translated into several languages, and still influences authors; the English version was *Battle of the Sea of Japan*, published in London in 1906). Klado actually set sail with the 2nd Squadron, but was dropped off to serve as an eyewitness at the international enquiry into the Dogger Bank affair; whether this was because he was notoriously shortsighted, or because he was a practised hair-splitter, or simply because Rozhestvensky wanted to get rid of him, is a question best left to the imagination. Also in Rozhestvensky's entourage was V. I. Semeonov, who had got himself appointed as unofficial historian of the voyage. His book (English version: *Battle of Tsushima*, London, 1906) has also been very influential. Neither Klado nor Semeonov are entirely reliable. Klado fancied himself as a Frenchified intellectual, and had the intellectual's weakness for the absurd, while Semeonov had several axes to grind (he was a staunch defender of Rozhestvensky, and also had some reason to feel that his own reputation was at stake; he had, after all, gone to Saigon in 1904 and fled from the field of battle with Rozhestvensky at Tsushima). Rivals in the service, rivals as authors, Semeonov and Klado had little affection for each other. After the war, in December 1905, *Novoye Vremiya* was enlivened by a running argument between these two in which, among other felicities, Semeonov referred to Klado as a 'dry-land sailor'.

2. *S eskadroi admirala Rozhestvenskogo* (Prague, 1930), p. 44. This is a collection of survivors' tales that have to be handled with some caution.
3. Interview published by *Petit Parisien*, 11 April 1904, marking Rozhestvensky's appointment to the 2nd Squadron.
4. See *Russian Review* (Stanford), January 1974, pp. 63–79.
5. The role of the Hamburg-Amerika Line is discussed in an article by L. Cecil in the *American Historical Review* (Washington, 1964), July, pp. 990–1005. For Germany and the war in general, see the same journal, Dec. 1970, pp. 1965–87.
6. This episode is treated, on an archival foundation, in *Morskoi sbornik* (Moscow, 1935), No. 6, pp. 96–108.
7. *Bristol Guardian*, 5 Nov., 1904.
8. The mutiny, such as it was, had been ended by the admiral, Felkerzam, who came aboard and persuaded the crew to ask forgiveness. Felkerzam died later during the voyage. The movement of this detachment is described in his diary by the son of Admiral Witgeft, who was serving in *Sisoi Veliky*. This diary was published in *Istoricheskii arkhiv* (Moscow, 1960), No. 4, the reference to the *Navarin* mutiny being on p. 121.
9. In a telegram to St Petersburg of 17 February, Rozhestvensky emphasised that '1st Squadron with 30 warships of different types and 28 torpedo craft proved insufficient to win command of sea. 2nd Squadron, with 20 warships and only 9 torpedo craft, now insufficient to gain command of sea because apart from Rossiya there is nothing left of 1st Squadron.' This message is quoted in *Morskiye zapiski* (New York, 1955), vol. 13, No. 1, p. 26.
10. *Russkaya starina* (St Petersburg, 1909), No. 4, p. 111. The officer is I. Ditlov, aboard *Ushakov*.
11. *S eskadroi admirala Rozhestvenskogo*, p. 118.
12. Rozhestvensky's true feelings may perhaps be gathered from a telegram he despatched between Singapore and Camranh Bay: 'If it is already too late to send Squadron to Vladivostok, then it must be brought back to Russia. It cannot exist without a base. I beg your Majesty's commands on further movement.' Nicholas replied 'Vladivostok open by land. Must proceed without awaiting Nebogatov. I have strong hope that God will help you do a great thing.' See *Morskiye zapiski*, p. 27.
13. A. Zatertyi, *Bezumtsy i besplodniya zhertvy* (St Petersburg, 1907), p. 25. After surviving Tsushima, Zatertyi became the successful Soviet novelist Novikov-Priboi. His long novel *Tsusima* (English edition: *Tsushima*, London, 1936) was based on his experiences, embellished with a touch of plagiarism. This novel has been used as source for several English-language books about the battle, whose authors do not always realise that it is a work of fiction. For more on the novel *Tsusima* and its sources and reliability, see the article by J. N. Westwood in *Slavic Review* (Seattle, Washington, 1969), vol. 28, No. 2, pp. 297–303.
14. Rozhestvensky later claimed (in a letter to *Novoye Vremiya* of 21 Dec. 1905, p. 4) that, knowing Togo would attack, he made his dispositions

so that he could easily deploy to meet an attack from any direction. Moreover he had confused Togo, for the latter had expected that the first Russian ships he would come upon would be the weaker column led by *Oslyabia*.

15. Witgeft, *Istoricheskii arkhiv*, p. 121.
16. Ditlov, *Russkaya starina*, p. 493.
17. Ibid.
18. Whether his story would have been coherent is another matter. He seems to have held several strange views. For example, he believed the British would have sent a squadron against him from Wei hei wei, if Togo had failed to defeat him (*Novoye Vremiya*, 21 Dec. 1905, p. 4).

## 9  PEACE AND ITS SEQUEL

1. P. A. Buryshkin, *Moskva kupecheskaya* (New York, 1954) describes how the war was felt in Moscow.
2. For Franco-Russian relations in general, see J. Long, 'Franco–Russian Relations during the Russo–Japanese War', in *Slavonic and East European Review* (London, 1974), No. 4, pp. 213–33.
3. E. von Baelz, *Awakening Japan* (New York, 1932), p. 288.
4. Much of this chapter is based on J. A. White, *Diplomacy of the Russo–Japanese War*, and S. Okamoto, *The Japanese Oligarchy*.
5. Admiralty, Intelligence Dept, *Reports from Naval Attachés* (BR815), not dated.

# Bibliography

The problem of sources for the study of the Russo–Japanese War is not scarcity of material, but rather its quality. At all levels the war aroused great interest in the west. Newly-literate populations found that the war made fascinating daily reading, and their demand was met by hosts of newspaper correspondents who descended on the battlefield. For the real enthusiasts, part-publications were issued, coming out in magazine form every few weeks to serialise the war. In the English-speaking world both the newspapers and the part-publications were grossly prejudiced in Japan's favour, so much so that the modern reader might well feel embarrassment at, for example, their contrast of the gentlemanly Japanese warriors with the brutal, cowardly or deceitful Russians. Many of the war correspondents wrote books after the war, as did other visitors to the conflict. At a higher level the military and naval staffs of the great powers were naturally anxious to discover whether modern war fulfilled their expectations, and appointed officers to accompany the forces of one or both the belligerents. In many cases the reports of these officers were published later for the enlightenment of their colleagues. Japan and Russia likewise published official histories of the campaigns. Ostensibly such histories were to enable future commanders to learn from the lessons of the past, but in practice they were often written in a discreetly partisan spirit, covering up or exposing mistakes according to the pressures put on their authors.

Foreign military observers, with their professional experience, are a useful corrective to the starry-eyed commentaries by journalists and others. It is interesting, for example, that the journalists' accounts of how the Japanese treated their wounded emphasised the high standard of hygiene that was obtained. One account which mentioned the filth and the flies that could be discovered around Japanese field hospitals was not by a journalist but by a high Royal Army Medical Corps officer (see p. 63). But army officers could have their own professional prejudices at a time when the nature of war was changing so rapidly that many military roles seemed threatened with obsolescence. For example, despite the poor showing by the cavalry of both sides, no foreign cavalry officer ventured the opinion that cavalry might be less important in modern warfare than had been thought. An Austrian cavalry officer (Wrangel) even wrote that 'the era of the sword, as well as that of the bayonet, is not passed.' Of the foreign official accounts the British *Official History* is by far the best. Unlike others, it includes naval affairs, and was the result of a long process. Using volumes of an earlier British official account, as well as multi-volume collections of *Officers' Reports* (made by officers attached to both sides), it was not until 1920 that the three volumes of text were completed. The authors succeeded magnificently in welding their often contradictory sources into a readable and comprehensible narrative. However, anyone familiar with the sources used by the authors soon realises that sometimes undeserved faith is placed in certain accounts by participants. On the naval side, for example, the accounts by Semeonov are taken at face value, even though Semeonov took great care to concoct convincing explanations for the doubtful actions of those whom he admired, or for his own activities.

Quite apart from participants who had axes to grind, many witnesses simply made mistakes, or (perhaps more often) simply saw what they expected to see. For example, there exist two accounts of the end of the battleship *Aleksandr III*; Taube describes the bridge as deserted apart from a solitary signaller, whereas Ditlov mentions two officers standing there, preparing to go down gallantly with their ship. In such cases the reader can only speculate about the discrepancy. Perhaps the two witnesses had different angles of view, or were a few seconds apart in time; or perhaps one or the other was inadvertently confusing the end of *Aleksandr III* with that of her sister *Borodino*; or did one wish to emphasise with artistic licence the pathos of the scene, while the other chose to give his readers an example of good officerly conduct?

Many diaries of participants were published between 1904 and 1914. These are illuminating, but again have to be treated with caution, for their authors could be prejudiced, and in any case would tend to view events from their own restricted angle. In many cases, too, the diaries show signs of amendment or elaboration between their ostensible date of writing and the time of publication; not everyone could resist the temptation to dress up hindsight as foresight. One diarist (Ditlov) hinted of such temptations:

> The second part of my diary, begun after Singapore, was lost. It would be strange to read it now. In it I described the junction of our squadron with that of Rozhestvensky, the energy and enthusiasm which he created with his Fleet Order, and its summons to 'wash away with blood the shame of our Motherland,' and the faith we felt in him and his capacity. Now, as a prisoner of war, all the comrades whom I meet tell me that nobody believed in success, that everybody knew with certainty that they were going to a useless death, and that they had always considered Rozhestvensky to be an upstart and careerist. But I can remember how people gloried in him and how the officers of his squadron shared their optimism with us.

The list that follows is far from exhaustive. A much more complete bibliography is M. Luchinin, *Russko-yaponskaya voina 1904–1905 gg: bibliograficheskii ukazatel'* (Moscow, 1940). However, even this is not definitive, although it includes non-Russian as well as Russian works. In particular, it is deficient in titles published by Russian emigrés.

Abamelek-Lazar, Prince ('A.N.A.'), *Boevaya rabota russkoi armii v voinu 1904–05gg* (St Petersburg, 1913).
Admiralty, Intelligence Dept, *Reports from Naval Attachés* (not dated), BR802/413 (Pakenham and Jackson reports, including Tsushima); BR803/

410 (includes diary of *Orel* seaman); BR815 (for *Mikasa* explosion).

Admiralty, Intelligence Dept, *The Russo–Japanese War: Technical Subjects* (London, about 1909).

Admiralty, War Staff, *Maritime Operations of the Russo–Japanese War* (London, 1914) (the 'Corbett and Slade Report').

Apushkin, V. A., *Kuropatkin* (St Petersburg, 1907)

Apushkin, V. A., *Mishchenko* (St Petersburg, 1908).

Apushkin, V. A. (ed.), *Voennaya entsiklopediya* (St Petersburg, 1911).

Baelz, E. von, *Awakening Japan* (New York, 1932).

Baring, M., *With the Russians in Manchuria* (London, 1905).

Barry, R., *The Events Man* (New York, 1907).

Bartlett, E. A., *Port Arthur* (Edinburgh, 1906).

Beklemishchev, N. N., *O russko-yaponskoi voine na more* (St Petersburg, 1907).

Belomor, A., 'Portarturskaya eskadra nakanuniye voiny', in *Russkaya Starina* (St Petersburg, 1907–08).

Belomor, A., *Portarturskaya eskadra nakanuniye gibeli* (St Petersburg, 1908).

Benckendorff, C., *Half a Life* (London, 1954).

Bompard, M., *Mon ambassade en Russie, 1903–08* (Paris, 1937).

Botkin, E. C., *Svet i teni russko-yaponskoi voiny 1904–1905gg* (St Petersburg, 1908).

Chegodaev-Sakonskii, A., *Na 'Almaze' vo Vladivostok* (Moscow, 1910).

Christie, D., *Thirty Years in Mukden 1883–1913* (London, 1914).

Committee of Imperial Defence, *Official History of the Russo–Japanese War* (London, 1910–20).

Committee of Imperial Defence, *Official History of the Russo–Japanese War* (initial edition), Part 3 (London, 1908).

Cyril, Grand Duke, *My Life in Russia's Service* (London, 1939).

Daveluy, R., *Les leçons de la guerre Russo–Japonaise* (Paris, 1906).

Ditlov, I. A., 'V pokhode in na boiu na bronenostse "Admiral Ushakov"', in *Russkaya starina* (St Petersburg, 1909), Nos 1–4.

Dobrotvorskii, L. F., *Uroki morskoi voiny* (Kronstadt, 1907).

Doenhoff, R. von (ed.), *The McCully Report: The Russo–Japanese War, 1904–05* (Annapolis, Maryland, 1977).

Druzhinin, K., *Issledovaniye dushevnogo sostoyaniya voinov . . . 1904–1905* (St Petersburg, 1910).

Dubrovskii, E. V., *Dela o sdache yapontsam (1) minonostsa 'Bedovyi' i (2) eskadry Nebogatova* (St Petersburg, 1907).

Egorev, V. E., *Operatsii vladivostokskikh kreiserov v russko-yaponskuyu voinu 1904–1905gg* (Leningrad, 1939).

Essen, N. O. von, *Les derniers jours du 'Sebastopol' à Port Arthur* (Paris, 1914).

German General Staff, *The Russo–Japanese War* (London, 1908).

Graf, G. K. *Moryaki* (Paris, 1930).

Gyubbenet, V. B., *V osazhdennom Port Arture* (St Petersburg, 1910).

Hamilton, I., *A Staff Officer's Scrapbook during the Russo–Japanese War* (London, 1905).

Hare, J. H., *A Photographic Record of the Russo–Japanese War* (New York, 1905).

Ienish, N., *Iz vospominanii minnogo ofitsera na bronenostse 'Petropavlovsk'* (St Petersburg, 1913).

Janin, P. T., *Aperçu sur la tactique des armées Russes et Japonaises* (Paris, 1909).

Japanese Naval General Staff, *Opisaniye voennykh deistvii na more v 37–38gg Meidzi (v 1904–05gg)* (St Petersburg, 1909); this Russian translation appears to be fuller than the French.

Japanese Naval General Staff, *Opérations maritimes de la guerre Russo–Japonaise* (Paris, 1910).

Kerst, G., *Jacob Meckel* (Gottingen, 1971).

Khudyakov, P. K., *Put' k Tsusime* (Moscow, 1907).

Kinai, M., *The Russo–Japanese War: Official Reports* (Tokyo, 1905–07).

Klado, N. L., *The Russian Navy in the Russo–Japanese War* (London, 1905).

Klado, N. L., *Battle of the Sea of Japan* (London, 1906).

Kokovstov, V. N., *Out of my Past* (Stanford, 1935).

Kononov, I. A., *Puti k golgofe russkogo flota* (Sao Paulo, 1961).

Kostenko, M. I., *Osada i sdacha kreposti Port-Artur* (Kiev, 1906).

Kostenko, V. P., *Na 'Orle' v Tsusime* (Leningrad, 1955).

Kuropatkin, A. N., *Otchet gen-ad. Kuropatkina* (Warsaw, 1905–07); four volumes.

Kuropatkin, A. N., *The Russian Army and the Japanese War* (London, 1909).

Kuropatkin, A. N., *Zapisi o russko-yaponskoi voine* (Berlin, 1909).

Kravchenko, V., *Cherez tri okeana* (St Petersburg, 1910).

Kvitka, A., *Journal d'un cosaque du transbaikal* (Paris, 1908).

Larenko, P., *Stradnye dni Port Artura* (St Petersburg, 1906).

Lensen, G. *Russia's Eastward Expansion* (Englewood Cliffs, New Jersey, 1964).

Lensen, G., *Korea and Manchuria between Russia and Japan 1895–1904* (Tallahassee, Florida, 1966).

Lensen, G., *The Russo–Chinese War* (Tallahassee, Florida, 1967).

Martynov, E. I., *Vospominaniya o yaponskoi voine* (St Petersburg, 1910).

Maurice, F. B., *The Russo–Japanese War* (Cambridge, 1910).

Morskoi general'nyi shtab, *Russko-yaponskaya voina 1904–1905gg* (St Petersburg, 1912–18): seven volumes.

Mukerjee, *A Poem on the Russo–Japanese War* (Calcutta, 1904–05).

Negrier, General de, *Lessons of the Russo–Japanese War* (London, 1906).

Nemirovich-Danchenko, V. I., *Na voine* (St Petersburg, 1904).

Nemits, A., *Istoriya russko-yaponskoi voine na more* (St Petersburg, 1914).

Nidermiller, A. G. von, *Ot Sevastopol' do Tsusimy* (Riga, 1930).

Nozhin, E. K., *Pravda o Port-Arture* (St Petersburg, 1906–07): two volumes.

Nozhin, E. K., *Konets osady Port-Artura* (St Petersburg, 1907).

Nozhin, E. K., *The Truth about Port Arthur* (London, 1908).

Nozikov, N., *Pokhod 2oi eskadry Tikhogo okeana* (St Petersburg, 1914).

Ogasawara, N., *Life of Admiral Togo* (Tokyo, 1934).

Ogawa, G., *Expenditures of the Russo–Japanese War* (New York, 1923).

Okamoto, S., *The Japanese Oligarchy and the Russo–Japanese War* (New York, 1970).

Ostrovskii, B. G., *Admiral Makarov* (Moscow, 1954).

Pfeil, R. and Klein-Elguth, R., *Ce que disent les Japonais de leurs succès maritimes* (Paris, 1911).

Planson, E. A., 'Dnevnik', in *Krasnii arkhiv* (Moscow, 1930), No. 41/42.

Pokrovskii, M. N. (ed.), *Russko-yaponskaya voina iz dnevnikov A. N. Kuropatkina i N. P. Linievicha* (Leningrad, 1925).

*Port Artur : Vospominaniya uchastnikov* (New York, 1955).

Rashevskii, S. A., 'Dnevnik polkovnika S. A. Rashevskogo', in *Istoricheskii arkhiv* (Moscow, 1954), No. 10.

Rerberg (Rehrberg, Rohrberg), F. P., *Istoricheskiye tainy velikikh pobed i neob'yasnimykh porazhenii* (Alexandria, 1925, on title page; Geneva, 1967, on title page verso).

Rostunov, I. I. (ed.), *Istoriya russko-yaponskoi voiny* (Moscow, 1977).

Rudnev, V. Boi '"Varyaga" u Chemulpo', in *Russkaya starina* (St Petersburg, 1907), No. 2.

Russian General Staff, *Guerre Russo–Japonaise 1904–05* (Paris, 1910).

Sakurai, T., *Human Bullets* (London, 1907).

Saligny, Captain de, *Essais sur la guerre Russo–Japonaise* (Paris, 1913).

Schwartz, A. von, and Romanovskii, Y., *Oborona Port Artura* (St Petersburg, 1908).

*S eskadroi admirala Rozhestvenskogo* (Prague, 1930).

Semeonov, V. I., *Battle of Tsushima* (London, 1906).

Semeonov, V. I., *Rasplata, or the Price of Blood* (London, 1909).

Smirnov, M. I., *Tsusima* (St Petersburg, 1910).

Sorokin, A. I., *Oborona Port Artura* (Moscow, 1954).

Sorokin, A. I., *Russko-yaponskaya voina 1904–1905gg* (Moscow, 1955).

Steer, A. P., *The Novik* (London, 1913).

Taube, G. N., *Posledniye dni vtoroi tikhookeanskoi eskadry* (St Petersburg, 1907).

Taube, M. de, *La politique Russe d'avant guerre* (Paris, 1928).

Terestchenko, S., *La guerre navale Russo–Japonaise* (Paris, 1931).

*The Times, The War in the Far East* (London, 1905).

Togo, Captain, *Naval Battles of the Russo–Japanese War* (Tokyo, 1907).

Tretyakov, N. A., *Nan Shan and Port Arthur* (London, 1911).

Ukach-Ogorovich, N. A., *Kuropatkin i ego pomoshniki* (Uman, 1914).

Veresaev, V., *Na voine* (St Petersburg, 1908).

Vineken, A., *Zametki ob yaponskoi armii v poslednuyu voinu* (St Petersburg, 1913).

Vyrubov, P., *Desyat' let iz zhizni russkogo moryaka* (Kiev, 1910).

War Office, *The Russo–Japanese War: Medical and Sanitary Reports* (London, 1908, etc.).

War Office, *The Russo–Japanese War: Reports from British Officers* (London, 1908, etc.).

Westwood, J. N., *Witnesses of Tsushima* (Tokyo, 1970).

White, J. A., *The Diplomacy of the Russo–Japanese War* (Princeton, New Jersey, 1964).

Witte (Vitte), S. Y., *Vospominaniya* (Moscow, 1960).

Wrangel, G., *Cavalry in the Russo–Japanese War* (London, 1907).

Yamata, K., *La vie du général Nogi* (Paris, 1931).

Zatertyi, A., *Bezumtsy i besplodniya zhertvy* (St Petersburg, 1907).

Zatertyi, A., *Za chuzhiye grekhi* (Moscow, 1907).

# Index